The Biblical Prophets In Outlined Notes

Compiled by

LEON D. STANCLIFF

B.A., M.A., ED.S.

GOSPEL ADVOCATE COMPANY

Nashville, Tennessee

1976

TABLE OF CONTENTS

To two women
who stand as spiritual examples,
my wife and my mother

And to my Saviour, JESUS CHRIST,
of whom the prophets bear witness
(Rev. 19:10)

PREFACE

The Biblical prophets have long held a fascination for the author. As a boy of fourteen he can recall reading from the book of Isaiah and wondering whether the statements there referred to the people of ancient Israel, or to the people of the twentieth century. Now some thirty-five years later he finds his interest growing stronger yearly.

For over twenty years as a high school and college science teacher there has been an increasing respect for logical processes. The gathering of evidence, and the evaluation of witnesses and their testimony holds a place of vital importance in both the science laboratory and the science classroom. The same mental characteristics which found the scientific method attractive were applied to the subject of Christian Evidences as manifested in the prophets.

And the prophets are Christian Evidence! To the people of the prophet's own time they were words of encouragement and hope and provided strength for the faithful and warning to the rebellious. But to the Christian of our time who can observe the promised impact of the Messiah and his Kingdom upon the world the prophets offer some of the most indisputable testimony mankind has ever viewed.

The testimony of Jesus is the spirit of prophecy. (Rev. 19:10.) This might be restated to say that both the Old Testament and the New Testament prophetic books are dead and meaningless unless one reads them as Christian testimony and witnesses to the divinity of the Son of God. Repeatedly the Scriptures refer to them as such. Jesus speaks of the Old Testament scriptures as "they which testify of me." (John 5:39.) Peter described prophecy as "a light that shineth in a dark place, until the day star arise in your hearts." (2 Pet. 1:19.) Again (Acts 10:43) Peter says, "To him give all the prophets witness." Surely it is true that "he hath not left himself without witness." (Acts 14:17.) If allowed free reign in the heart of an honest man "the testimony of the Lord is sure, making wise the simple." (Psa. 19:7.)

There is a unity manifested throughout the books of prophecy which stamps them as one work. The theme is the BATTLE OF THE AGES. God desires a people who recognize him as sovereign of the universe. In turn he will recognize them as his people with all the blessings attendant to this relationship. Satan works to prevent this relationship. He attacks through heathen nations without and through apostasy within. Over and over again Satan succeeds in corrupting God's chosen nation of Israel. But God has known the ultimate outcome from before the foundations of the earth. When the *Mystery of God* is completed Satan and his forces will have been vanquished.

Repeatedly it looks as if Satan is to be the victor. Only a remnant of the chosen people remain true. Yet the remnant never disappears. From the faithful remnant the Messiah enters. This results in the ultimate confrontation with the love of Christ providing the knockout blow as he offers himself willingly upon the cross. It is then only a matter of time before the death throes of the Serpent end in the lake of fire.

Strangely enough, it is in the study of the prophets that some Christians lose their faith. The reason may lie in the demand that these books make for one to either accept or reject the supernatural. If axeheads cannot float on water (2 Kings 6:6) Elisha becomes either a fabrication or an impostor. If there is no possibility of predictive prophecy Isaiah spends an enormous amount of time in silly gibberish about a suffering servant who is to become a ruler. One comes face to face with the question, "What think ye of Christ?" The testimony of the prophets is clear. He is the Messiah of the coming Kingdom of God. To reject their witness is to declare oneself incompetent as a judge. The prophets will stand. The man who denies their truth will die. Some try to deny the supernatural elements and accept the moral truths. This cannot be done. The doing and the teaching are one.

As can be seen from the previous comments the author is strictly conservative and fundamental in viewpoint. It is his firm conviction that God has two great books. One is the book of nature from which one may discover his existence and his majesty. The other is the Bible, revealed and providentially protected for our guidance. Only the greatest concern can be felt for those who chop the Book of books to pieces retaining only those portions which fit their preconceived notions. Only the Divine hand could have woven the book of Revelation from the strands and fibres presented one by one in the Old Testament. It is far from chance or human wisdom which includes a reference to Isaiah in every chapter of the final book of the Holy Scriptures.

The present book was finally precipitated by the writer's need for text materials to use with a class on the Biblical Prophets in a school of Bible and Preaching in Murfreesboro, Tennessee. It was not difficult to find commentary type material on the minor prophets written by those with a sound respect for plenary verbal inspiration. The difficulty lay in finding a single work which handled all four of the major prophets' writings as well as the minor prophets. Apparently the possible length of such a book had been an obstacle. The only answer seemed to lie in an outline commentary which stood somewhere between a strict outline and a full commentary. And so over a period of five years the present work was completed.

At some points, as in the book of Revelation, each verse is handled separately. At other places several verses may be examined together. It was deemed advisable on some scriptures to present a variety of explanations from various sources. Still, again a single explanation appeared to be adequate.

There is an increasing interest in prophetic materials. It is highly likely that preachers are going to be asked by their congregations to prepare lessons along this line. Schools of preaching are in need of just such presentations as this one. With much condensation, yet covering the vast majority of points which might come up, it is believed this volume can render a valuable service. We might add that Bible teachers in Sunday morning and Wednesday evening classes should give consideration to series of lessons on the prophets. Enthusiastically and accurately presented they can be very inspirational.

Honest errors have been a matter of great concern to the writer. He is acutely aware of the warnings in the Scriptures about adding to or taking away from them. If one is guilty of misleading the children of the Father in Heaven the condition is serious. It is tempting to avoid the responsibility by keeping thoughts out of print. But this seems to be a coward's way out. The same dangers exist when the spoken word is used, and God commands, "Go preach the Gospel." The solution seems to be in presentation of the work and a sincere caution to the reader to forever remember that the works of men must always be checked against the works of God, not vice versa. We are but an earthen vessel and must be careful not to contaminate the precious water of life.

Our gratitude must be expressed to those earnest students in the Murfreesboro School of Bible and Preaching, and to Harvey Clark and Charles Locke, the directors, for the inspiration they have provided. Also a special word of thanks should be spoken to Homer Hailey of Temple Terrace, Florida and to several teachers of the Sunset School of Preaching in Lubbock, Texas, for books and tapes which provided much valuable research material.

GENERAL INTRODUCTION
to the Prophets

1. *There has been a general neglect in study of the prophets.*
   A. Perhaps because of their location in the Old Testament.
      1. But the things written aforetime were written for our learning, that we through patience and comfort of the scriptures might have hope. (Rom. 15:4.)
      2. And the law was our schoolmaster to bring us unto Christ that we might be justified by faith. (Gal. 3:24.)
   B. Even the book of Revelation which is New Testament prophecy, is avoided.
   C. It may be that the questions of the critics have alarmed some.
   D. Again, abuse of the prophets and wild speculation and schemes of interpretation are discouraging.
2. *But there are very valid reasons for studying the prophets.*
   A. They are a primary source of historical records.
      1. Political activities of their times are revealed.
      2. Social conditions of ancient Palestine are shown.
      3. The impact of religion upon that society can be seen.
   B. Problems similar to those they faced exist today.
      1. Sins of justice, compassion and hypocrisy are common to men of all ages.
      2. God's plan of action may change but his attitudes toward the obedient and the disobedient do not. (Rom. 11:22)— Behold the goodness and severity of God—
      3. Every newspaper, every newscast and article from *Newsweek* or *Time* take on vital significance.
         a. Not because we can find every event in Old Testament prophecies. b. But because we may react with full confidence that God is overseeing the affairs of men.
   C. The prophets may provide inspiration for us.
      1. They possessed a courage of their convictions which we need every day.
      2. Their dynamic messages can breathe life into our own efforts to speak God's Word.
      3. Their loyalty to God rather than self can strengthen ours.

1

D. The prophets provide a strong line of evidence for the Divinity of Jesus Christ.
   1. There are several lines of evidence.
      a. Type and antitype—Moses, The brazen Serpent, etc.
      b. The life and teachings of Jesus. c. Prophecy.
   2. The prophets all pointed to Christ. (Rev. 19:10.) THE TESTIMONY OF JESUS IS THE SPIRIT OF PROPHECY.
   3. The apostolic preaching used prophecy freely.
      a. Peter in Acts 2. b. Philip in Acts 8. c. Stephen referred to the promise to Abraham. (Acts 7:1-5.)

3. *The place of prophecy in Israel*
   A. Prophecy takes its place with history and religion.
      1. History—shows God's power and glory.
      2. Religion—shows God's character and holiness.
      3. Prophecy—shows God's constant planning.
   B. God's eternal purpose is gradually manifested. (Eph. 3:11.)
   C. They did more than speak to the signs of the times.
      1. Higher critics see them as "moral reformers."
      2. These critics would deny miraculous prediction.
         a. They would have two Isaiahs. b. One could then speak after the event.
      3. The signs of the times would not allow:
         a. Isaiah to call the name of Cyrus. (Isa. 44:28.) b. Micah to name Bethlehem as Christ's place of birth. (Mic. 5:2.)
   D. While calling out *turn or burn* the prophet was also unrolling God's *scheme of redemption.*

4. *A prophet was a spokesman for God.*
   A. God has provided at least five classes of speakers.
      1. Lawgivers—Moses and Christ. (Neh. 9:13, 14; James 1:25.)
      2. Wise men or elders. (Jer. 18:18; Ezek. 7:26.)
      3. Priests—taught the law and tended the sacrifices. (Lev. 10:8-11.)
      4. Psalmists. (Neh. 12:45, 46.)
      5. Prophets. Not extenders of the law but proclaimers.
   B. Names applied help to explain the spokesman role.
      1. They were Ro'eh or *seers.*
         a. This implies special insight. b. They had answers from a higher source. (Heb. 1:1.) c. The word above is used eleven times.

2. They were Chozeh or *gazers*.
   a. This word speaks of the method of gaining information.
   b. This word is used twenty-two times.
3. They were Nahbi, or *proclaimers*.
   a. This time the function is in behalf of another. Example: Aaron was Moses' prophet. (Ex. 7:1; Deut. 18:18.) b. This word is used over three hundred times.
4. The Greek original is "prophetes," one who speaks for another.
5. Other terms applied to the prophets were:
   a. Man of God. (1 Kings 17:18.) b. Servant of God. (1 Kings 18:36.) c. Watchman. (Ezek. 3:17.)

5. *There were certain basic marks of a prophet.*
   A. They were uncompromising individuals. (Amos 7:12-17.)
   B. They were conscious of a Divine call. (Amos 7:15.) (1 Sam. 3:8; Jer. 20:9.) "Fire shut up in my bones."
   C. They spoke all in the name of God. (Deut. 18:19, 20.)
   D. They spoke only by inspiration.
      1. "Thus saith the Lord" over 1500 times.
      2. "My words in his mouth." (Deut. 18:15-19.)
      3. This is different from modern day "prophets."
         a. God's prophets received—*God* gets the credit. b. Modern day prophets discover—*They* take the credit. See also Numbers 12:6.
   E. They were men of spotless character.
      1. Enemies usually bring out one's faults.
      2. The prophets are nearly free of aspersions.
   F. They often accompanied their preaching with miracles.
      1. Moses. (Ex. 4:1-9.)
      2. Samuel. (1 Sam. 12:16.)
   G. Their message harmonized with the rest of God's Word.
      1. Deuteronomy 12:32-13:5 is an example of disharmony.
      2. The old prophet of 1 Kings 13:11 should have remembered this passage from Deuteronomy.
   H. The prophet's message was confirmed by events.
      1. Jeremiah forecast a yoke—It was worn. (Jer. 28.)
      2. Ahab to die said Micaiah—Ahab died. (1 Kings 22:24-37.)
   I. The moral quality of the message distinguishes the true prophet.
   J. They were a people of communion with God.

3

      1. Men of prayer.
      2. Often lonely.
  K. They were men who stood out from the crowd.
      1. A "peculiar people."
      2. Persecuted and mocked. (Matt. 23:37.) "Thou that stonest the prophets (them that are sent unto thee)."

6. *God dealt often with false prophets.*
  A. The true prophet was bound to present only God's message. (Deut. 13:1-5.)
  B. False prophets departed for two reasons primarily.
      1. Like Balaam they left the truth for gifts. Also, Micah 3:5-11.
      2. Like those of 1 Kings 22 they wanted the favor of the kings and rulers.
  C. God gives a test for the false prophet.
      1. His prophecy must come to pass. (Deut. 18:20-22.)
      2. It must not contradict loyalty to God. (Deut. 13:1-3.)
      3. Jeane Dixon claims only 60 percent. (Not good enough.)
  D. God's true prophets opposed false prophets vigorously even when they erred through ignorance.

7. *God's use of the prophet's mind is interesting.*
  A. Some of the earlier prophets went into a trance.
      1. Music played a part. (2 Kings 3:14, 15; 1 Sam. 10:5.)
      2. Saul is said to be turned into another man. (1 Sam. 10:6.)
  B. A number of scriptures indicate strong control by outside sources such as the Holy Spirit. (1 Sam. 10:11; 2 Kings 2:9, 15, 16; Ezek. 2:2; Jer. 1:4-11.)
  C. Still the prophet retained his identity.
      1. Isaiah is poetic.
      2. Micah is blunt.
      3. And THE SPIRITS OF THE PROPHETS ARE SUBJECT TO THE PROPHETS. (1 Cor. 14:32.)
  D. The messages are imprinted on the prophets' minds through diverse manners.
      1. By direct communication
         a. To Moses, Exodus 33:11. b. To Samuel, 1 Samuel 3:10-14. c. To Daniel, Daniel 9:20-23 (through Gabriel, an angel).
      2. By dreams
         a. Joseph, Genesis 37:5-11; b. Gideon, Judges 7:13-15.
      3. By visions
         a. Isaiah, Isaiah 6; b. Ezekiel, Ezekiel 8:3 and 11:24 c. Zechariah, Chapters 1-6.

E. A number of passages show inspiration.
   1. 2 Chronicles 15:1—"The Spirit of God came upon Azariah."
   2. Isaiah 38:4—"Then came the Word of Jehovah saying."
   3. Joel 1:1—"The Word of Jehovah that came to Joel."
   4. Jeremiah 1:2—"Jeremiah to whom the word of Jehovah came."
   5. 2 Peter 1:21—"Men spake from God being moved by the Holy Spirit."
   6. 1 Timothy 4:1—"The Spirit saith expressly—"
F. Like preachers there seem to be three kinds of prophets:
   1. Those who have something to say.
   2. Those who have to say something.
   3. Those who have something to say and say it.

8. *There are certain principles of interpretation in dealing with prophetic material.*
   A. Prophecy is more sure than eye witness. (2 Pet. 1:18-21.)
   B. Old Testament prophecy pointed to the first coming of Jesus Christ.
   C. New Testament prophecy points to the second coming.
   D. Much Bible prophecy cannot be understood fully until it has been fulfilled.
      1. This creates continuous curiosity and excitement with attention drawn to God's Word.
      2. The fulfillment of the prophecies provides new evidence for the existence of Divine power and providence.
      3. The obscurity before the fact prevents deliberate human efforts to bring about the fulfillment.
   E. Some Biblical prophecy can be understood previous to fulfillment.
      1. Daniel understood when the captivity was to end. (Dan. 9:1, 2.)
      2. The scribes told Herod where Christ was to be born.
   F. The three main figures of speech used in prophecy are:
      1. The *allegory*—the obvious meaning carries a secondary meaning which is really the message intended. "Break up your fallow ground, and sow not among thorns" speaks not of tillage but of repentance. (Jer. 4:3.)
      2. The *parable* applies some real truth through the use of a narrative carrying a secondary meaning. Example: The vineyard story of Isaiah 5:1, 2.
      3. The *metaphor* gives individual words a meaning which they do not ordinarily carry.

Example: The prophets shall become wind. (Jer. 5:13.)
G. Figures of speech are taken from four areas of life.
1. Natural—animals, mountains, heavenly bodies, etc.
2. Occupations—husbandry, building, metallurgy, etc.
3. Religion—sacrifices, type of clothing, etc.
4. History—flood, resurrection, judgment, etc. See Adam Clarke, Vol. 4 for further elaboration here.
H. One should not depart from the primary meaning unless the original sense is less suitable to the context, or is contrary to other scriptures.
I. Certain terms are consistently applied in the same manner by more than one prophet.
1. Mountains—power concentrations
2. Earthquakes—turmoil in governments
3. Stars—important personages
4. Cedars—persons of importance
5. Briars and thorns—common people
6. Latter days—gospel dispensation
7. A city—organized people
J. In *some* cases a day stands for a year. (Ezek. 4:6; Num. 14:34.)
1. Barnes and others stand heavily upon the year-day principle.
2. Yet their application in several places is suspect.
K. One technique of the prophets is the *prophetic past.*
L. In many cases there is double prophecy.
1. A first obvious sense refers to a present situation.
2. A second mystical sense refers to later events. Example: Isaiah 22:22 refers to Eliakim, son of Hilkiah. But it refers also to Jesus Christ. (Rev. 3:7.)
M. Prophecy may be conditional.
1. God pronounces an evil upon a people.
2. They repent and he does the same. (Jer. 18:5-11.)
N. The Scriptures themselves are an infallible interpreter.
1. "This is that which was spoken . . ."
2. "As it is written in the prophet . . ."
9. *The list of prophets extends throughout the Old Testament.*
A. There were prophets in the time of the patriarchs.
1. Enoch prophesied. (Jude 14.)
2. Abraham was a prophet. (Gen. 20:7.) Note also Psalm 105.

6

3. They extended from Abel to Zacharias. (Luke 11:49-51.) In the Hebrew Bible this was from beginning to end.

B. Moses was a prophet and Miriam a prophetess. (Deut. 18:15-18; Ex. 15:20.)

C. There were prophets in the times of the judges.
   1. Deborah was a prophetess. (Judg. 4:4.)
   2. Samuel was both a judge and a prophet.

D. During Samuel's time "schools of prophets "were organized.
   1. These were interested persons gathered around a great prophet to learn from him.
   2. These students were called "sons of the prophet." (Amos 7:14.)
   3. Saul met a company of prophets. (1 Sam. 10:9-12.)
   4. One headquarters for such a school was Naioth. (1 Sam. 19:18-23.)
   5. These schools performed three functions.
      a. Learning. (2 Kings 4:38.)   b. Worship. (1 Sam. 10:5.)   c. Preaching and service. (2 Kings 9:1.)

E. There were non-literary prophets in the Kings period.
   1. Nathan—for David and Solomon. (2 Sam. 12:1.)
   2. Ahijah—for Jeroboam. (1 Kings 11:29.)
   3. Shemaiah—Rehoboam. (1 Kings 12:22.)
   4. Elijah and Elisha—Ahab. (1 Kings 16-2 Kings 13.)

F. Then we have the writing or "literary prophets."
   1. Four major prophets.
   2. Twelve minor prophets.

10. *A list of important prophets and their times*

Name of Prophet	Date of Prophecy	Place and Condition
Abraham	1900 B.C.	General
Moses	1500 B.C.	General
Samuel	1140 B.C.	United Kingdom—Saul
Sons of the Prophets	1100 B.C.	United Kingdom
Elijah	870 B.C.	Northern Kingdom—Ahab
Elisha	850 B.C.	Northern Kingdom—Ahab
Joel	830 B.C. (?)	Southern Kingdom—Amaziah
Jonah	800 B.C. (?)	Nineveh
Amos	760 B.C.	Northern Kingdom—Uzziah
Hosea	745 B.C.	Northern Kingdom—Jeroboam II
Isaiah	740 B.C.	Southern Kingdom—Ahaz, Hezekiah
Micah	735 B.C.	Southern Kingdom—Ahaz, Hezekiah

7

ASSYRIAN CAPTIVITY OCCURRED—722 B.C.

Zephaniah	630 B.C.	Southern Kingdom—Josiah
Jeremiah	625-585 B.C.	Southern Kingdom—Before and during the captivity
Nahum	625 B.C.	Southern Kingdom—Josiah
Habakkuk	610 B.C.	Southern Kingdom—Jehoiachim

BABYLONIAN CAPTIVITY OCCURRED—605 B.C.

Obadiah	587 B.C. (?)	During captivity
Ezekiel	592 B.C.	During captivity
Daniel	605-535 B.C.	During captivity

RETURN FROM BABYLONIA OCCURRED—535 B.C.

Haggai	520 B.C.	Jerusalem—Darius
Zechariah	520 B.C.	Jerusalem—Darius
Malachi	435 B.C.	Jerusalem—Medo-Persians

11. *Methods of classifying the prophets*

A. According to the dates of the prophets as we have done under Section 10.

B. According to the recipient of the message
   1. To Israel—Hosea, Amos
   2. To Judah—Joel, Isaiah, Micah, Zephaniah, Jeremiah
   3. To Nineveh—Jonah, Nahum
   4. To Babylon—Daniel
   5. To the Exiles—Ezekiel
   6. To Edom—Obadiah

C. According to the Hebrew text
   1. Major prophets—Isaiah, Jeremiah, Ezekiel
   2. Minor prophets—The Twelve
   NOTE: Daniel and Lamentations are in the Writings.

D. According to the Septuagint
   1. Major prophets—Isaiah, Jeremiah, Lamentations, Ezekiel and Daniel
   2. Minor prophets—Hosea, Joel, Amos, Obadiah, Jonah, Micah, Nahum, Habakkuk, Zephaniah, Haggai, Zechariah, Malachi

E. According to chronological periods
   1. Pre-exilic
   2. Exilic—Daniel, Ezekiel
   3. Post-exilic—Haggai, Zechariah, Malachi

F. According to the great empire dominating at the time
   1. Assyrian period—Obadiah, Joel, Jonah, Hosea, Amos, Isaiah, Micah, Nahum
   2. Babylonian period—Zephaniah, Jeremiah, Habakkuk, Daniel, Ezekiel
   3. Persian period—Haggai, Zechariah, Malachi

MOSES

1. *Moses held a unique place among the prophets*
   A. Numbers 12:1-8 speaks of this uniqueness.
      1. Aaron and Miriam are both called prophets.
      2. They decided to speak against Moses.
      3. God tells them he normally speaks to prophets in dreams and visions.
      4. But in Moses' case he made more personal contact.
         a. Mouth to mouth.
         b. Not in dark speeches.
   B. Other passages agree with the above.
      1. Exodus 33:11—"And the Lord spake unto Moses face to face as a man speaketh to a friend."
      2. Deuteronomy 34:10—"And there arose not a prophet since in Israel like unto Moses, whom the Lord knew face to face."
      3. The rich man was told "They have Moses and the prophets." (Luke 16:29.)
   C. Moses' deliverance from bondage appears to be a beginning point for a special prophetic assistance.
      1. Jeremiah 7:25—"Since the day that your fathers came forth out of the land of Egypt unto this day I have even sent unto you all my servants the prophets . . ." See also Luke 24:27. (Important)
   D. Moses stands closer to Christ than other prophets.
      1. Deuteronomy 18:17—The prophet like unto Moses is Jesus.
      2. Hebrews 3:5, 6—Jesus is the son and Moses is the servant in the house, yet they both held a special place.
      3. It was Moses and Elijah who were seen with Christ on the Mount of Transfiguration.
   E. The key to the special place of Moses is his position as both *prophet* and *lawgiver*, as was Jesus Christ.
2. *The background for Moses' prophecy.*
   A. Political
      1. The Hyksos Kings had been replaced by new rulers "who knew not Joseph."

9

    2. The Israelites had been reduced to slavery.
    3. Some think this was the time of Rameses II.
    4. Egypt was the dominant power in the western world.
    5. The Hittites were growing rapidly.
    6. The Assyrians were just beginning to awaken.

B. Social
    1. Hebrews lived in poverty and hard labor.
    2. Children were executed to prevent population growth.
    3. Egyptian rulers rolled in luxury.
    4. The educational opportunities were magnificent for the privileged nobility.
    5. Moses spent forty years in close contact with both the slaves and the nobility.

C. Religious
    1. Undoubtedly some of the teachings of earlier days had been neglected during slavery.
    2. Initiative and independence must have been almost non-existent.
    3. At the same time they were surrounded by the idolatry of Egypt.

3. *The man, Moses.*

A. Moses' life can be divided into three periods.
    1. In Egypt. (40 years)
        a. Education. b. Choice of Israelites over Egyptians. c. Flight.
    2. In the wilderness of Sinai. (40 years)
        a. Marries. b. Herds sheep. c. Hears the call of Jehovah. d. Returns to Egypt with Aaron.
    3. Leading the Israelites. (40 years)
        a. The Red Sea. b. Receiving and teaching of the law. c. Fails to give God the glory. d. Death.

B. God prepared Moses for his task through:
    1. Training in the home of Amram and Jochebed.
    2. The opportunity to see the evil of bondage.
    3. The opportunity to see the corruption of luxury.
    4. Exposure to the finest possible education in the world at his time.
    5. The discipline of the wilderness.
    6. A knowledge of the wilderness country.
    7. Confidence through the vision that he would have God's continuing assistance.

C. Certain outstanding characteristics can be seen.
1. Moses was strong as a leader.
2. He had great confidence in the plan of God.
3. He is said to be exceedingly meek.
    a. This probably has to do with God rather than man. b. When Miriam and Aaron spoke against him God immediately defended him.
4. Twice he lost patience with the followers.
    a. Once when he came down from the Mount of Sinai. b. Again when he spoke unadvisably in obtaining water for them. (Psalm 106:33.)

4. *The message of Moses.*
A. Arise from bondage.
B. Place your lives in God's hands.
C. Listen to the direction of God's law.
D. God has a covenant.
1. You keep your part of the covenant.
2. He will keep his promises.
E. The Ten Commandments and the entire law are the message of Moses as he speaks for the one God, Jehovah.

5. *Practical lessons for today.*
A. God does not like excuses.
B. With God one man may overcome an empire.
C. Communion with God brings power.
D. Seemingly trivial mistakes bring serious consequences.
E. God has a work for you to do.
F. He will prepare you for it and see you through it.

SAMUEL

1. *Samuel is sometimes considered as a second Moses...*
   A. Jeremiah 15:1 places them side by side.
   B. Both found God's people in ignorance, slavery, and despair.
   C. The efforts of both resulted in release from the oppression.
   D. Each ushered in a new era.
      1. Moses brought the law.
      2. Samuel anointed the first king.
   E. An interesting question is, "Which prophet was the beginning point?" (Compare Jer. 7:25; Luke 24:27; and Acts 3:24.)

2. *The background for the prophecy of Samuel.*
   A. Political
      1. Three hundred years from death to Moses to birth of Samuel.
      2. Philistines controlled much of the territory of the promised land.
      3. The tribes of Israel were not united.
      4. There were invasions by Syrians, Moabites, Canaanites, Midianites, Ammonites and Philistines.
      5. Judges such as Gideon, Deborah, and Samson had been raised up but the difficulties continued.
      6. The glory of the Egypt of Joseph and Moses' day had dimmed.
      7. Assyria was a mighty power but had not troubled Israel.
   B. Social
      1. The Philistines had placed Israel in slavery.
      2. Poverty was a way of life.
      3. There was no lasting effort at unification.
   C. Religious
      1. They had been without religious instruction for a major part of three hundred years.
      2. They were surrounded by idols, heathen rites, and superstition.
      3. They lived among low moral standards and immorality.
      4. Eli's sons had brought about a loss of respect for the priesthood.
      5. One bright note was a number of young men who showed a burning interest in the true religion.

3. *The man, Samuel*
   A. He was an answer to a mother's prayer.
   B. He was promised to the Lord by his mother.
   C. He was trained under a Godly man.
   D. He was called unmistakably to God's work.
   E. He never knew the meaning of resignation.
   F. He continued to grow spiritually for a lifetime.
   G. Major points in his life. (1 Sam. 1-25.)
      1. His birth. (1:1-8.)
      2. His apprenticeship under Eli. (2:11-36.)
      3. His call by the Lord. (3:1-21.)
      4. His Nazarite vow. (1:11.)
         a. No intoxicating drinks. b. Self-denial. c. Separation from sensual indulgence. d. No haircut. e. Avoidance of dead bodies—See Numbers 6.
      5. The Philistines capture the Ark. (4:1-21.)
      6. The Ark among the Philistines. (5:1-12.)
      7. Israel reforms and is victorious. (7:1-12.)
      8. Israel demands a King. (8:1-22.)
      9. Saul is anointed by Samuel. (9:1-10:27.)
      10. King Saul defeats the Ammonites. (11:1-15.)
      11. Samuel chastises the people for wanting a king. (12:1-25.)
      12. Samuel chastises Saul for not destroying all of the Amalekites. (15:1-34.)
      13. Samuel anoints David. (16:1-23.)
      14. Samuel's death is lamented. (25:1.)
      15. Samuel appears to Saul at Endor. (28:11-20.)
4. *Practical lessons from the life of Samuel*
   A. One man can do wonders when he allows God to direct.
   B. A good mother is invaluable.
   C. One must be ready when God calls.
   D. One must freely move into action for God.
   E. As God's servant you may rejoice in preparing a younger man who will be more popular than yourself.
   F. There can be no compromise with evil.
   G. To obey is better than the offering of sacrifices.
   H. Rebellion and stubbornness are like idolatry. (15:22, 23.)
5. *It was Samuel who originated the school of the prophets.*
   A. Saul would see a band of prophets. (1 Sam. 10:5-13.)
   B. As a Nazarite there is a connection. (Amos 2:11, 12.)
   C. Samuel stands as their head. (1 Sam. 19:18-24.)
   D. We shall see more of the Sons of the Prophets in the life of Elijah as well as Elisha.

ELIJAH (ELIAS)
(My God Is Jehovah)

1. *The prophet Elijah is of great importance to the Jew.*
   A. An empty chair is placed for him at certain feasts.
   B. It was he who appeared with Moses and Christ. (Luke 9:28-30.)
   C. John was asked if he was Elias. (John 1.)
   D. Jesus said that John was the fulfilment of the prophecy that Elias would come. (Mal. 4:5, 6; Matt. 11:14.)

2. *The background for the prophecy of Elijah*
   A. Political
      1. There had been seven kings in 58 years since Solomon died.
         a. Jeroboam—an idolater. (1 Kings 12:28-32.) b. Nadab—Did evil. (1 Kings 15:26.) C. Baasha—Murdered Nadab. (15:27.) d. Elah—A drunkard. (16:8, 9.) e. Zimri—Committed treason. (16:20.) f. Omri—Wrought evil. (16:25.) g. Ahab—Did evil. (16:30, 31, 33.)
      2. Moab broke away from Israel and the Moabite stone was set up in commemoration.
      3. Ahab was putty in the hands of his wicked wife.
      4. Jehoshaphat ruled in Jerusalem (Southern Kingdom) while Elijah prophesied in the north.
   B. Social
      1. There was severe drought.
      2. The king lived in luxury at the expense of others.
      3. Jezebel had no qualms about confiscating property.
   C. Religious
      1. As far back as Solomon his wives had brought in idolatry.
      2. Ahab had now married Jezebel from Tyre of Phoenicia where Baal was worshipped.
      3. The people were turning to the worship of Baal in an adoration of *power*.
      4. The priests and prophets of Baal were numerous and Jehovah's prophets were persecuted.
      5. There was corruption of the leaders and the morality of the people required God to introduce a prophet.

14

3. *The man, Elijah*
   A. He has no more history than Melchizedek. (1 Kings 17:1.)
      1. Gilead was a desolate area east of the Jordan.
      2. It tells us that he was a Tishbite.
   B. He immediately appears before Ahab.
      1. He speaks in the name of Jehovah.
      2. He announces a drought with neither dew nor rain.
   C. He is then sent to the brook Cherith. (17:2-6.)
      1. There he is to hide.
      2. There he is to be nourished by ravens.
   D. When the brook dries up God sends him to Zarephath. (17:9-24.)
      1. Meets a widow about to starve with her son.
      2. Implores her to feed the man of God before self.
      3. She does so and her food supply continues throughout the drought.
      4. The widow's son falls sick and dies.
      5. Elijah prays and revives the child.
   E. Elijah is commanded to return to Ahab. (18:1-18.)
      1. On the way he enounters Obadiah.
         a. Obadiah had been sent by Ahab to find grass. b. But Obadiah was not in favor with Ahab because he had protected prophets of Jehovah. c. Elijah instructs Obadiah to tell Ahab of his whereabouts. d. Obadiah fears for his life if Elijah is not there when he returns. e. He finally agrees and Ahab went to meet Elijah.
      2. It is interesting that Elijah did not go to Ahab.
   F. Elijah meets the prophets of Baal. (18:19-46.)
      1. Ahab asks, "Are you the one who troubles Israel?"
      2. Elijah is absolutely fearless in his answer. (Verse 18.)
      3. Elijah sends for the people and the prophets of Baal.
         a. If he fails it will be 100 percent. b. But God supports those he assigns duties.
      4. The sacrifices are made ready.
      5. Baal's prophets are given first chance to call for their God to help.
         a. They call for half a day. b. They leap about and cut themselves.
      6. Elijah suggests they holler louder, he might be asleep!
      7. Then he prepares his sacrifice.
         a. Twelve stones for the twelve tribes. b. Barrels of water soak the sacrifice three times.
      8. Elijah prays and fire consumes his sacrifice.

15

9. The prophets of Baal are killed.
10. Elijah prays again and rain comes upon the earth.
11. Ahab and Elijah both go to the house of Jezebel.
    a. Ahab to tell of the death of her prophets. b. Elijah at the hand of the Lord.

G. Elijah is forced to flee for his life.
1. Jezebel threatens to kill him.
2. He pleads for God to take his life for he is alone.
3. God provides food whose nourishment lasts forty days while he travels to Mount Horeb.
4. God speaks to him in a still small voice.
   a. He is not alone—there are seven thousand others. b. He is to anoint Jehu king. c. He is to anoint Elisha to be his successor.

H. Elijah returns to Ahab with another denunciation. (21:1-29.)
1. Ahab has coveted Naboth's vineyard.
2. Jezebel says, why worry about it—go take it.
3. Naboth is accused of blasphemy and stoned.
4. Elijah pronounces a terrible curse upon Ahab and Jezebel.
5. Ahab repents but Jezebel dies as Elijah predicted.

I. Elijah rebukes Ahaziah for turning to Baal-zebub. (2 Kings 1.)
1. Ahab had died and been replaced by Ahaziah.
2. Ahaziah became sick and sent for Baal-zebub instead of Jehovah.
3. The messengers of Ahaziah are killed twice before the third captain pleads for his life from the man of God.
4. Ahaziah dies just as Elijah predicts he would.

J. Elijah is taken up in a chariot of fire. (2 Kings 2:1-2:13.)
1. God sends Elijah to Bethel and Elisha follows.
2. The Sons of the prophets ask Elisha if he knows Elijah will be taken away that day.
3. They are told not to worry, Elisha knows.
4. They move to Jericho and the question and answer are repeated.
5. They come to the Jordan and Elijah parts the waters.
6. When Elijah offers a favor Elisha asks for a double portion of Elijah's power.
7. A chariot and horses of fire appear and Elijah is taken up into heaven by a whirlwind.
8. Elisha catches the mantle which fell from Elijah, and he grieves and tears his clothes.

16

4. *Lessons from the life and teachings of Elijah*
   A. There is but one God and he is Jehovah.
   B. God's enemies are to be completely vanquished.
   C. There is satisfaction in training a successor.
   D. Prayer is the key to tremendous powers.
   E. A god of power and greed is a false god.
   F. No man of God ever stands completely alone.
   G. Sometimes God restores our confidence with new tasks.
   H. Communion with God can provide nourishment unknown to others.
   I. Caves and juniper bushes are alright for a momentary rest but the man of God must face the people.

ELISHA
(God Is Saviour)
(2 Kings 2-13)

1. *The background for the prophecy of Elisha*
   A. Political
      1. Much the same as that of Elijah.
      2. The Syrians sometimes attacked cities of Israel.
      3. Moab Jehoram, son of Ahab, reigns in Israel.
      4. Jehoshaphat reigns in Judah.
      5. Moab is in a state of rebellion against Jehoram.
   B. Social
      1. Famine is present.
      2. Conflict and turmoil leave a confused people.
   C. Religious
      1. Baal worship must still be fought.
      2. The Sons of the Prophets are mentioned often.

2. *The man, Elisha*
   A. Prophesied through the reign of four kings. Jehoram, Jehu, Jehoahaz and Joash. (Perhaps 50 years.)
   B. Was bald-headed and wore the mantle of Elijah.
   C. As compared with Elijah.
      1. Elijah denounced—Elisha taught.
      2. Elijah retreated to the wilderness—Elisha had a chamber built for him.
      3. Elijah was more solitary—Elisha was social.
      4. Yet both performed some similar miracles.
   D. The transfer of power from Elijah to Elisha
      1. Elijah find Elisha plowing with oxen. (1 Kings 19:16-20.)
      2. His mantle is thrown over Elisha and Elisha severs all ties and follows Elijah.
      3. Elisha associates with the Sons of the Prophets.
      4. When Elijah is taken up Elisha possesses his mantle.
      5. He receives a double portion of Elijah's spirit. (2 Kings 2.)
   E. Elisha's advice sought in battle with the Moabites. (2 Kings 3.)

18

1. After Ahab's death Mesha, King of Moab, rebelled.
2. Elisha is called for but says he will only help because of the king of Judah, not the king of Israel.
3. A minstrel plays and the hand of the Lord comes upon Elisha.
4. Moab is delivered into the hands of Israel.

F. Two boys are saved from slavery. (2 Kings 4:1-7.)
1. One of the Sons of the Prophets' wives is about to sell her sons because of poverty.
2. Eisha provides oil which the widow can sell.

G. The Shunammites' son (2 Kings 4:8-37.)
1. Elisha makes friends with a rich family of Shunem.
2. A room is built for h'm when he passes that way.
3. The woman has been barren and Elisha promises a son.
4. The boy goes to the field after his father, becomes ill and is laid on Elisha's bed.
5. Elisha first sent his servant in response to the family's call.
6. Later he went himself, prayed, administered aid and the child who was dead became alive again.

H. Death in the pot
1. There was a famine in the land.
2. Elisha commanded to gather herbs for the Sons of the Prophets to eat.
3. Poisonous materials are found in the pot after it has been cooking.
4. Elisha asked for some meal which he threw into the pot rendering the food safe to eat.
5. While with the Sons of the Prophets someone brings food to Elisha.
6. He commands that it be given to the Sons.
7. When told that there is not enough for a hundred he says, "Give it to them, and there will be some left over."—There is.

I. Naaman the leper is cleansed. (2 Kings 5:1-19.)
1. A small maid of Israel is captured by the Syrians.
2. The captain of the Syrian army in whose home she served becomes leprous.
3. In sympathy the maid suggests that the captain, Naaman, go to consult Elisha in Israel.
4. Elisha's instructions to Naaman are to dip in the Jordan River.
5. Naaman hesitates, but when he obeys he is cleansed.
6. Naaman offers gifts which Elisha rejects.

7. Gehazi, a servant, lies to Naaman and takes the gifts.
8. Elisha causes the leprosy to afflict Gehazi.

J. An axe head floats.
1. The Sons of the Prophets begin building homes by the river.
2. A borrowed axe head comes off and falls into the river.
3. Elisha causes the axe head to float on the water.

K. An invisible army.
1. The Syrians attack Israel but fail.
2. The king of Syria believes that there is a spy.
3. He is told that Elisha can read his thoughts and inform the king of Israel.
4. He gathers a great host and prepares to take Elisha.
5. When Elisha's servant becomes worried Elisha opens his eyes to a mountain covered with horses and chariots of fire.

L. Samaria is besieged.
1. Ben-hadad, King of Syria besieges Samaria.
2. The famine becomes so great that women eat children.
3. Jehoram the King of Israel blames Elisha.
4. Elisha promises food by the next day.
5. By the intervention of God the Syrian army became afraid and fled leaving the food behind.

M. Graveyard inspiration.
1. Elisha died and was buried.
2. The Moabites invade and cast a man into Elisha's open grave.
3. When he touched the bones of Elisha he revived and stood upon his feet.

3. *Lessons from the life and teachings of Elisha.*
   A. The rich may also have sympathy with God's cause.
   B. God provides nourishment which never fails.
   C. When God's men nourish themselves the food must be pure.
   D. God's instructions must be followed to the letter.
   E. There are spiritual armies at the side of the faithful.

OBADIAH
(Servant of Jehovah)

1. *The background for the prophecy of Obadiah*
   A. Obadiah (21 verses) is the shortest book in the Old Testament.
   B. The book is a reaction to an invasion of Jerusalem.
   C. The theme is a condemnation of Edom for her part in the plunder.
   D. This is just one of the evidences of the malice felt between Israel and Edom.
      1. It began with the matter of the birthright. (Gen. 25:30-34.)
      2. Although Jacob and Esau reconciled their descendants experienced strife.
         a. Saul fought Edom. (1 Sam. 14:47.) b. David subjected Edom. (2 Sam. 8:13, 14.) c. Edom rebels again. (1 Kings 11:14-22.) d. Freedom achieved under Jehoram in 845 B.C. (2 Kings 8:20-22.)

2. *The date of the incidents recorded in the book*
   A. There is great difficulty in deciding between two dates.
      1. 587 B.C.
      2. 845 B.C.
   B. The evidence seems stronger for the 845 B.C. date.
      1. There were several invasions of Jerusalem.
         a. Invasion by Shishak of Egypt. 926 B.C. (1 Kings 14:25, 26.) But Edom was subject to the Hebrews at that time. b. The Philistines and Arabs invaded in 848-844 B.C. (2 Chron. 21:16) during Jehoram's reign. c. Jehoash invaded it in the days of Amaziah. 780 B.C. But these invaders are "strangers." (Verse 11.) d. Nebuchadnezzar destroyed it in 586 B.C.
      2. The two invasions which may be considered are those in 845 B.C., and in 587 B.C.
      3. Other prophets referring to Nebuchadnezzar's invasion call the Chaldeans and even Nebuchadnezzar by name but Obadiah does not.

4. In describing this invasion Obadiah does not mention:
   a. The razing of the walls. b. The burning of the palace.
   c. The burning of the temple. d. The deportation of
   the King. e. Movement of the entire nation.
5. But these things are all mentioned in the 586 B.C. invasion.
   (2 Kings 25.)

C. Jeremiah writes before 586 B.C. and the two books contain
   material in common. See Jeremiah 49:7-22.
D. Thus we believe this invasion to be that by the Philistines and
   Arabs in 848-844 B.C.

3. *The man, Obadiah*
   A. There are numerous Obadiahs mentioned in the Old Testa-
      ment.
      1. 1 Kings 18:3—Officer in the house of Ahab.
      2. 2 Chronicles 17:7—A prince to teach the law in Judah.
      3. 2 Chronicles 34:12—An overseer in the repair of the tem-
         ple.
      4. Nehemiah 10:5—A priest in the time of Nehemiah.
   B. Obadiah was sensitive enough to be hurt by the lack of broth-
      erly love manifested by Edom.
   C. He was fearless enough to denounce these neighbors who had
      at times held the territory where he lived.
   D. He was confident that "The kingdom shall be Jehovah's."

4. *A brief outline of the book of Obadiah*
   A. Edom is to be destroyed.
      1. The nations are called for this purpose.
      2. There is no possibility of escape.
      3. Her destroyers will carry away her treasures.
      4. Her present allies will turn against her.
      5. Her wise and mighty men will be useless.
   B. The reasons for Edom's destruction are:
      1. The violence done to Jacob.
      2. The neglect of Edom to help.
      3. The glee over Jacob's plunder.
      4. The sharing of the spoils by Edom.
      5. The selling of Jacob's people as slaves.
      6. Edom's haughty and self-sufficient attitude.
   C. A day of the Lord will come.
      1. All nations shall be judged.
      2. Jacob will be restored and God's Kingdom exalted.

5. *Notes on the text of Obadiah*
   1—Obadiah has seen a vision from *God*.
   He will tell the meaning.
   A messenger is to call the heathen against Edom.
   2—Here is the burden of Edom.
   Everyone will despise her.
   Other prophets speaking of judgment upon Edom are: Isaiah
   34:5; Ezekiel 25:12-14; Amos 1:11, 12; Jeremiah 49:7.
   3—Edom's pride-filled heart is the prime reason.
   They have trusted in their natural defenses.
   Though living in the plains they could retreat to rocky cliff
   fortresses such as Petra.
   Eisenhower's motto was "Power for peace." (Not enough.)
   America is in danger today because of our sin and pride.
   4—One cannot flee to the highest cliffs as the eagle and escape
   from God.
   It is more dangerous to fall from high places.
   Who shall bring me down? "If among the very stars *I* will
   bring thee down."
   5—Even thieves in the night leave a little.
   Even the laborers in the harvest field leave gleanings.
   6—Edom depends upon her riches.
   But even the hidden riches shall be all taken.
   Edom, Babylon and Rome all fell.
   May we depend upon the stronghold of wealth in the U.S.?
   7—Edom will not be able to depend upon her allies either.
   Those whom she encouraged to plunder Israel will now turn
   upon her own borders.
   The bread, or foreign aid Edom offered them was eaten
   while plans were laid for thievery.
   8—Wisdom and understanding will not deliver Edom.
   Colleges without God are creators of Frankensteins.
   The wisdom of men is foolishness before God.
   9—Military might will be confused.
   Note Psalm 20:7 "Some trust in chariots and some in horses,
   but we will remember the name of the Lord, our God."
   Christianity is the common man's religion.
   "Not many mighty, not many noble are saved."
   10—There is a sin of neutrality.
   There is such a thing as meddling.
   (Be careful about interfering in matrimonial quarrels.)

On the other hand sometimes interference with Scriptural teaching is called for.

When the Church is attacked, do you defend?

Some believe this passage teaches physical defense should be exerted against an attacker of those we love.

Edom is as guilty as the strangers for the violence done to Israel.

She shall be destroyed completely.

This prophecy was fulfilled when Edom suffered the same fate as Israel at the hands of Nebuchadnezzar, yet Israel remained identifiable—Edom did not.

11—Edom is counted as one of the thieving strangers since she bid them Godspeed.

12—Three should nots.
    Should not have looked on.
    Should not have rejoiced.
    Should not have spoken proudly.

13—Three more should nots.
    Should not have taken their goods.
    Should not have gone into their city.
    Should not have enjoyed their calamity.

14—Two more should nots.
    Should not have blocked Israel's escape.
    Should not have turned the stragglers to invaders.

15—The day of the Lord is a time of final destruction upon all evil nations.
    Whatsoever a man soweth, that shall he also reap.
    But every farmer knows that more is harvested than is sown.
    —Give unto her double. (Rev. 18:6.)
    Neither is it wise to sow wild oats and expect a crop failure!

16—The drunkenness is over the disaster which has befallen Israel.
    They drink to their own destruction. They shall be as though they had never existed.

17—While Mount Seir of Edom is due for destruction Mount Zion which is God's mountain shall be restored.
    The coin will soon be turned over. The last shall then be first.

18—Fire consumes stubble.
    The process is very rapid.
    Nothing shall remain of Edom when consumed by the flame of Jacob and Joseph.

24

19—No invader will remain in Israel, but Israel will possess Edom to the South, Ephraim to the north, the Philistines to the west, and Gilead to the east.

20—Those taken captive from Israel shall be released and these released shall captivate their captors.

No one is sure about the place called Sepharad.

21—This bringing of Saviours to Judah with the conquest over Edom has a Messianic fulfilment.

Numbers 24:15-19 refers to Christ as morning star. (Rev. 22:16.)

The remnant of Edom mentioned in Amos 9:11, 12 is conquered through Gentiles becoming Christians as shown in James' reference to it in Acts 15:15-17.

6. *Vital lessons from the book of Obadiah*
   A. There are no defenses against the wrath of God.
   B. Pride goeth before destruction.
   C. To gloat over the misfortune of another is sinful.
   D. Through Christ God's Kingdom will be triumphant.

JOEL
(Jehovah Is God)

1. *Background for the prophecy of Joel*
   A. The enemies of Israel are Philistines, Phoenicians, Egyptians and Edomites.
   B. The boy king is probably still growing up.
   C. Hazael is then king of Syria and is beginning to make trouble for Israel.
   D. Shalmaneser III of Assyria is advancing in a drive to conquer the west.
   E. There is a terrible plague of locusts.
   F. Famine, drought and poverty abound.

2. *The date of the book of Joel*
   A. There is no mention made of Assyrians, Babylonians, or even kings of Judah.
   B. It is placed by the Hebrews with the early prophets.
   C. Amos seems to quote from Joel. Compare Joel 3:16 with Amos 1:2.
      1. We could presume that the quote went the other way except that Amos appears to have used Joel as a text to expand upon.
      2. This is not unusual among the prophets.
   D. In dating Joel several conditions must be met.
      1. The temple stands.
      2. The city walls are intact.
      3. There is no idolatry.
      4. There is no king to mention.
   E. Liberals say this did not exist until after the exile.
   F. But these conditions did exist in the time of the minority of Joash.
   G. One evidence for a later date is some language in the book which seems to be of later date.
   H. The majority of evidence seems to point to about 830 B.C.

3. *The man, Joel*
   A. He is a son of Pethuel.

26

B. He shows a good knowledge of the temple and its worship.

C. He knew full well how to take advantage of the occasion to preach repentance to the people.

D. His language is bold and picturesque.

4. *The nature of the book*

   A. The book contains 73 verses.

   B. The book begins in gloom and ends in joy and gladness.

   C. There are a number of connections with other books.
   Joel 1:15—Isaiah 13:16.
   Joel 2:2—Zephaniah 1:15.
   Joel 2:3—Isaiah 51:3; Ezekiel 36:35.
   Joel 2:10—Isaiah 13:10.
   Joel 2:32—Obadiah 17.
   Joel 3:10—Isaiah 2:4; Micah 4:3.
   Joel 3:16—Amos 1:2; Isaiah 13:13.
   Joel 3:17—Ezekiel 36:11; Isaiah 52:1.
   Joel 3:18—Amos 9:13.
   Joel 2:28-32—Acts 2:17-21; Numbers 11:29.

   D. There are shadows of Revelation in Joel.
   Joel 2:31—Revelation 6:12. Moon turned to blood.
   Joel 3:13—Revelation 14:17. Judgment as a harvest.
   Joel 3:13—Revelation 14:20; 19:15. The winepress.
   Joel 2:1-11—Revelation 9:3-11. The locusts.

   F. The central theme is the "Day of Jehovah."

5. *Outline of the book*

   A. Devastation of the land of Judah.

   B. A call to repentance.

   C. Blessing promised to Israel.

   D. Judgment pronounced upon the nations.

   E. A final spiritual glory described.

6. *Comments upon the text*

   Chapter 1

   1:1—Not the word of Joel, but that of God.

   1:2—Nothing like this has been known by present men.

   1:3—From the grandfathers to the grandchildren it stands as a horror.

   1:4—The plague of the locusts leaves nothing in its path. These may be stages of the metamorphosis of the locust. Deuteronomy 28:38 had foretold of locust curses for disobedience.

27

But this plague is not the worst, it is only a forewarning of the "Day of Jehovah."

1:5—The sleepy drunks will wake up to find no wine.
The locusts have cut off the supply.

1:6—Most scholars agree that this is a nation of locusts and is not humans.
Proverbs 30:35, "The ants are a people, not strong."
Proverbs 30:27, "The locusts have no king."
Have you ever tried to count jumping grasshoppers?

1:7—Joel speaks of what he sees around him.
Then he tells them, "There are *bad days* ahead!"

1:8—There is little more sorrowful than a young bride or engaged woman who loses her husband.

1:9—Now the priests add their lamentation to the drunkards and the virgins.
The sacrifices are cut off with no meat or drink offering to offer.

1:10—The wine, the oil and the wheat now join the barked fig tree.

1:13—This desolation requires action in the form of repentance.

1:14—They are already fasting by necessity.
Now they are to sanctify the fast and gather for a cry of repentance to God.
Could Peter have been familiar with this passage as he told the Jews at Pentecost to "Repent and be baptized . . .?"

1:15—The Day of the Lord is a day of destruction.

1:16—Nothing will grow.
The barns fall down from disuse.

1:18—The flocks and herds are starving to death.

1:19—It is likely that fire has broken out after the vegetation has become dry and dead.

1:20—All creation seems to groan.
Compare Romans 8:22

Chapter 2

2:1—Trumpets sound for different reasons.
This trumpet sounds a warning.
Something *worse* is coming.

2:2—The Day of Jehovah will see
Darkness and Clouds. An invading horde will spread over the land like the dawn spreads over the mountains.

2:3—The land will turn from an Eden to a wilderness.

2:4—This still seems to describe the locusts.

28

They are not people since they are said to be *like* people.

2:9—There is no more way to avoid the Day of Jehovah than there is to avoid the hardes of locusts.

2:10—The effects here could be caused by the swarms of locusts.

2:11—This is the Lord's army formed for the purpose of executing his Word.

This is like telling a man with a migraine headache that one of these days he is liable to have a real bad headache.

2:12—There is still hope but it will require complete change of heart.

2:13—Outward rending of garments will not be enough.

When men truly repent God also repents of the wrath they could suffer.

2:14—Repentance could actually restore the offering and fellowship which had been taken away because of their sin.

2:15—Now another trumpet sounds but this time to call assembly rather than give alarm.

2:16—Even the ones who would normally be excused are to be included.

2:17—Indication that the priests are weeping before God because there is nothing to offer on the altar.

See 2 Chronicles 8:12.

2:18—Repentance is implied between verses 17 and 18.

The Lord has changed because they have changed.

2:19—The material blessings now begin to flow.

The corn and oil is restored.

The reproach is taken away.

2:20—The locusts will be driven out to the Dead Sea and the Mediterranean.

2:23—A call comes to rejoice.

Gratitude is to be expressed to God.

2:25—When God's army has brought about repentance the damage done will be undone.

2:26—Praise to God means a happy and unashamed population.

2:28—This is the first undoubted prophecy of the Messiah.

Peter quotes it nearly in full. (Acts 2.)

This verse is the beginning of Chapter 3 in the Hebrew Bible.

The categories here simply mean that God will now

not restrict the outpouring of his Spirit to specific times and places but will distribute it to both Jew and Gentile, bond and free, young and old.

Material blessings had already been described.

Now spiritual blessings are outlined.

2:30—Compare Luke 21:25 signs in the sun, moon and stars.

Compare Mark 13:24, 25 signs in the sun, moon and stars.

Compare Matthew 24:29 signs in the sun, moon and stars.

The destruction of Jerusalem seems to be a sort of end of the world for the Jewish nation.

This destruction of Jerusalem may also be a type of the final end when time shall be no more. See also Revelation 6:12.

2:32—The Day of Jehovah need bring no terror to the heart of the remnant who call upon the name of Jehovah. (God's remnant is an interesting topic.)

Chapter 3

3:1—Those days are the days of the spiritual outpouring.

Judah shall escape from captivity.

3:2—Jehoshaphat means Jehovah's judgment.

God's chosen will be released from their despised position.

3:3—God's chosen have been treated as property to be bartered for almost nothing.

3:4—The Phoenicians of Tyre and Sidon were known as slave traders.

3:5—The miseries which have been visited upon God's chosen will be returned upon the heads of the persecutors.

3:9—God challenges those who would oppress his people to prepare for confrontation with his forces.

3:10—They are to mobilize every effort toward fighting against him.

Compare the reverse of this in Isaiah 2:4; Micah 4:3.

3:11—The mighty ones here may well mean angels.

Recall that God speaks of war in heaven and conflict between Michael and his angels with the Devil and his angels. (Rev. 12:7.)

Notice also the similarity between this whole confrontation and that of Revelation 19 and 20.

3:12—God will be the judge in the valley of decision.

Does your picture of Christ include this part?
If not—enlarge it! Sword—Rod—Winepress.
3:13—God is ready for the harvest.
Compare with Revelation 14:15-20.
See Isaiah 26:9—"When thy judgments are upon the
earth—then men learn righteousness."
3:14—Vast numbers will feel the consuming vengeance of God
Almighty as they oppose him in the valley of decision.
3:15—The brightness of the Jewish nation shall be dimmed—
The ruling powers will be replaced.
3:16—The old dominion and its territory will become a new
heaven and a new earth. The new ruler is the Christ
and refuge will be found for his people.
Compare this passage with Hebrews 12.
A remnant is preserved.
3:17—New Jerusalem come down from God out of heaven.
No one can break into the present city of God. (Rev.
21:27.)
3:18—A day of gladness, blessing and joy for those once bowed
down under their enemies.
3:19—Those who were once enemies shall be no more. He
does not mention the Assyrians and Babylonians here.
Violence against God's people is not wise.
3:20—The promised land and the Holy City shall abide forever.
3:21—Their sins will be forgiven.
"I shall dwell with them, and I will be their God, and
they shall be my people." (Rev. 21:3.)

WE ARE TALKING ABOUT THE CHURCH!!

A FEW REMARKS ABOUT ZION

Zion comes into history as a Jebusite stronghold. (2 Sam. 5:6.)
It changes from a Jebusite stronghold to the City of David. (2
Chron. 11:4.)
It is now the place of the ark indicating God's presence. (2 Sam.
6:12.)
It is a combination of the City of David and the place of the Ark.
(1 Kings 8:1.)
Jehovah is against the *nations* from Zion.
It is a holy hill from which the *Son* judges. (Psa. 2.)
The City of our God—his holy mountain. (Psa. 48.)
Jehovah's holy habitation. (Psa. 132:13, 14.)
Sit at my right hand. A rod of iron out of Zion.

31

Dashed in pieces.

How big is your picture of Jesus? (Psa. 110.)

The rod of uprighteousness is used to judge. (Heb. 1:8, 9.)

Out of Zion comes judgment, but out of Zion also comes the law.
—All nations flow into Zion.

Clearly the rod of uprighteousness is the Word of the Lord.

Peace will abide in Zion. (Isa. 2.)

Escape will be found in Zion. (Obad. 17.)

Parallels the above scripture. (Joel 2:32.)

No physical mountain no—But:

> Heavenly Jerusalem.
> Mount Zion.
> City of God.
> Angels.
> Church of the firstborn.
> Spirits of just men. (Heb. 12:18-21.)

Israel cast out to be replaced by those coming from the east and the west in the Church. (Matt. 8:10-12.)

The Lamb is on Mount Zion with 144,000.

They are the *purchased*.

They are without *blemish*.

These are the Church on earth.

Revelation 7:1-8 tells that they are *sealed*. (Rev. 14:1-5.)

See the following verses for those sealed.

> Ephesians 1:13, 14; 2 Corinthians 1; Ephesians 4:30; 2 Timothy 2:19.

See the following verses for the purchased.

> 1 Peter 1:18, 19; Revelation 5:9, 10.

See the following verses for the spotless.

> Ephesians 5:32; 2 Corinthians 11:3; Colossians 1:22.

The Church follows the lamb wherever he goes.

> John 21:22.

The Church is the firstfruits unto God.

> 1 Peter 1:23; Hebrews 12:23: James 1:18.

God lives with his whole family in heaven and on earth.

> Ephesians 1:10; Ephesians 3:15.

> *And thus the Prophecies of Zion are fulfilled*
> *in the Church of Christ.*

A FEW REMARKS ON "THE DAY OF THE LORD"

1. *The Day of the Lord is known by a variety of titles.*

    A. Day of visitation, 1 Peter 2:12.

    B. Day of redemption, Ephesians 4:30.

C. Day of salvation, 2 Corinthians 6:2.

D. Day of wrath, Ezekiel 7:19.

E. Day of judgment, Matthew 10:15.

2. *It is a day of cosmic upheaval.*

A. A day of darkness, Joel 2:30.

B. The moon turns to blood, Joel 2:31.

C. The sea and the waves roar, Luke 21:25.

D. The powers of heaven shake, Luke 21:26.

3. *It is a day of victory for God in battle.*

A. He will send a great army, Joel 2:1-22.

B. The wicked shall be defeated, Isaiah 13:1-22.

C. God will be magnified, Ezekiel 38:19-23.

D. He shall be King of all, Zechariah 14:1-9.

4. *It will be a day of terror for the unbelievers.*

A. Jesus shall appear taking vengeance, 1 Thessalonians 1:8.

B. The flesh of kings shall be eaten, Revelation 19:18.

C. There shall be no place to hide, Revelation 6:15-17.

5. *It is a day of joy to the believers.*

A. The dead shall be raised, 1 Thessalonians 4:16.

B. The Lord shall claim his own, 1 Thessalonians 4:17.

C. The righteous shall be rewarded, Matthew 16:27.

6. *There are several days of the Lord.*

A. Individual nations of heathens meet their day of doom, Obadiah 15.

B. The Jewish nation is destroyed in A.D. 70, Matthew 24.

C. The end of time when Christ appears in final judgment, Romans 2:16.

ALL THE LESSER DAYS LEAD TO THE
ONE GREAT JUDGMENT DAY!!

7. *Practical lessons from the book of Joel.*

A. People in trouble sometimes listen to the Lord better.

B. There is no escape from judgment.

C. Judgment may be either joy or terror as you choose.

D. Genuine repentance may be followed by restored blessings.

E. God's Spirit is to be available to all men.

JONAH
(Dove)

1. *Background for the prophecy of Jonah*
   A. Two powerful kings ruled in Palestine.
      1. Jonah prophesied to Jeroboam II in Israel. (2 Kings 14:25.)
      2. Uzziah ruled in Judah at the same time.
   B. The Jews had reached a period of ascendency.
      1. Israel had pushed her enemies back in the north.
      2. Judah had pushed her enemies back in the south.
   C. There was only one dark cloud on the horizon.
      1. Assyria was beginning to oppress the surrounding nations.
      2. The wicked capital called Nineveh had become known afar.
   D. The Jews were characterized by:
      1. Luxurious living.
      2. Narrow nationalistic views.

2. *The man, Jonah*
   A. From Gath-Hepher in Galilee near Nazareth.
   B. The son of Amittai.
   C. A preacher of good news for Israel.
   D. Effective in delivering his message.
   E. A very unwilling missionary.
   F. One who thought God was mistaken at times.
   G. A contemporary of Amos, Hosea, Isaiah and Micah.
   H. Jonah's reluctance to preach to Nineveh is understandable.
      1. God had restricted Israel from social connections with other nations.
      2. Assyria had proven herself to be a tyrannical people.

3. *The book of Jonah*
   A. The book is about Jonah rather than by Jonah.
   B. The material is mostly biographical with little preaching.
   C. Yet the lessons are very important.
   D. Main theme—God is not willing that any should perish.
   E. There have been two tragic interpretational methods.

    1. Jonah should not be considered a myth.
    2. Nor should it be considered a parable.
F. The book of Jonah is historical fact.
    1. It presents itself in this manner.
    2. The Jews such as Josephus believed it so.
    3. Jonah is recorded as a real man. (2 Kings 14:25.)
    4. Christ considered these matters as history. (Matt. 12:38-41; Luke 11:29-32.)
G. Jonah provides a preview of two New Testament incidents.
    1. Peter's hesitation in going to the Gentiles.
    2. The elder brother's attitude toward the penitent prodigal son.
H. The date of the book is during the reign of Jeroboam II and thus about 800 B.C.
I. Outline of the book.
    1. Jonah runs away from God—Disobedience.
    2. Jonah runs to God—Repentance.
    3. Jonah runs with God—Obedience.
    4. Jonah runs ahead of God—Complaint.

4. *Comments upon the text of Jonah*
Chapter 1
    1:1—Not Jonah's word—God's Word.
    1:2—Nineveh may have been as large as 600,000.
        See Jonah 3:3 and 4:11.
        Nahum spoke of Nineveh wickedness. (Nah. 2:8.)
        Capital of the Assyrian empire.
        Two hundred fifty miles north of Babylon.
        Very old. (Gen. 10:10.)
      A city which Jonah despised.
    1:3—Many think Tarshish was a city in Spain as far away as Jonah could get.
        Jonah paid the fare—but he did not know how much the trip would really cost.
        It is not possible to escape from the Lord. (Psa. 139.)
    1:4—This is the first of several things the Lord prepared.
        This was not just a normal Mediterranean storm.
    1:5—When professional sailors fear and pray it is bad.
        Interesting that these sailors backed their prayer with action.
        Jonah may have been exhausted from the emotional strain.
    1:6—Should a man of God sleep while heathen pray?

1:7—In Old Testament times God sometimes directed casting of lots. (Prov. 17:33.)

Matthias was chosen to replace Judas in this manner.

1:9—Jonah was one preacher who admitted, (I am the problem.)

Did he really fear the Lord as he said?

1:14—By this time the sailors are praying to Jonah's God.

1:15—Was the calming of the storm an answer to sinners' prayers?

1:16—By this time the sailors are offering sacrifices of gratitude.

With the aid of the Lord Jonah had converted a boatload of sailors.

1:17—Here is the second thing the Lord prepared.

The word used here could be translated appointed.

Some see a difference between an act of God and a miracle.

The blowing of the wind is considered an act of God.

Jonah's preservation in the fish's belly a miracle.

The same God who created man to breathe oxygen could certainly sustain his life without it.

Chapter 2

2:1—Now Jonah is grateful and penitent.

The next few verses are his prayer.

2:2—Out of the hidden depths. (Sheol)

2:4—The temple was standing at this time.

2:5-10—Jonah is not the first man who turned to God in response to chastisement.

However, there are those who will curse God to the end.

There may have been time for word of this event
To reach Nineveh before Jonah got there!!

Chapter 3

3:1—Jonah was fortunate to receive another opportunity.

3:2—The recipe for successful preaching—"Preach the preaching that God bids thee."

3:3—Some say Nineveh was about 54 to 60 miles around the wall.

Three days' journey could have been the amount of time it would normally have taken for Jonah to have preached to the entire city.

3:4—The city repents before Jonah can get the job half done.

What a strange sermon!

No long argument.

No miracle—unless the "sign of Jonah" had preceded.
And from an unwilling heart.
An unenthusiastic heart often produces brief sermons.

3:5—*Everyone* repents

3:6-8—From the king to the lowly beasts they are covered with sack cloth.

3:9—God does not repent of sin, but does change his course of action when we change ours.

Jonah really got results—first a boat full of sailors, and now an entire city.

Preachers today would call this "visible results."

Chapter 4

4:1—Not many preachers would be angry if even one third of their audience responded.

But Jonah was afraid from the beginning that this would happen.

He just figured God might not destroy Nineveh in less than forty days when Jonah had prophesied such a destruction.

4:3—Jonah wishes he could die for the very opposite reason that some men of God have desired this.

4:5—Jonah sets up the east side anti-Nineveh building.

4:6—Now God prepares the third thing—a gourd plant to shade Jonah from the sun in his grief.

And Jonah is proud and grateful for his gourd plant.

4:7—Now God prepares the fourth thing—a worm.

It cuts down Jonah's gourd plant and Jonah wants to die again.

4:8—God prepares the fifth thing—a vehement east wind.

It is more than Jonah can take.

4:9—Jonah now runs ahead of God. "I do well to be angry."

4:10-11—God informs Jonah that he has a strange set of values.

He mourns and grieves over a gourd plant which has only been around a brief time.

But he is angry that 120,000 innocent children in Nineveh have been saved from God's punishment.

5. *Practical lessons from the book of Jonah*

A. God can turn men's mistakes into good influence. (Jonah's influence on the sailors.)

B. It is futile to resist God's will.

C. God seeks the salvation of all men of every nation.

D. People are more important than gourd trees.

E. God has his own methods of working behind the scenes.

37

AMOS
(Burden Bearer)

1. *Background for the book of Amos*
   A. Political background.
      1. The king of Syria had kept Israel in subjection for awhile.
      2. Then Assyria had conquered Syria, thus giving Israel a degree of freedom which lasted until Tiglath-Pileser began his rule of Assyria.
      3. Israel had peace from 805-740 B.C.
      4. Jeroboam began to reign in 783 B.C.
      5. Jeroboam restored the borders to what they were in the days of David and Solomon.
      6. Uzziah did likewise in the land of Judah.
   B. Social background.
      1. Prosperity.
      2. Injustice.
      3. Ease and luxury.
      4. Greed.
   C. Religious background.
      1. Abundant religious rites but little righteousness.
      2. Idolatry at Dan, Beersheeba, Gilgal and Bethel.
      3. Feasting and revelry.
      4. Bribery and contempt for holy things.
      5. Moral decay.

2. *The man, Amos*
   A. A herdsman from Tekoa six miles from Bethlehem.
   B. A man of the outdoors who had learned first hand about:
      1. The roar of the lion.
      2. The ears left in a trap.
      3. Orion and the Pleides.
      4. Horses running on rocks.
      5. Separation of wheat and chaff.
      6. A theology far higher than that in the king's chapel.
   C. A man who prophesied at the command of God, and not trained in the schools of the prophets.

D. One who was probably young while Jonah was old.

E. Amos undoubtedly provided inspiration for Isaiah and Micah, also contemporary with Hosea.

F. The "Golden Age" of prophecy.

3. *The nature of the book of Amos*
   A. Nine chapters
   B. Theme—D-O-O-M for Israel
   C. Some suggest the book to be a complete sermon.
   D. Date—About 755 B.C. in the overlapping of Jeroboam and Uzziah.

4. *Outline of the book*
   A. Punishment for nations bordering Israel.
      1. The heathen nations.
      2. Judah.
   B. Punishment for Israel.
   C. Reasons for the punishment.
   D. Overthrow and a "Day of Jehovah."
   E. Five visions related to Israel's judgment.
   F. The Messianic promise.

5. *Comments on the text of Amos*
   Chapter 1
   1:1—The date is in the days of Uzziah and Jeroboam II, two years before the earthquake. (Zech. 14:5.)
   1:2—This is the Lord speaking.
   1:3-5—*Damascus* is to be judged for cruelty in war.
   The bar of the city will be broken for entry.
   The people of Syria will be taken captive.
   1:6-8—*Gaza* is to be judged for slave traffic.
   God's turning away is for repeated transgressions, not for just three or four.
   Even the remnant of the Philistines will perish.
   1:9-10—*Tyre* shall be judged for not remembering the brotherly covenant. (Perhaps 1 Kings 5:12.)
   Devouring fire shall be sent upon the Phoenicians.
   1:11-12—*Edom* will be judged for stubborn hatred of his brother.
   Devouring fire shall be sent upon the rulers.
   1:13-15—*Ammon* will be judged for cruelty in war.
   Fire and tempest will be sent and the king and his princes will be taken captive.

Chapter 2

2:1-3—*Moab* shall be judged for lack of respect for a dead king.

Devouring fire shall be sent in the midst of tumult and confusion.

2:4-5—*Judah* shall be judged for their religious corruption.

2:6-8—Judah will be followed by judgment of *Israel.*

Israel has oppressed the poor.

Through fleshly lusts it has profaned the name of Jehovah.

They have sought satisfaction in other gods.

2:9-11—God had done much for Israel.

He had destroyed the Amorites before them.

He had brought them out from the land of Egypt.

He had raised up speakers of the truth.

2:12—Israel's reaction had been to corrupt and stifle God's messengers.

2:13-16—The day of the Lord shall come upon them.

They shall be pressed down like soil under a loaded cart.

No one shall be swift enough or strong enough to escape.

Even the most courageous shall be ashamed and fearful.

Chapter 3

3:1-3—Israel has been favored above all the earth.

To whom much is given much will be required.

God finds it necessary to punish them.

He can no longer walk with them in their sin.

3:4-6—Israel is helpless before her punishment.

Israel is like the prey of a lion.

Israel is like a bird in a snare.

Israel is like a city in danger of attack.

3:7-10—The people will be warned by the prophet.

God does not punish without proper warning.

God has roared a warning as a lion.

The people should fear.

The prophet must prophesy the message.

They have rejected God's Word and no longer know good from evil.

3:11-15—God will send an adversary.

Their power shall be broken.

Their riches shall be taken.

Their luxurious living shall be removed.

Only a trace shall remain of once proud Israel. (Like the ear of an animal in a trap.)

Their idolatrous altars shall be broken down.

The entire picture is one of nearly complete destruction.

Chapter 4

4:1-3—The women will share in the punishment.

They are like fat cows lolling in a pasture.

They crush the needy and instruct their husbands to feed their drunken appetites for luxury.

They will be dragged forcefully away even through the gaps in the walls of their fine houses.

4:4-5—Their religious ceremonies are abominable.

They bring their sacrifices regularly.

But everything they do is done because it pleases *them*, not Jehovah.

4:6-10—God has chastised them but it has done no good.

He brought drought and took away the harvest.

He made it necessary for one city to go to another for water and still they were thirsty.

He brought blasting, mildew and pestilence upon crops and people.

The young men have been slain in battle.

They have been plucked from the fire of punishment just before complete destruction.

Yet they will not repent and return to God.

4:12-13—God will not forever strive with man.

They are to prepare to meet him.

Let him that is filthy be filthy still. (Rev. 22:11.)

Chapter 5

5:1-3—The beauty of Israel is no more.

God will leave her in such condition that she shall not be able to be lifted up.

Ninety percent of her shall be taken away.

5:4-6—There may be individual salvation but not city-wide.

Bethel, the house or abode of God will be of no meaning any more.

The unquenchable fire was to be Assyria.

5:7—Individuals are to seek the Lord and turn away from a host of evil actions.

They have made judgment as bitter as wormwood.

Have taken from the poor to build fine houses.

Have opposed the prophet Amos or anyone else who tried to speak for righteousness.

41

They have taken bribes and turned a deaf ear to the poor.

5:16-20—The Day of the Lord will be one trouble after another.

There shall be paid wailers.

God will no longer pass over—he will pass *through*.

Those who are in this condition and look forward to the Day of the Lord are to be shocked and surprised.

A man runs from a lion to a bear or a serpent.

To the righteous the Day of the Lord is a day of light—but not to these evil ones.

5:21-27—Israel's religious offerings are useless.

Their feasts, sacrifices and music are a stench in the nostrils of Jehovah.

After God's care through forty years in the wilderness they have now turned to gods made by their own hands.

THEY WILL THEREFORE BE SENT INTO CAPTIVITY BEYOND DAMASCUS. (Thus into Assyria.)

Chapter 6

6:1-6—Other nations had been brought down who had as much strength as Israel.

Israel has not the slightest idea of concern over either the plight of the poor, or of a Day of Jehovah.

They stretch out in idleness.

They eat the animals while they are fat and tender.

They listen to musical instruments.

They drink from the finest containers.

They spread perfume upon themselves.

6:7-11—Israel shall go into captivity.

God shall see that the great houses are emptied.

Ten men in one house shall not be enough to defend it.

6:12-14—It would be stupid for horses to run on rocks or to plow upon rocks with oxen.

Still Israel has acted just as foolishly by perverting justice.

They have rejoiced in the calf at Bethel.

They have depended upon the power of their own strength.

But God will bring an enemy nation upon them.

They will be invaded from one end of Israel to the other.

Chapter 7

7:1-3—God showed Amos grasshoppers which were to annihilate the land.

The prophet pleads for Israel because it is so small in comparison with Jehovah.

The Lord postpones the destruction.

7:4-6—Amos is shown a great fire which devoured the sea and was about to devour the land.

Again Amos beseeches the Lord because Israel is so small.

Again Jehovah postpones the destruction.

7:7-9—God showed Amos the Lord standing upon a wall with a plumbline in his hand.

Israel does not fit the plumbline and therefore places of false worship will be laid waste. God will set himself against the house of King Jeroboam II.

7:10-12—Amaziah speaks against Amos to the king.

He tells Amos to go back to Judah and get out of the king's chapel.

7:14-17—Amos replies that he is there at God's command.

He can but prophesy—therefore hear the Word of the Lord.

The king's wife shall be a harlot.

His sons and daughters will be killed by the sword.

The land shall be divided by invaders.

He will die in a spiritually polluted land.

Israel will be taken out of their land and into captivity. (Beyond Damascus—See 5:27.)

Chapter 8

8:1-3—God showed Amos a basket of summer fruit.

Israel is as ripe for harvest as the fruit.

The songs of worship shall turn into wailing.

The dead shall be scattered everywhere.

8:4-7—Israel's corruption is again detailed.

They have valued the poor no higher than a pair of shoes.

They have caused the poor to feed upon the chaff of the wheat.

God will not overlook such behavior.

8:8-10—A bitter day is to come.

The light of Israel shall go out when it should be a time of brilliance.

Joy shall be turned into mourning.

The sorrow can be compared to the loss of an only son.

8: 11-14—A spiritual famine is to come upon them.

Then they shall look for the nourishment of God's Word and it shall not be found.

Those who depend upon the false gods who do not live shall fall and *never rise again*.

Chapter 9

9: 1-3—Amos sees God standing upon the altar.

Everything about their false worship shall be destroyed.

There is no place to hide in hell or heaven.

9: 4-7—Even among the enemies as captives they will suffer evil at God's hands.

At God's command both the earth and the sea shall punish the people of Israel.

Israel is no better than the Philistines and the Syrians. They will be punished.

9: 8-10—God is going to remove Israel as a nation. Yet he will not destroy the righteous. Not a single kernel of true wheat will fall from God's careful hand.

But the evil of death by the sword will come upon every sinner.

9: 11-15—The Day of the Lord will bring joy to the righteous.

David's rule shall be reestablished.

Israel shall captivate its captors. (Acts 15: 16.)

Great prosperity shall abound.

Israel shall be planted firmly and no one shall have power to uproot them.

3. *Practical lessons from the book of Amos*

A. God abominates worship not backed by righteousness.

B. God is patient and longsuffering warning repeatedly.

C. God will not continue to warn forever.

D. An easy luxurious life easily separates men from God.

E. The most awful kind of famine is famine of God's Word.

F. Solitude may help to prepare one to deliver the message of Jehovah.

G. The manner in which we treat those at our mercy is important to God in determining his treatment of us.

HOSEA
(Salvation)

1. *Background for the book of Hosea*
   A. Historical and political
      1. Amos had had little effect upon wicked Israel.
      2. Historians might have seen a healthy nation.
      3. But the prophet of God saw the signs of decay.
      4. After Jeroboam II died anarchy began.
      5. There was rebellion against constituted authority.
      6. Kings ruled for short periods and were assassinated.
      7. There was extreme dependence upon human wisdom.
   B. Social
      1. The courts were corrupt.
      2. The rulers were immoral.
      3. Where Amos had seen ease Hosea sees violence.
      4. The family is disrespected.
      5. There is much inequality of wealth.
      6. Drunkenness abounds.
      7. Fear rules.
      8. Among the moral corruption are lying, thievery, adultery, murder, and deceit of every kind.
   C. Religious
      1. Jeroboam I had introduced calf worship long before.
      2. This had turned into Baal worship.
      3. The golden calf at Bethel was abomination to God.
      4. The priesthood led the people *away* from God.
      5. So called "holy women" served as temple prostitutes.
   D. Once proud Israel is now more like a poisoned rotten tooth.

2. *The man, Hosea*
   A. His name is parallel to Joshua and Jesus. (salvation)
   B. He seems to be a native of the Northern Kingdom.
      1. He speaks of "our king."
      2. He knows the land and the people.
   C. He is a man willing to follow God's commands at all cost or he would have not have married Gomer.
   D. He is a man with unusual patience and compassion.

45

E. He is a man with the ability to draw comparison between his own plight and that of Jehovah.

3. *The nature of the book of Hosea*
   A. The main theme is a mixture of God's longsuffering and his wrath.
   B. There are two main divisions.
      1. Hosea's own experiences with Gomer, Chapters 1-3.
      2. God's experiences with Israel, Chapters 4-14.
   C. The book is a little difficult to read because there is little logical continuity.
   D. There are dozens of analogies such as that Israel is like "a cake not turned."
   E. Hosea does not pull punches but calls a whore a whore, etc.
   F. Hosea shows the real depths of God's love, with only Jesus surpassing him.
   G. The date is shortly after the year 750 B.C. just before Tiglath-Pileser takes the throne of Assyria.

4. *Outline of the book*
   A. Gomer as an example of Israel's whoredom. (Chapters 1-3.)
   B. The ungodly character and punishment of Israel.
      1. National guilt. (Chapter 4.)
      2. Widespread corruption. (Chapter 5.)
      3. Insincerity. (Chapter 6.)
   C. Corrupt political conditions. (Chapters 7 and 8.)
   D. Religious apostasy. (Chapters 9-11.)
   E. God's faithfulness. (Chapters 12-13.)
   F. Israel's conversion and pardon. (Chapter 14.)

5. *Comments on the text of Hosea*
   Chapter 1
   Hosea declares that he speaks the Word of God.
   He is told to take a wife of whoredoms.
   Three children are born to Gomer
       The first is Hosea's—Jezreel—(scattered)
       The second is a daughter—Lo-ruhamah—(no pity)
       The third is another son—LoAmmi (not my people)
   Still the time will come when those not God's people shall become his people. Compare 1 Pet. 2:9, 10 and Rom. 9:24-27.
   Judah and Israel shall be combined under *one head.*
   Chapter 2
   Gomer had failed to play the part of a wife.

46

She had made the mistake of going after lovers, whom she believed gave her the best gifts.

When she finds that the fine things she had did not come from her lovers but from her husband she will perhaps repent.

Baal was considered the father of the gods.

This was the god of the Canaanites when Israel entered the country.

The worship of Baal was a licentious fertility ceremony with temple prostitutes.

Jehovah will go after the unfaithful Israel to make a new covenant.

The evil shall be removed from her and those who were not God's people shall become his people.

Chapter 2:14-23 is Messianic in nature.

Chapter 3

Hosea is told to go and buy his wife back from adultery.

This is helpful in his understanding of God's attitude toward adulterous Israel.

Gomer shall be kept from her adultery but she will not act as his wife for many days.

So Hosea does buy her back for the price of a gored slave. (Ex. 21:32.)

Just as Gomer was kept from her husband for many days, so Israel will not have king, sacrifice, nor idolatrous image for many days.

At a later date Israel would seek the Lord, David, their king and the goodness of Jehovah.

Chapter 4

Israel went through a series of steps to her downfall.

1. Lack of knowledge, 4:6.
2. Pride, 5:5.
3. Instability, 6:4.
4. Worldliness, 7:8.
5. Corruption, 9:9.
6. Backsliding, 11:7.
7. Idolatry, 13:2.

God will destroy Israel for her lack of knowledge.

His people have turned to divining.

They have sacrificed wherever was convenient to their taste.

Judah is warned not to follow the path of Israel.

Ephraim is joined to idols, let him alone.

Ephraim is the ruling tribe of Israel since the first king of the Northern Kingdom was taken from Ephraim.

Ephraim is therefore put for Israel.
When both the North and the South are spoken of it is Jacob which is used.

Chapter 5

Israel's pride testifies to its unfaithfulness.
They have begotten strange children, not the Lord's.
God will be to them like a moth or rot.
They will try to heal their wounds through other nations but this will not help.
God will tear Ephraim as a lion and they shall not find any to rescue.

Chapter 6

His people speak of repentance but their goodness lasts only as long as a morning dew.
God desires more than formal worship and sacrifice.
He wants knowledge of him and resulting goodness.
Just as in the case of Adam their transgressions will result in expulsion from the land.
The priests have led the people into corruption, 6:8-9.

Chapter 7

Samaria was the capital of the Northern Kingdom.
Thieves and robbers collaborate with the king in wicked plots.
Then they deceive the king with whom they planned.
Ephraim is like a cake not turned.
Burnt on one side toward evil
Raw on the other side toward God.
Absolutely worthless for any purpose.
Spent in strength and turning gray without knowing it.
Ephraim is like a silly dove.
He flits from Egypt to Assyria but will not return to God.
God will bring the net upon him and chastise him.
They howl upon their beds in difficulty but refuse to seek God.
They are like a deceitful bow which breaks when pulled.
This shall take them back into bondage.
Egypt here actually stands for the bondage which threatens from the north in Assyria.   See Chapter 8, verse 9.

Chapter 8

The calf of Samaria must go!
They have sown the wind of nothingness.
Now they must reap the whirlwind of destruction.
The independent ass of Ephraim shall now go to Assyria.

Ephraim shall be in the same position as Gomer, lost among her hired lovers.

Israel hath forgotten her maker. Compare Isaiah 1:2-3.

Chapter 9

Israel had loved her material things more than the living God. (Loved a reward upon every cornfloor)

They rejoice now but they will eat the bread of mourning.

Return to bondage of an *Assyrian Egypt* O Ephraim which was born in bondage!

They will then realize their prophets have been fools.

The prophets of Ephraim were watchmen against God and not for him as in Ezekiel 3:17.

Though once desirable as grapes in the wilderness or first ripe figs they had now turned to Baal and were fit to be cast away. See Numbers 25:1-9 for Baal.

Israel would now be cast away to wander among the nations until God saw fit to buy her back through the blood of Jesus Christ.

Chapter 10

The golden calf will be carried away to be a present for the king of Assyria.

Thorns will grow upon the altar.

The people will call for the mountains to cover them and for the hills to fall on them. See Luke 23:30 and Revelation 6:16.

Unlike the tribe of Benjamin which was reduced to 600 men, the Northern Kingdom will be destroyed.

They are still told to repent
Break up the fallow ground.
Sow in righteousness.
Reap in kindness.

The Assyrian flood shall overwhelm the land which is:
Sown in wickedness.
Reaped in iniquity.

Chapter 11

Jehovah has led Ephraim as an infant son.

Now he has turned in complete ingratitude.

Verse 1 is quoted in Matthew 2:15.

The king of Assyria shall be their king in a new Egypt.

They have been *bent* on backsliding.

They call on the Lord but make no effort to rise to a purer life.

God, will destroy and yet not destroy.

This shall come about because God is God and not man.

He will destroy the earthly kingdom—but will redeem a remnant through the Kingdom of Christ.

They shall come out of Egypt (Assyria) like doves or pigeons returning to their homes.

But these homes shall be in the new City of God. Compare 1:11; 2:23; 3:5; Hebrews 12:22; Philippians 3:20.

Chapter 12

Ephraim has fed upon nothingness and made covenants with Assyria.

They should have found the same strength in God that Jacob of old did when he found God in Bethel.

Ephraim's false balances may fool some, but they will not fool God.

Their altars shall be turned into heaps in the fields.

Jacob had served for seven years keeping sheep for his wife.

Ephraim merely provoked God.—How different!

Punishment must be expected.

Chapter 13

Ephraim had lost his life in worshipping Baal.

They had been blessed by God over Manasseh. (Gen. 48:18-20.)

Ephraim stood tall among the tribes in the time of the judges. (Judges 8:1-3; 12:1.)

Ephraim was the first tribe from which a king of the ten tribes was chosen. (1 Kings 11:26; 12:20.)

They had fallen through calf worship to Baal worship.

Ephraim would disappear as:

1. The morning dew.
2. The chaff in the wind.
3. The smoke from a chimney, verse 3.

From the time of Jeroboam I to Hoshea there had not been a king of Israel who led the people to Jehovah.

But Israel shall be ransomed from the power of the grave.

Ephraim which indicates "double fruitful" will now become waste.

The Assyrians will spoil everything of value.

Israel's capital, Samaria, would become a desolation.

Chapter 14

There will be a day of return to the Lord.

Note the following Messianic passages:
  Chapters 1-3
  Chapter 11:10-11
  Chapter 14
The time will come when Israel will turn away from:
  Allies, military power, and false gods or idols.
Then times of refreshing shall come from God.
Ephraim will again be fruitful.

5. *Practical Lessons from the book of Hosea*
  A. God's love is never quenched.
  B. For men to desert God is the same as for a wife to desert her husband.
  C. Marriage is sacred.
  D. Sin destroys the conscience.
  E. A nation tends to follow its corrupt leaders.
  F. When men repent God will forgive.
  G. Nothing is more dangerous to a nation than spiritual corruption.
  H. When God destroys a nation he always watches for his remnant.

MICAH
(Who Is Like Unto Jehovah)

1. *Background for the book of Micah*
   A. Historical
      1. Assyria had now become a world power.
      2. In 745 *Tiglath-Pileser* began his westward march.
      3. By 738 his armies were in Syria and Israel.
      4. The kings of these nations are forced to pay tribute.
      5. Rezin of Syria and Pekah of Israel revolt.
      6. Jotham and Ahaz, his son, of Judah will not join the revolt and Judah is attacked by the other two.
      7. Ahaz calls upon Tiglath-Pileser to aid him.
      8. Tiglath-Pileser attacks Damascus which falls along with much of Israel. 732 B.C.
      9. Hoshea is made a vassal king ruling from Samaria.
      10. Hoshea rebels and *Shalmaneser* who succeeded Tiglath-Pileser punishes him by taking Samaria in 722 B.C.
      11. *Sargon* II then became ruler of Assyria and reigned until 705 B.C.
      12. Meanwhile new revolts were developing against Assyria.
      13. Ahaz refused to join, but Hezekiah took the throne and began to turn to Egypt for aid.
      14. In 705 when Sargon died *Sennacherib* took the Assyrian throne.
      15. Sennacherib's armies came in 701 B.C. to defeat Judah and the armies of Egypt, taking all but the city of Jerusalem.
      16. God protected Jerusalem by smiting 185,000 of the Assyrians, after which Sennacherib returned home with his forces. (2 Kings 19:34-36.)
      17. THESE WERE THE DAYS OF MICAH AND ISAIAH.
   B. Social
      1. Judges judged for bribes.
      2. Prophets prophesied for reward.
      3. Princes devised evil against their people.
      4. Business transactions were corrupt.
      5. Greed and degradation were guiding the people of God to bondage.

C. Religious
  1. The religion was shallow and self-centered.
  2. The people wanted prophets who would tickle their ears.
  3. There was much witchcraft, idolatry and superstition.
  4. No one could be trusted, even one's own wife.
  5. The prophets "made war" on any who would not go along with their mercenary ways.
  6. Among the sins were:
     a. Oppression, 2:2, 8-9. b. Abuse of power, 2:1-3:10. c. Dishonesty, 6:12; 7:2-6. d. Scorn of true religion, 3:5-8; 5:12-14. e. Love of false prophets, 3:5, 7, 9-11. f. Greed, 7:3.

2. *The man, Micah*
  A. Micah was from Moresheth-Gath, 20 miles from Jerusalem.
  B. His home was near the great highway which ran from Assyria to Egypt.
  C. With the help of God's Spirit he has a keen insight into the meaning of world events.
  D. He shows some of the same antagonism for cities as did Amos.
  E. He and Isaiah prophesy primarily to Judah while Amos and Hosea prophesied to Israel.
  F. He was very forceful through use of figures of speech.
  G. Though he can be majestic like Isaiah he tends to be strong through his simple clearness.

3. *Nature of the book of Micah*
  A. Seven chapters.
  B. The theme is well stated in Micah 6:8.
     Justice—Mercy—A humble walk with God.
  C. The book has unity but it must be looked for carefully.
  D. Micah makes six predictions.
     1. Samaria is to fall.
     2. Jerusalem and the Temple are to be destroyed.
     3. Judah is to go captive to Babylon.
     4. They are to be restored from captivity.
     5. The Messiah is to be born in Bethlehem.
     6. The Messiah is to bring peace.
  E. Micah's picture of God.
     1. He is a God of justice.
     2. He is a God of ethical righteousness.
     3. God will convert the world through Zion.

4. He is a God of peace.
5. He is a God of hope.
F. Micah combines the justice of Amos with the love of Hosea and the fellowship of Isaiah in his great passage of 6:8.

4. *Outline of the book*
A. Judgment for Samaria and Jerusalem.
1. Announcement of judgment.
2. Causes of judgment.
3. Promise of restoration.
B. Present corruption to give way to righteousness.
1. Present leaders are corrupt and Godless.
2. The Messiah will bring a better day.
C. The outcome of Jehovah's case against Israel.
1. Jehovah declares his case.
2. But the remnant will see salvation.

5. *Comments on the text of Micah*
Chapter 1
Micah prophesied for a long period of time.
As usual the prophet speaks only through God.
God is to come forth from his Holy Temple.
When he comes the earth will quiver from his presence.
The sins of the people center in the capitals of the Kingdoms of Israel and Judah.
Samaria, the capital of Israel will be judged.
The very foundations of the city will be dug up.
The treasures and idols will be removed.
Samaria's sickness has reached all the way to Jerusalem.
Now there is a play on words.
In Akko (weep town) weep not.
In Gath (tell town) tell it not.
In Shaphir (pretty town) walk in naked shame.
Samaria is to tear out their hair in grief over such sin.

Chapter 2
God is displeased with those who plot mischief.
Compare verse 1 with the first verse of Psalm 1.
These plot evil while lying awake at night.
Then they practice it simply because they are able.
Because of this God will devise evil against them.
Their prophets shall not prophesy.
Their inheritance shall not pass to them.
Their sins against God's true people are grievous.
They steal the clothing.

54

They cast out women and children.
They seek prophets who will advise strong drink.
God's true remnant will go out from such sin.
He will gather them together like sheep.
They will break out through the gates.
God will be their leader.

Chapter 3

The ones who should be shepherds of the people betray them.
Instead of shearing the sheep they skin them and eat their flesh.
The time will come when they shall feel judgment.
Then they will cry to the Lord, but he will not hear.
The prophets have lied to the people and they shall be punished.
They shall receive no vision.
They shall not perceive truth and shall be in darkness.
They shall be ashamed and cover their lips.
Micah is not among these false prophets.
He is full of the Spirit of God.
He will declare Israel's transgressions.
The leaders are a sorry lot.
The judges seek reward.
The priests teach for hire.
The prophets divine for money.
Then they declare that God is with them and there shall be peace for no evil can come.
Because of this Jerusalem and the temple will fall.

Chapter 4

The Lord will bring forth a new day.
The mountain of his house will stand above all.
People from all nations shall flow into his house.
He will teach and his people will listen.
His laws shall spread from Jerusalem and Mt. Zion.
God will judge all nations.
His people will seek peace and not war.
There shall be prosperity and not fear.
His people will walk in his name eternally.
Those who now must be punished will provide a remnant.
A new Israel will be produced, strong and proud.
God shall reign over it from Zion.
This new Kingdom will be like the first dominion under David.
The present punishment is only a labor of birth.

They must now go into the land of Babylon to await later
delivery.
The nations who now rejoice at their pain will then be de-
feated.
God will gather these nations to rejoice at Israel's sorrow.
But then Israel will arise to thresh them to pieces.
Israel will have a power like an iron horn.
She shall tread upon them with feet of brass.
The meek shall then inherit the earth.

Chapter 5
A challenge is given to those who live by force to smite the
true Judge of Israel. (God)
But Jehovah will bring against them a powerful Messiah.
He will be born in Bethlehem of Ephrathah.
His efforts are only a continuation of that which he has al-
ways been doing.
When the delivery of the Man-child has been accomplished
he will bring a new and complete Israel together.
He (the Messiah) will feed them as a good shepherd.
His sheep will be safe in his care forever.
There shall be no fear from the enemies when the Good
Shepherd protects their peace.
There shall be enough good rulers to meet any enemy.
The remnant of God will be a great blessing.
Like refreshing dew or showers to the nations.
The remnant will tear in pieces and tread down the ene-
mies.
Yet they will accomplish it in an unusual manner.
They will not use weapons like horses and chariots.
They shall not depend upon city strongholds.
Witchcraft and soothsaying magic will not be used.
Idols and graven images will not be needed.
God himself will execute vengeance in his own way.

Chapter 6
God now calls Israel to account.
The very mountains are to hear his case.
He asks what excuse they have for their evil.
His blessings are then recalled.
He delivered them from Egypt.
He provided Aaron, Moses and Miriam.
He caused Balaam to bless them.
Israel can only plead guilty and ask for mercy.
Should she sacrifice rams?

Should she sacrifice rivers of oil?
Should she offer her most precious firstborn?
God seeks more than formal sacrifice.
She must do justly.
She must love mercy.
She must walk humbly in fellowship with God.
The man of wisdom will hear this wisdom and respect it.
There are some who still will not hear.
They give scant measure with false scales.
They practice violence, lying and deceit.
God will punish them.
They shall eat but still be hungry.
They shall labor but not be able to deliver.
They shall take with the sword and God will take it away again.
They shall sow and cultivate but not harvest.
Since they persist in following the principles of wicked and idolatrous Omri and Ahab they shall be made a reproach.

Chapter 7

God looks in vain for righteousness.
He desires full grapes but they are like a field already harvested.
The good are all gone and the evil abound.
They do evil with all their energy.
They are like briers and thorns.
One cannot trust even his friends.
A man's wife will even betray him.
There is utter lack of respect within the family.
Micah grieves over his solitude in such wickedness.
But the Lord will bring light to his darkness.
The wickedness shall be defeated one day.
God will build a new city with walls of his own divine protective presence.
His people shall come from every part of the earth.
His flock shall be fed in luxurious pastures such as those of Bashan and Gilead.
Nations who would oppose the people of God shall meet defeat.
Consider—Rome and Hitler's Germany.
WHO IS LIKE UNTO JEHOVAH?
Who pardons iniquity?
Who does not remember sin forever when men repent?
Who delights in being merciful to his own?

Who casts sins beyond sight and beyond reach?
Who will keep his promise of blessing to the world through Abraham, Isaac and Jacob?

6. *Practical lessons from Micah*

   A. One cannot separate sacrifice from justice, mercy, and a humble walk with Jehovah.

   B. There comes a time when God brings conniving men to account.

   C. God will triumph over all opposition through his Messiah.

   D. God continues beyond our understanding to warn and chastise men to repentance.

   E. There will always be God's remnant.

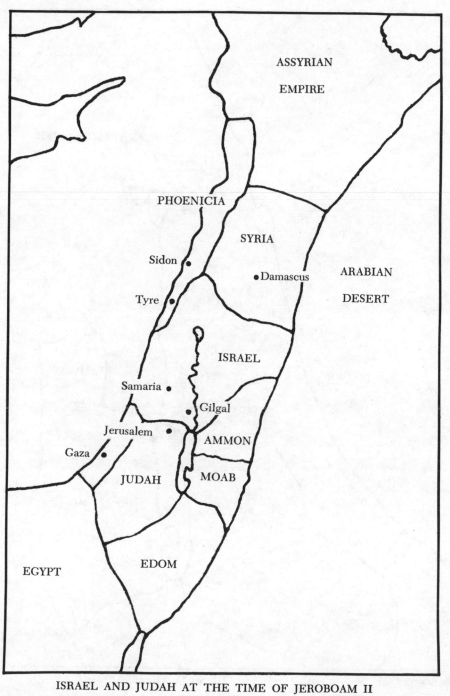

ISRAEL AND JUDAH AT THE TIME OF JEROBOAM II
785-745 B.C.

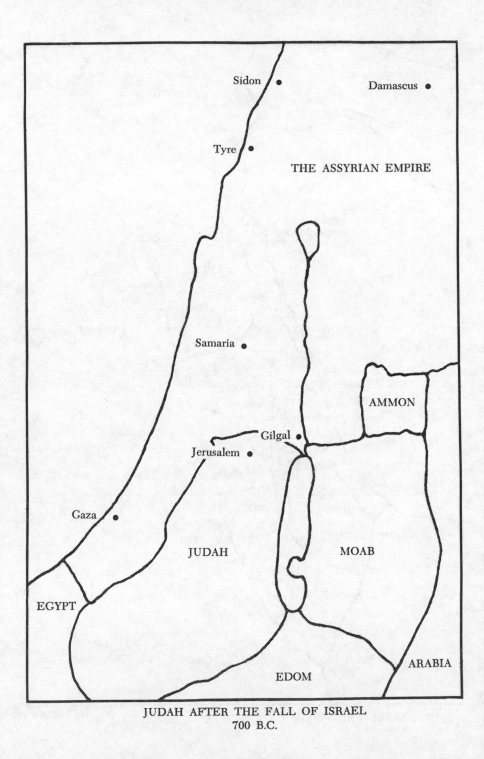

Sidon •

Damascus •

Tyre •

THE ASSYRIAN EMPIRE

Samaria •

AMMON

Gilgal •

Jerusalem •

Gaza •

JUDAH

MOAB

EGYPT

ARABIA

EDOM

JUDAH AFTER THE FALL OF ISRAEL
700 B.C.

ISAIAH
(Jehovah Saves)

1. *Background for the book of Isaiah*
   A. Historical.
      1. During the reigns of Uzziah, Jotham, Ahaz and Hezekiah.
      2. Jereboam in Israel and Uzziah in Judah had brought about prosperity and security.
      3. As is often true affluence brought decay.
      4. Israel was more willing to trust human alliances than Jehovah.
      5. Greece and Rome were still in their infancy.
      6. Babylon would not reach world supremacy for another one hundred years.
      7. But Egypt and Assyria were contending for power in Isaiah's day.
      8. Palestine lay directly between them.
      9. To protect against Assyria Israel and Syria made an alliance and asked Judah to join.
      10. Judah refused and they attacked her to force compliance.
      11. Judah appealed to Assyria for assistance.
      12. Assyria proceeded to conquer both Syria and the Northern Kingdom and made Judah pay tribute, conquering all the way to Jerusalem.
      13. God intervened and 185,000 Assyrians died.
      14. The Assyrian army under Sennacherib returned home.
   B. Social conditions
      1. There was practically no middle class.
      2. The rich unmercifully oppressed the poor.
      3. Land grabbing was common.
      4. Laziness, drunkenness and indifference were prevalent sins.
      5. Justice was perverted as the law was used to mistreat rather than to protect.
   C. Religious conditions
      1. Israel was to have transformed others. Instead she had been conformed to Canaan's sin.
      2. Baal and Moloch were worshipped.
      3. Even the prophets had turned to drunkenness.

4. Ethical standards were almost non-existent.
5. Women had become coarse and sensual.
6. They had turned to soothsaying and superstition.
7. Religion had been divorced from everyday life.

2. *The man, Isaiah*
   A. He was the son of Amoz (not Amos).
   B. He seems to have been born into high rank, since he had access to the royal court.
   C. He served as historian to the king.
   D. Early in his life he saw a vision of the Lord and never forgot it.
   E. He was a statesman of faith.
      "Do not ally with Egypt."
      "Do not ally with Assyria."
      "Make God your helper."
   F. While Micah was prophesying in the countryside Isaiah was in the court in the palace.
   G. It is likely that he was acquainted with Micah in the Southern Kingdom and Amos and Hosea in the Northern Kingdom.

3. *The nature of the book of Isaiah*
   A. The book is strongly Messianic and presents pictures of several phases of the life of Christ.
      1. His birth.
      2. His divinity.
      3. His reign.
      4. His trial and suffering.
      5. His death.
   B. There are four predominating themes.
      1. God's providence overrules.
      2. Redemption through a Messiah.
      3. Hope survives in God's remnant.
      4. There will be a new creation.
   C. There are several outstanding chapters.
      Chapters 1, 6, 9, 11, 40, 49, 50, 53, 55.
   D. The date of the book
      1. Probably written over several decades of Isaiah's life.
      2. From the last year of Uzziah's reign, 1:1
      3. 2 Chronicles 32:32 says Isaiah wrote the history of Hezekiah.
      4. 2 Chronicles 37:28 speaks of recording the death of Sennacherib which occurred in 681 B.C.

5. Since Uzziah died in about 740 B.C. this would extend Isaiah's efforts over 60 years.
6. Tradition tells us Isaiah was sawn apart with a wooden saw. (Compare Hebrews 11:37.)

E. Authorship of the book
1. Liberals believe Isaiah wrote only a portion of the first 39 chapters.
2. Chapters 40 to 66 are called "Second Isaiah."
3. Some critics have even spoken of a "third" or "fourth" Isaiah.
4. Much of this stems from an unwillingness to admit the possibility of the prophet speaking of conditions occurring in Babylonian captivity after his death.
5. Some of the critics would go so far as to deny Isaiah portions of chapters 11, 12, 13, 14, 15, 16, 21, 24-27 and 34-39 leaving him as author of only about one third of the book.

BUT

6. The Dead Sea Scrolls include all 66 chapters.
7. The Septuagint ascribes all 66 chapters to Isaiah.
8. Both of the above date back to at least 200 B.C.
9. Other prophets known to have written before the captivity allude to portions of the latter chapters. Zephaniah 2:15—Isaiah 47:8; Nahum 1:15—Isaiah 52:7; Jeremiah 31:15—Isaiah 51:15.
10. And the New Testament quotes from the latter chapters. John 12:38—Isaiah 53:1; Luke 4:17—Isaiah 61:1; Acts 8:30—Isaiah 53.
11. If one accepts the inspiration of the New Testament there is no difficulty.

4. *Outline of the book*
A. Prophecies of judgment.
1. Prophecies concerning Judah and Jerusalem.
   a. Condemnation of Israel's corruption. b. A new rule after judgment. c. Isaiah's vision of the Lord. d. Prophecies about the Messiah.
2. Prophecies of judgment against the nations.
   a. Babylon. b. Assyria. c. Philistia. d. Moab. e. Damascus. f. Ethiopia. g. Egypt. h. Jerusalem. i. Tyre.
3. The new Kingdom established.
   a. Establishment of the new Kingdom. b. Beauties and blessings of the new Kingdom. c. The song of the redeemed. d. Israel triumphant.
4. Prophetic warnings against Samaria and Judah.

  a. Samaria will fall. b. Jerusalem will be besieged and delivered. c. The Egyptain alliance is denounced. d. The Messianic reign—a rebuke and a promise. e. Assyria to be chastised and Jerusalem delivered.
 5. A new day to come.
  a. The Day of the Lord. b. Blessings of the new Kingdom.
 6. A historical transition.
B. Prophecies of consolation.
 1. Comforting promises of restoration.
  a. Restoration promised. b. Cyrus will deliver God's servant Israel. c. The Messiah's work will be effective. d. God will redeem his servant. e. Babylon's gods will fall along with Babylon. f. Israel will be delivered.
 2. Salvation will come through God's servant, the Messiah.
  a. The Messiah's commission and work. b. The Messiah's humiliation and steadfastness. c. A promise of salvation to Zion. d. The Messiah's suffering and his glory. e. Promise of Israel's future restoration.
 3. Warnings, Prophecies and Future Glory of Israel.
  a. Unfaithfulness rebuked and righteousness commanded. b. The glory of Zion and the new Kingdom. c. The Messiah will overthrow Israel's enemies. d. A prayer for redemption and deliverance. e. The reply of the Lord.

5. *Comments upon the text of Isaiah*

Chapter 1

The book is directed primarily to Judah and Jerusalem.

It is the result of divine vision.

God has provided extreme care for his chosen children.

Yet dumb animals are more grateful than are they.

They can be described as sick and full of untreated sores.

They are like temporary shacks in a field, soon to be removed.

God will however leave a remnant.

He is nauseated with their hypocritical sacrifices.

He will turn his face away from their outstretched bloody hands.

Jerusalem is a harlot city, having committed adultery with created riches.

God's children have committed all sorts of social injustices.

But God will purge their sins and create a new Zion of righteousness.

Then she shall be ashamed of her idolatry.

God will use the strong as kindling for his purging fires.

There shall be no escape since none can quench the purifying fire.

Chapter 2

There shall come a time when God's house will be an establishment of unshakeable exaltation.

It will extend hospitality to persons of all nations. Compare Micah 4:1-5 and Daniel 2:35, 44.

Men's ways will then become secondary to the will of God.

The Heavenly Jerusalem will provide a center for the outspreading of the truth.

Swords and spears will give way to the Word of God as controlling forces.

Agriculture shall occupy the talents of men rather than armaments.

NOTE: This does not necessarily mean that all violence shall disappear from off the earth. (2 Tim. 3:13; 2 Pet. 3:2-4.) However, those who truly subject themselves to the Prince of Peace will follow his example.

Israel must get ready for this wonderful destiny by walking in God's light now.

They have been depending upon soothsayers.

They have worshipped non-entities.

Their land is full of idols and material security.

The Day of the Lord shall come.

Then the proud shall be humbled.

They shall hide in the holes of the rocks.

They shall cast away their golden idols as useless.

They are warned to cease from depending upon men.

It was God who breathed the breath of life into the nostrils of those upon whom they depend.

Chapter 3

There will be a breakdown of law and order.

Capable leadership will disappear.

Children shall rule over them.

The situation will become so bad they cannot get anyone to accept rulership.

Instead of being ashamed of sins they parade them.

Women will rule and children shall oppress.

The women shall manifest a haughty attitude.

Compare Verse 16 with Amos 4:1-3.

But God will turn their beauty into ugliness, their clothing into nakedness, and their perfume into foul-stinking.

Their men will be taken away and they shall sit in lamentation. Compare Revelation 18:14-16.

Chapter 4

The women shall compete for the few men who are left.

The BRANCH of God shall bring forth fruit as the land is rejuvenated.

When the filth is removed that which is left in the new Jerusalem will be HOLY.

God's fire and cloud shall indicate his Divine presence among his people in the new Zion.

He shall be a protecting tabernacle spreading his protective covering over them.

Chapter 5

This is an actual song in the Hebrew language.

God had blessed Israel, his vineyard, in a very special way.

He now had the right to expect a very special harvest.

Instead his beautiful vineyard had produced "Wild Grapes." Compare Deuteronomy 32:32, 33.

A number of woes are pronounced:
1. Upon those who join house to house.
2. Upon those who follow after strong drink.
3. Upon those who draw sin around like a cart on a rope.
4. Upon those who call evil good, and good evil.
5. Upon those who are wise in their own eyes.
6. Upon those who take bribes from the wicked.

Because of this evil fruit God's vineyard is to be destroyed.
1. An invader will appear.
2. He shall not stumble.
3. His weapons shall be very sharp.
4. He shall carry away prey.
5. Darkness and sorrow shall cover the land.

Chapter 6

Uzziah died about 740 B.C.

He had been a good king for about 50 years.

Now with his death the land is in turmoil.

Isaiah is sent to bring instruction from God.

Isaiah sees a vision of the Lord.

This brings an awful realization of his own sin.

God touches his lips and purifies him.

And he is told to go preach.

He wonders how long he is to continue.

It is to be until the land becomes desolate!

However, after the desolation a tenth will remain as a remnant through which God will act.

This remnant shall be God's Holy seed.

Chapter 7

King Rezin of Syria and King Pekah of Israel decide to conquer Ahaz of Judah and force him to make alliance with them against Tiglath-Pileser.

Ahaz' heart and that of his people tremble as the leaves in the wind.

Isaiah is sent with his son Shear-jashub to give Ahaz strength and comfort.

NOTE: Shear-jashub means—The remnant shall return. Isaiah tells Ahaz that Syria and Israel are like two smoking firebrands about ready to burn out.

They have even decided upon a man to take Ahaz' place.

But they shall fail because they are mere men and they are pitting their power against Judah and the plans of Jehovah.

If Ahaz would believe, God would support him, if not he would not receive personal support.

Ahaz is told to ask for a sign either in the heights or the depths.

Within sixty-five years Syria and Israel will fall.

But Ahaz refuses to ask for a sign proving he will not trust Jehovah.

As a representative of the House of David he is told a sign will be given anyway.

A virgin will conceive and bear a son.

His name shall be called Immanuel—God with us.

He shall eat butter and honey and thus shall know good from evil.

But before he is old enough to know good from evil Syria and Israel will have lost their kings.

The Holy Spirit tells us who the virgin was in Matthew 1:23.

The sign was not to Ahaz only but to the House of David.

Both the king of Syria and the king of Israel were taken away long before the Messiah had reached the normal age of accountability.

The Hebrew word used in 7:14 for virgin is ALMAH.

This word is used in six other places in the Old Testament and always means an unmarried maiden. (Gen. 24:43; Ex. 2:8; Ps. 68:26; Prov. 30:19; Song of Sol. 1:3 and 6:8.)

The other word which is sometimes said by the critics to be the logical one if a true virgin were intended is BETHULAH.

The word Bethulah is used in Joel 1:8 where a young woman is lamenting over her husband.

It would seem wise to let the scripture determine the proper interpretation and to all sincere believers in the authenticity of the Bible. Matthew 1:23 decides the matter.

But there is a bad part of the sign which Ahaz himself will see.

God will call for the Egyptian and the Assyrian and they shall cover the land of Judah like insects.

Ahaz is willing to hire the razor of the king of Assyria, but now the manliness of Judah shall disappear before that same razor.

Land thriving now with a thousand vines shall be covered with briers and thorns.

The remnant shall eat butter and honey, but the arrow and the bow shall strike king Ahaz and his land.

Chapter 8

Isaiah is told to put up a sign and write on it in clear fashion Maher-shalal-hash-baz.

This means—The spoil speedeth—The prey hasteth.

In other words Judah's problems will soon appear.

Two witnesses are taken to see the sign erected.

Thus it will be apparent to all that the prophecy was made before the event occurred.

Each of the names here marked points of time before which certain events were to occur. (See 7:16; 8:4.)

God's people had refused the gentle refreshing water of Shiloh's blessings.

Now they would be overwhelmed by the raging waters of an Assyrian flood.

It will go even to the neck—but will not finish. (Verse 8.)

They need not oppose and form confederacies but should sanctify the Lord.

God will become to them either: A stone of stumbling—or A sanctuary. (Compare 1 Peter 2:8; Acts 4:11; Isa. 28:16.)

Many of the Jews should fall over the stone of God. (See Luke 20:17-18.)

The law and the testimony of God's prophecy shall be clear to those who wait as his disciples.

Any soothsayer or wizard who disagrees does not have the light of God's truth.

When men look to other sources than God they shall only behold trouble, anguish and darkness.

Chapter 9

This chapter makes a change from gloom to hope.

Out of what is later called Galilee there shall come illumination to ease the darkness.

Zebulun and Naphtali in the north had been particularly looked down upon by the people of Jerusalem but now light is promised from this area.

Jesus is later called:

1. Sun of Righteousness. (Mal. 4.)
2. The True Light. (John 1.)
3. The Light of the World. (John 1.)
   See the quote in Matthew 4:16.

Now we have more about the infant born in 7:14.

1. He shall break the rod of the oppressor.
2. He shall be given the authority of government. (Matt. 28:18; Eph. 1:22, 23; Col. 1:12.)
3. He shall be a Wonderful Counsellor—Wisdom.
4. He shall have Divine characteristics.
5. His reign shall last forever.
6. His shall be a reign of peace.
7. He shall both establish and order his Kingdom.

How is it then, that evil men and seducers wax worse and worse? (2 Tim. 3:13.)

The emphasis here is on the spiritual Kingdom.

Even though the number of persons living were to be brought to nearly zero, as long as any are being added to Christ's Kingdom it is increasing because the dead are still to be counted.

Still there shall be some who will oppse God.

God will strengthen the enemies of these.

The Syrians and Philistines shall punish them.

The punishment will extend from head to tail.

The wise man and the prophet lead to destruction.

The young men, widows and orphans shall all feel the consequences of the nation's arrogance.

It shall be burned as a world aflame.

In the darkness of confusion they shall consume one another.

As God chastises they will not repent and therefore his outstretched arm continues to point to their folly.

Chapter 10

Judah is scolded for social injustice.

They make unjust laws to cheat the poor.

They make prey of the fatherless and the widow.

Three questions are asked of them.
1. What will you do when God takes account?
2. To whom will you turn for help?
3. What will happen to your glory?

Because of all these sins God does not draw back his outstretched hand of wrath.

Assyria will be used as a "rod of correction."

Assyria is not aware of this in his heart.

Assyria boasts much.

But the Lord will punish his proud heart.
Compare Nebuchadnezzar's experience.

Assyria claims to have: eliminated nations' boundaries; robbed their nests of riches; forced them not to make a peep.

Assyria is as stupid as an axe which believes itself independent of the hewer.

God shall burn up the glory of the king of Assyria like thorns and briers in a holocaust.

The Assyrian cannot destroy all for there will be a remnant of God's people left.

God's people are not to fear the Assyrian.

"Yet a little while and the indignation shall cease." (This is strangely like the passage in Revelation 6:11.)

It was some thirty years from Tiglath-Pileser to Sennacherib. This was also a little while.

God's own power shall be delegated to the remnant.

The king of Assyria shall be allowed to come as far as the city of Nob.

There he will shake his fist at Jerusalem.

God will then lop off the haughty and the high of both Assyria and Judah through the power of his mighty one.

Chapter 11

From that which is cut down a fresh BRANCH will shoot forth.

This is the same child:
Born, 7:14; Described, 9:6, 7.

There are six characteristics grouped in pairs:
Wisdom and understanding—perception; counsel and might —ability; knowledge and fear—relationship to God. (See Colossians 2:9; Isaiah 61:1.)

He will not depend upon his five senses for information since it will come directly from God.

The poor shall be reinstated through his reign.

His teaching shall destroy the wickedness of the earth.

He shall be clothed in righteousness and faithfulness, and thus he can be recognized.

We are also to be clothed in the Gospel armor.

Through the efforts of the BRANCH peace shall be the order of the day.

The most violent of enemies shall be united.

There shall be no evil intent in Mount Zion.

This shall come about only as the knowledge of the Lord covers the earth.

And it shall only be true of the Holy Mountain.

The BRANCH, or root of Jesse, shall serve as a banner for all nations who will seek his rest and peace.

He shall first gather a remnant from Babylonian captivity—then a second time gather from the four corners of the earth.

God shall himself remove all obstacles to the return of his remnant to Zion.

Chapter 12

Here is a song which could be called "In That Day."
In Christ there shall be:

1. Righteousness.
2. Punishment of the wicked.
3. Faithfulness to duty.
4. Peace.

There shall be *wells of salvation*
66 of them (Water of Life)

Inhabitants of Zion are members of the Church.

Chapter 13

This is the beginning of ten chapters dealing with God's judgments upon the nations.

A burden is something which one must carry.

We speak of "burdensome."

Babylon is today a short distance from Baghdad and is very disappointing to the sightseer.

God is now giving the orders to muster his forces.

The Medes and Persians were used to punish Babylon.

Men may oppose God but he will use them at his will.

In the Day of the Lord all resistance will melt.

Babylon will fall before the Medes and Persians.

It will become uninhabited.

Arabs hesitate today to go into the ruins.

Tyre was built back, but Babylon was not.

This was a BOLD prophecy.

Chapter 14

Verse 1 is possibly Messianic.

Babylon's fall means peace for Israel.

Isaiah is told to instruct the King of Babylon.

She is to be reduced from her great power.

All nature will rejoice at her collapse.

The word Lucifer means DayStar. *Lucid, Luciferin*

The king of Babylon has considered himself as the great light-giver. (Compare Revelation 22:16.)

The Lucifer spoken to here is a *man*. (See verse 16.)

Yet he may be symbolic of the Prince of Darkness.

Lucifer shall be brought down from his lofty place.

Today there are *no Babylonians*.

There are Egyptians, Syrians and Jews, but *no Babylonians*.

The overthrow of the Assyrian will show the later destiny of Babylon.

When the Assyrian serpent falls the Babylonian adder will replace it.

Babylon would also fall, but Israel would live on.

Chapter 15

Moab was a desert country with fierce warlike people.

An enemy will overrun Moab and cause great grief.

The grief shall extend to the shaving of the beards.

Isaiah feels pity for them.

The wailing and howling shall reach from border to border.

Chapter 16

Moab is given advice.

They have parted friendship with Israel.

They need to reinforce that old friendship.

The throne of David would offer aid.

But Moab is too proud and turns to false Gods.

All but a remnant of Moab will be ruined.

This shall happen in precisely three years.

Chapter 17

Damascus is one of the oldest cities.

It was known in the time of Abraham. (Gen. 15:2.)

Though Damascus is to be destroyed there is no reference to its never being rebuilt.

Ephraim had allied with Syria and so the burden includes reference to Ephraim.

There shall be a complete harvest with only gleanings left.

There shall be a partial repentance.

But most will be destroyed because they have forgotten God.
They shall plant desirable plants.
But their harvest will be despicable.
The nations shall rush upon them as a flood.
The troubles shall come upon them in one night.

Chapter 18

Today's Ethiopia is not the same as that of the Old Testament.
Ethiopia is hurriedly sending messengers in preparation for the Assyrian invasion.
But God will prune the Assyrian branches and Ethiopia shall be spared.
Their bodies shall be left to the birds and beasts.
185,000 Assyrians found this to be true.
Ethiopia will then send gifts to the place where the name of the Lord is found. (Mt. Zion: See 1 Kings 8:29; 2 Kings 23:27.)

Chapter 19

Egypt will collapse.
The Assyrians will gain control.
False gods will be no help.
A cruel lord will arise and rule over Egypt.
God's judgment will include drought and invasion.
Their wise men will become as fools.
The entire nation will reel as a drunk.
But the false worship will be replaced by true worship.
And unity of the nations shall come through a Messiah. (See verses 23-25; John 14:6; Matthew 7:13-14; Luke 1:79; Psalm 119:35 and Isaiah 35:8.)
We note that Alexandria, Egypt later became a center for Christianity.

Chapter 20

Isaiah now walks barefoot and naked to show the certainty of the King of Assyria taking captives from Egypt and Ethiopia within three years.
This provides a warning for Judah.
Judah cries, "How shall we escape?"

Chapter 21

Babylon is to fall.
The picture is so tragic Isaiah wants to turn away.
Instead of turning to Jehovah men are seen banqueting.
Remember Daniel's picture of Belshazzar's banquet.
Edom is the same as Dumah.

The watchman is asked how long the night will last.

It will come to an end but unless they repent it will be of no use.

The princes of Arabia will fall within a year.

Jehovah's judgment marches on and only repentance could change it.

But there are not many who repent.

Chapter 22

The valley of vision refers to the fact that the prophetic visions had come out of Jerusalem.

Judah was under siege but they had made material preparations without turning to Jehovah.

They should have repented.

Instead they had a party.

Death would be the result.

The chief treasurer Shebna was second in power even to the King.

But Shebna had abused the keys to the Kingdom.

He would be replaced with a more faithful steward called Eliakim, who would use the key of David more appropriately.

This verse is referred to in the Revelation description of Jesus. (Rev. 3:7.) See also 2 Kings 18:19.

Chapter 23

Tyre was a center of shipping and materialism.

Returning ships would find the port gone.

Sailors would receive the news in Cyprus beforehand.

Egypt depended upon Tyre's ships and so would grieve.

In a period of seventy years Tyre should go from the one nation to the other in attempts at fornication.

Ultimately she will see the Lord's people inherit.

Chapter 24

The preceding have been specific for individual nations.

Now the warnings turn general in nature.

God will shake the entire earth.

No individual will be too big or important to feel the consequences. See Revelation 6:14-17; 20:12.

The reason is given as the breaking of the laws, statutes and commandments of God's eternal laws.

One cannot afford to ignore either God's:
1. Natural laws.
2. Spiritual laws.

The land has become polluted or profane.

The merrymaking ceases and the houses must now be shut up or locked.

All the confused rebellion shall be broken down.

The remnant which shall be left will be as the few olives left after the harvest.

The survivors shall rejoice in the Glory of God.

But Isaiah cannot rejoice as he feels the sorrow of the harvest of punishment.

The entire earth will reel as a drunken man.

Some see the host of the high ones in verse 21 as principalities and powers in heavenly places.

After the turmoil God shall reign in Mount Zion.

Chapter 25

This chapter is a hymn of thanksgiving.

God is praised for his destruction of the city of confusion.

While he destroys the proud he protects the humble.

In Mount Zion there shall be many blessings.

Death, tears and shame shall be removed from his people.

Those who trust in him will rejoice in their salvation.

Those who build walls against him will find them brought down into the dust.

Chapter 26

God provides a strong city for his own.

Those within are protected by the walls of salvation.

Only those who keep the faith may enter in. See 2 Timothy 4:6-8.

Those who do enter in shall find perfect peace.

When God's judgments strike there are some who learn of righteousness.

There are some who will not see even when the Lord's hand is lifted up.

The nation of Israel had brought forth nothing in her labors until the remnant recognized God.

Now they shall bring forth and the dead shall come to life.

While God's own find protection the wicked shall be punished.

Chapter 27

The dragon, the serpent and leviathan may all be the same monster.

See Job 41:1; Psalm 104:26; Revelation 12; 20:2.

God now promises to make the useless vineyard of Chapter 5:1-7 a fruitful place which will provide fruit throughout the earth.

73

Jacob will take root and no briers and thorns will be able to choke him out.

The defenced city shall present no obstacle to God as he gathers his own from both Egypt and Babylon.

This gathering probably has reference to both Babylonian exile and to the ingathering begun at Pentecost.

When the outcasts return to God they shall worship at Mount Zion and Jerusalem.

Chapter 28

This chapter begins a series of woes against rebels.

1. Woe to the drunkards of Ephraim, 28:1-29.
2. Woe to Jerusalem, 29:1-14.
3. Woe to those who hide counsel from God, 29:15-24.
4. Woe to those who trust in Egypt, 30:1-33.
5. Woe to those who seek help from Egypt, 31:1-32:20.
6. Woe to Assyria, 33:1-24.

The tribe of Ephraim is drunken and not fit to rule.

The Assyrian storm will soon destroy their pride.

They are like figs ready to be picked.

Even the religious rulers are drunken.

The tables are covered with vomit and there is no clean place.

They are bored with God's presentation of his Word:

1. Line by line.
2. Precept by precept.
3. Here a little—there a little.

Since they will not understand God will speak to them in Assyrian and Babylonian terms.

They rule by falsehood and lying.

God will provide a true foundation and will measure their lies with the plumbline. See Amos 7:7-8; Romans 9:32-33; 10:11; 1 Peter 2:6-10; Matthew 16:18; 21:42-44; Ephesians 2:19-20; 1 Corinthians 3:11.

God's true foundation of rule is: a stone, tried; a corner, sure.

The line and the plummet are justice and righteousness.

The Assyrian storm will sweep away the part that does not meet the plumbline.

The measuremnts they have been making are "way off."

There is no way to be comfortable with them.

Like the farmer who uses the truth to get a harvest those who hear his Word will share his workmanship.

Chapter 29

Now Isaiah turns to the city of Ariel (Jerusalem).

This is the city where David dwelt and where the sacrifices to God are offered.

Ariel means "Hearth of God."

Ariel shall be distressed and brought to the ground.

There shall be but a whisper left of her strong voice.

Most of those who dwell there are strangers whom God will blow away as chaff and dust.

Also the enemies of Ariel shall disappear as a dream does in the morning.

Ariel has blinded itself.

How did God pour out the spirit of deep sleep?

See Romans 11:8-10, 20-22.

It is done as they come into contact with the truth and shut their eyes.

Carnal minds do not grasp the truth. See Romans 8:5-8; 1 Corinthians 2:14.

The book of God is sealed to them, with the learned and the unlearned in the same condition.

Compare Matthew 15:8-9 and 1 Corinthians 1:19-20.

They tend to memorize God's truth in a mechanical manner.

And then they add their own traditions.

They are like the clay which claims to be wiser than the potter.

God will bring about a complete change:
1. Blind will see;
2. Poor will rejoice;
3. Meek will be blessed, Luke 4.

Israel shall become free from fear.

There shall be a resurgence of understanding.

Some of the murmurers will accept his book and teaching.

Chapter 30

They have been trusting in Egypt rather than God.

Trust in bombs and alliances are pure foolishness.

Ten righteous would have saved Sodom.

Jerusalem was not conquered until God allowed it.

The strength of Egypt will bring only shame.

Perhaps verse 8 is speaking about the book of Isaiah.

God's children have asked for false prophets who will speak only smooth things which they like to hear.

They are like a rotten wall ready to buckle.

They have turned from the quietness of God to the supposed strength of horses and chariots.

See Leviticus 26:8, 36; Deuteronomy 28:25; 32:30.

75

God will one day bless the remnant: they must be patient; they must listen to his Word; they must reject their idols.

They will then be restored and returned to Zion.

The proud Assyrians will be stopped by God-not Egypt.

The *tophet* is a place for the burning of bodies.

Some connect this with hell.

Chapter 31

Woe to those who not only trust in Egypt, but seek help there.

To trust in man is to distrust God.

The Egyptians are only men and their horses and chariots are material rather than spiritual.

Jehovah will protect his own as:

1. A lion protects its prey.
2. A mother bird protects her young.

The Israelites need to turn back to the only One who is capable of saving them.

They must reject the idols of silver and gold made with their own hands.

The Assyrians shall fall by the sword of the Lord, not by that of a mighty or vicious man.

God's fiery furnace in Zion and Jerusalem will strike fear into the hearts of the Assyrians.

Chapter 32

Here is a promise that the future shall be better.

A marvelous new king shall reign in righteousness and justice.

Some believe this king to be Hezekiah. See 2 Kings 18:3-6.

Many believe the reference to be to Christ.

See Jeremiah 23:5; Isaiah 9:6-7; Daniel 7:14; Acts 2:30-33; Luke 1:31-33.

It may well have dual application.

Men shall become a blessing to others rather than a curse: A hiding place from the wind; a refreshing stream in a dry land; a shadow of a rock in weary days.

There shall be a spiritual awakening: Eyes shall see; ears shall hear; hearts shall understand; tongues shall speak plainly.

Compare 1 Corinthians 3:12.

Evil and good shall not be confused. The vile person shall not be called liberal; the liberal man shall truly be liberal. Compare 5:20.

Notice the different meaning of the term "liberal."

Women have been overconfident in their ease.

They will have reason to repent for the land will be turned from pleasant fields to briers and thorns.

After this the Spirit shall be poured out and conditions will be reversed.

See 11:2; 44:3; 59:21; Ezekiel 39:39; Joel 2:28; Acts 2:17-21.

Peace, quietness and righteousness shall then be found.

The people of God shall be interested in sowing and reaping as opposed to oppression and injustice.

Chapter 33

Woe unto Assyria.

Assyria was spoiling and dealing treacherously with the people of God.

God will use her to chastise and then will punish her.

Assyria will flee at the exaltation of Jehovah.

The Israelites will swarm over the remains like locusts and caterpillars. See 2 Kings 18-19.

When conditions seem the worst God will exalt himself.

Those who oppose shall see bad times.

They shall have stubble for offspring.

They shall be consumed with fire as the thorns.

Only the righteous in Zion will be saved.

1. Who despise the gain of oppression.
2. Who do not take bribes.
3. Who do not like to hear of violence.
4. Who turn away their eyes from evil.
   See Romans 8:28

The righteous shall see a King in his beauty.

Since the land they see is afar off it would seem to be the Kingdom of Heaven.

The righteous must look beyond the Assyrians who speak with tongues they do not understand to see a new Zion which shall never be overcome.

They must trust in Jehovah who will provide a river of refreshment with no turbulence of warships.

Jehovah must be: Judge, Lawgiver, Savior.

Chapter 34

Chapters 34 and 35 are companion chapters.

Chapter 34 speaks of the doom of God's enemies.

Chapter 35 speaks of the exaltation of Zion.

Edom is used as a prime example of the enemies of Jehovah.

All the nations are called to attention.

God's indignation is about to become apparent.

The upheaval will include both heaven and earth:

1. The mountains melt in the heat of the bloodshed.
2. The stars of heaven remove from their places.

We are reminded that mountains and stars are both highly symbolic in the prophetic books.

It may be that the prophet speaks of the breaking down of the power and the rulers of Edom.

Those who have attempted to destroy Zion will now come to destruction.

Edom shall become uninhabited and desolate.

The desolation shall be of eternal nature.

These prophecies are to be written down so that men of all the ages may read them and know of God's ability to move in the affairs of nations.

Chapter 35

The Israelites who are so dry and barren in Isaiah's day are some day to blossom and be fruitful.

This chapter could easily be connected to chapter 40 since after the interlude of chapters 36-39 the scene of this chapter is elaborated upon. See Romans 7:4.

They are exhorted to be faithful and strong.

Compare Hebrews 3:13; 12:12; 10:24-25 and Romans 5:3-5.

The miracles of Jesus are said to be fulfillment of the words of verses 5-7. See Matthew 11:2-5; 13:15-17.

There is to be a highway available for those who *choose* to come out of bondage.

It is however only for the Holy.

Only the redeemed will pass over it. See Titus 2:14.

It may be found by the simplest of intellects.

Upon this highway there can be no real danger: One may be attacked physically or spiritually. But no force can tear away the faithful from the Highway of Holiness which leads to Glory. See James 4:7; Romans 8:31-39; 16:20.

Chapter 36

This chapter and the next three provide a transition between the two major portions of the book.

Chapters 36 and 37 show the end of Assyrian threat to Jerusalem.

Chapters 38 and 39 introduce the encounter with Babylon which takes place in the chapters to come.

King Sennacherib of Assyria was ransacking the kingdom of Judah at this time.

2 Kings 18:13-16 tells of Hezekiah's offer to pay tribute to him.

The following account indicates the reason for his fear.

"As for Hezekiah the Jew, who did not bow in submission to my yoke, forty-six of his strong walled towns and innumerable smaller villages in the neighborhood I besieged and conquered by stamping down earth-ramps and then bringing up battering rams, by the assault of foot soldiers, by breaches, tunneling and sapper operations. I made to come out from them 200,150 people, young and old, male and female, innumerable horses, mules, donkeys, camels, small and large cattle, and counted them as spoils of war. He himself I shut up like a caged bird within Jerusalem, his royal city."

Sennacherib sent Rabshakeh, a high officer to talk Hezekiah into surrender.

At the time Hezekiah stood by a water conduit which had been prepared to prevent the Assyrians from getting water during the siege.

In 1880 archeologists identified this conduit in the city of Jerusalem by an inscription on its wall.

Hezekiah sent messengers to the city wall to talk with Rabshakeh.

Rabshakeh makes several arguments for surrender.
1. Egypt is like a broken reed and cannot defend Jerusalem.
2. Hezekiah has offended Jehovah and so they need not turn to him.
3. I can offer 2,000 horses *if* you can provide riders for them.
4. The Lord himself has sent us to conquer you.

Hezekiah's messengers are afraid and tell Rabshakeh not to speak in the Jewish language where the guards on the city wall might understand him.

Rabshakeh then cries out in defiance and makes more points before the guards.
1. Don't let Hezekiah make you believe the Lord will protect you.
2. The king of Assyria can bring peace and security to all of you.
3. No god of any land has been able to deliver from my king.

The messengers of Hezekiah did not answer, but returned to Hezekiah with rent clothing and the bad news.

Chapter 37
Hezekiah grieves and goes to the temple sending the messengers to Isaiah the prophet.

Isaiah informs them that they are not to fear the king of Assyria since he will return to his own land and fall by the sword there.

Hezekiah then receives another message by letter from Rabshakeh placing more pressure upon him.

79

Hezekiah decides to pray to Jehovah and spread all the matter before him.

His prayer makes an excellent model for others.

See Philippians 4:6; James 5:13, 16.

God hears and answers the prayer:
1. Assyria has been foolish to blaspheme itself and exalt itself against the Holy one of Israel.
2. Jerusalem will shake its head and laugh at the Assyrian king.
3. He is through with Assyria now and will put a hook in her nose and a bridle in her mouth.
4. Assyria will be turned around in her tracks.

It will be a sign to Jerusalem that in a two-year period they will be able to sow in the fields surrounding the city.

In the night the angel of the Lord strikes the Assyrian camp killing 185,000 men.

Sennacherib returns home to dwell at Nineveh.

He is killed by two of his sons while worshipping in the temple of a false god.

Another son, Essar-haddon reigns in his place.

Interesting records are found among the Egyptians as to how the Assyrian army was defeated in an unexpected manner.

Chapter 38

Hezekiah now becomes sick and is informed he is to prepare for death.

He beseeches God to remember his righteous life.

God informs Hezekiah that Jerusalem will be protected from any further Assyrian invasion, and that he will add fifteen years to Hezekiah's life.

Hezekiah sings a song of praise and thanksgiving:
1. He describes his feelings when about to die.
2. He praises God for his assistance.
3. He describes the procedure used to cure him.

A sign was given to Hezekiah that he might know with confidence that God would keep his promise.

The sun was to return ten degrees on the sundial.

Chapter 39

The king of Babylon then sent a present to Hezekiah when he heard of Hezekiah's recovery.

Hezekiah in his happiness and pride showed the messengers all the riches and armaments of the kingdom.

Isaiah asks Hezekiah what the men have been shown and where they were from.

When told they were from Babylon and that they have been shown everything he scolded Hezekiah: Isaiah told Hezekiah that the riches shall be carried away to Babylon; the men of the kingdom shall become servants to the king of Babylon.

Hezekiah understands but seems not to be very worried because God has promised the security of Jerusalem during his own days.

Remember that this prophecy takes place over a century before the actual fulfillment occurs.

It is very easy to confuse the two major enemies of Jerusalem —the Assyrians of Isaiah's own day—and the Babylonians of whom he prophesies.

Chapter 40

Beginning with Chapter 40 the material is a message of comfort and hope of deliverance to a people in Babylonian captivity.

They have ignored the message of the prophets in the past.

Now they are under chastisement for their neglect.

But there is reason to take hope for God has not forgotten and there will be a remnant restored.

A voice is to cry out about a highway of deliverance in the wilderness.

Compare with Matthew 3:3 as applied to John the Baptist.

There is much dual application in the last 26 chapters of Isaiah.

The voice cries that though men pass away the Word of God abides forever and his promises will never fail.

Chapter 41

God calls all nations to listen to his evidences.

God who is the first and last has been working in the affairs of the nations from the beginning.

The nations may have tried to strengthen each other in their fear of Jehovah's purposes.

Yet Israel is his servant and is chosen from among all peoples of the earth.

God will uphold Israel in the face of her foes.

Opposition shall be blown away like chaff before the glory of the Holy One of Israel.

The enemies who see Israel restored will have evidence that God is with his servant Israel.

Nations with false gods are challenged to bring them forth to make the same kind of predictions that Jehovah is able to make.

Their gods are *nothings* and cannot answer a word.

81

Chapter 42
    This is the first of four "servant" passages.
    The apostles considered it a privilege to be a servant of God.
    Other servant passages are: 49:1-7; 50:4-9; 52:13-53:12.
    Israel is sometimes the servant.
    Other times Christ is clearly meant.
    It is likely that as the Son of man Christ is considered a part of
        spiritual Israel, or the People of God.
    Some have suggested that Cyrus or even Isaiah is the servant.
    Some of the descriptions cannot apply to either, or to any ex-
        cept Jesus Christ.
    Each of these at one time or another is related to the main
        theme of service.
    Jesus is obviously the center of Isaiah 53 because it was this
        passage where the eunuch was reading when Philip began to
        preach unto him Jesus.
    God's Spirit was given to Jesus without measure.
    The work of Christ was done in a gentle manner without force.
    The heart was to be changed.
    Jesus and his blood provide a covenant for us now.
    All the creation is to give praise to the Lord of Glory.
    For covenant passages see Jeremiah 31:31-34; Isaiah 49:8.
    Christ will release those in the captivity of sin.
    Joy and sight for blind eyes will be provided.
    Crooked paths will be made straight.
    God's servant had been blind and deaf to his presence.
    He had therefore allowed them to be spoiled and captured.
    God's anger has been poured out upon the foolish servant.
Chapter 43
    Now Israel has served long enough and will be redeemed.
    Israel shall be flooded but not drowned.
    They shall be burned but not consumed.
    It will cost the lives of men but God would bring Israel back.
    The spiritually blind and deaf will be provided with sufficient
        testimony that there is one God, that they will have no ex-
        cuse for their actions.
    The nation of Israel when restored will act as his witnesses.
    There will be a new creation which will make the earth bloom
        in a way that no false god could ever do.
    The blessings God was prepared to give were far better than
        his people deserved.
    Rather than bringing him acceptable sacrifices they had wea-
        ried him with their sins.
    Their sin is responsible for their captivity.

Chapter 44

They are to hope and not to fear.

Jesurun means—the upright one.

See Deuteronomy 33:5, 26; 32:15.

Refreshing times were to come.

The life-giving spirit would be poured out as a flood upon dry ground.

Both Jew and Gentile will be proud to call themselves by the name of the Lord.

The foolishness of worshipping idols is shown: A man cuts a tree; he burns part of it to warm himself; he uses part of it to cook his food; he takes the rest and carves out a useless image; he has deceived his own heart and holds a lie in his hand in the form of the completed idol.

Through his redeeming power God would glorify himself in Israel.

The same God who had done all the things of verses 24-27 predicts that Cyrus will decree the rebuilding of the temple and the city of Jerusalem.

Though the prediction is made over a century beforehand it came true even to the name of Cyrus.

There is some discussion over the name Cyrus, since its meaning is "Lord."

There are strong similarities between the delivering power of Jesus and that of Cyrus.

Chapter 45

To be anointed is to be appointed to a responsibility.

God would see that opposing kings would be caught unprepared before the march of Cyrus.

It is to become evident to Cyrus through mysterious blessings that Jehovah is with Israel.

God has even given Cyrus his name though Cyrus did not know him.

God creates darkness and evil by producing goodness and light.

As soon as one comes into existence the other is a reality.

Righteousness is a characteristic from heaven itself since man cannot make himself righteous when he has sinned.

No man has the power to contend with his creator.

The temple shall be rebuilt and the captives shall be released through the deliverer.

Even the African nations shall produce converts to the true God.

All other nations shall be confused but Israel who trusts in the Lord shall not be.

No idol can predict like the God who tells of Cyrus.

Sometime every knee shall bow and every tongue confess. See Romans 14:11 and Philippians 2:10-11.

Chapter 46

Bel and Nebo were Babylonian gods.

Bel is found in the name Bel-shazzar.

Nebo is found in the name Nebuchadnezzar

Bel is the Babylonian form of the god Baal.

These gods cannot deliver.

They will be overthrown.

They will be carried into captivity themselves.

These gods must be carried about on weary beasts.

The true God carries men; he is not carried by them.

Again the challenge is made to the false gods to predict the end from the beginning if they can.

Jehovah will provide salvation in Zion and this will separate him from false gods.

Chapter 47

Beautiful and pampared Babylon will be brought down to sit in the dust.

She sounds here exactly like the fallen Babylon harlot of Revelation.

She will sit in darkness, silence and ugliness.

She who trusted in wickedness will be brought down in a moment.

No false source of wisdom will save Babylon: enchanters, stargazers, astrologers, nor sorcerers.

They shall fall before Jehovah's wisdom as chaff in the fire.

Nothing shall save Babylon.

Chapter 48

Israel provided a lot of lip service to Jehovah.

God had given them abundant evidence of his power.

Yet they had hard heads (brass brows).

God will complete his plan of deliverance in spite of Israel's weakness.

He will do it for future generations and the glorification of his name.

God desires that they should have listened to his commandments.

Now Israel must be called forth from captivity in Babylon because of their indiscretion.

They will then sing Jehovah's praises.

But there will be no peace for those who fail to respect the voice of the Lord.

Chapter 49

Here the servant has a mission to Israel and thus cannot be Israel.

The servant has the ability to speak with penetrating truths like a sharp sword. See Hebrews 4:12-13.

The servant shall provide light to the Gentiles to bring salvation to all nations.

The servant will be preserved and will act as a covenant with God's people.

There shall be food, freedom and light for those who have been hungry, bound and confused.

God's people shall come from every direction to Zion.

God has not forgotten his own any more than a woman can forget her tiny suckling infant.

His children will not be left in Babylon.

Those who oppress God's people will be persuaded that he is the Holy One of Israel.

Chapter 50

God had not wanted to put away unfaithful Israel.

They had rejected him like an unfaithful wife.

But the servant will deliver them.

The servant would speak in a clear and effective manner.

The servant has several characteristics:
1. He listens to God.
2. He meekly suffers for God's people.
3. He is determined and never confused.

Those who would kindle their own fires for light will not receive assistance from the God they have rejected.

They shall lie down in sorrow.

Chapter 51

Israel is to look back to the rock that carried them through former days for present comfort.

Through Zion God's salvation shall be presented and it shall be everlasting.

The wicked shall be destroyed as garments before moths and wool before worms.

The foundation for a new creation is being laid.

Jerusalem has been as foolish as a drunken fool.

But God will finish his chastisement of them and then turn to Babylon.

The cup of God's wrath shall be taken away from their lips and placed before the lips of Babylon who now enslaves them.

Chapter 52

Jerusalem was like a fallen woman who must arise now and put on fresh and attractive garments.

No one is then to enter Jerusalem with an unholy nature.

Here is a strong dual prophecy.

It is unpleasant to God that his people are ruled over and made to howl with their condition.

They shall come to the realization that he is God.

The feet of those who carry the Gospel of God are beautiful to the one who believes and responds to the message.

They will sing with joy when they are released.

All of the earth shall see the salvation of the Lord.

Once cleansed they are to remain separate from the defilements of the world.

God would go both ahead of them and before them if they were interested in salvation.

Verse 13 begins the fourth and last servant passage.

The servant who delivers Israel will be a most unusual person:
1. Wise.
2. Very high and exalted.
3. His face and form disturbed by suffering.
4. He should sprinkle many nations in purification.
   (This is done through his blood. See 1 Peter 1:2.)
5. Kings shall stand in awe of his wisdom.

Chapter 53

The Jews will not believe his report because he is not as they expect.

He grows up unexpectedly as a root or shoot of Jesse rising up out of the dry ground of the Jewish nation.

There is nothing about his physical stature which would account for the impressiveness of his teachings.

He is despised and rejected by all, and this includes even the apostles who lived with him for over three years.

He knew the meaning of grief and sorrow, weeping with Mary and Martha over Lazarus and crying out, "O Jerusalem, Jerusalem."

He had more to give than any man who ever lived, yet we esteemed him not for his true worth.

His body was wounded and bruised as our own souls received healing.

86

It was his responsibility to take the punishment for all God's
sheep who have strayed.

He therefore went to the sacrifice as a lamb without a struggle.

His life was cut off and he could never have descendants.

Yet God provides him with children every time a person obeys
the Gospel.

His spoil as a conqueror will be the saved souls of men.

To him we will turn for one to plead our case with God.

Through knowledge of him men shall be able to stand in righteousness before their God.

Chapter 54

Now the sorrow of the previous suffering servant turns to joy
and singing.

Barren Israel will bear many children.

Her blessings will be far greater than could be expected.

Any present suffering will turn into joy because Israel's husband is Jehovah.

There will be a new covenant which will be everlasting.

The very mountains will be removed before this covenant be
ended.

A New Jerusalem is to be built and will outlast every onslaught.

Their wisdom will not depend upon the frailty of human
priests.

They will be established through righteousness.

Any who gather together against God's servant shall fall.

Chapter 55

Salvation is considered to be a great feast.

It cannot be bought with money.

Listen to God's invitation and the promises to David will be
yours.

But it is important to listen while he can be found.

The time will come when men will seek and not find.

God's ways and thoughts are far higher than man's.

God's Word is powerful and effective and will accomplish its
purpose.

At the release of Israel from bondage all nature will ring out
with praise to God.

Chapter 56

All distinctions among men shall fall.

Those who once were excluded from the worship will now be
included—the eunuch—the stranger.

They shall be given a new name.

All who are faithful will be allowed in God's house.

Even so the present leaders of Israel are like watchdogs who lie asleep.

They look to their own ways rather than the ways of God.

They look to drunken pleasures of the moment instead of the eternal pleasures of God's righteousness.

Chapter 57

When a righteous man dies men of Israel do not take notice because they do not know the difference.

Too many of them have become idolators and adulterers.

They have gone to the extent of sacrificing their own children to idols.

They shall come to destruction.

On the contrary the meek shall inherit Mount Zion.

God will revive their spirits and hearts.

When they become contrite and humble he will cease to chastise or contend with them.

God will heal the penitent but there will never be peace for the wicked.

Chapter 58

The people of Israel must be made to see their sin.

This will not be easy because they have become accustomed to shallow "ceremonial" type worship.

Their religious services were planned to please themselves rather than God.

They wonder why God does not respond to their shallow worship.

When they will allow God to affect their daily lives God will respond to their worship.

If they will respond to others God will lift them.

When this happens they will receive great blessings.

Chapter 59

It was Israel's sin which had separated them from God.

God gives a list of sins of which Israel is guilty.

In this condition there will be no peace.

Israel is groping like the blind in darkness.

There is no justice and they are like dead men.

Jehovah cannot depend upon depraved earthly Israel for the spreading of salvation.

A Redeemer is to come!

A new covenant will be created.

God's Word will be brought through the lips of the Redeemer. The Spirit of God will provide power for conquest through the Word.

Chapter 60

Darkness shall cover the earth but the glory of the Lord will shine through the people of God.

The Gentiles shall come to the light of God.

There will be a City of God.

And there shall be a Mountain where God dwells.

All nations will flow into the House of God.

The gates shall always be open to those who are obedient.

Compare the description of God's city here with that of Heaven in Revelation 21:22-27.

Chapter 61

The captives shall be freed from Babylon which is typical of the bondage of sin worldwide.

Verses 1 through 3 are quoted by Jesus in Luke 4 and applied to himself.

There shall be a kingdom of priests.

They shall be called ministers of God.

There shall be rejoicing in salvation and righteousness instead of gold and pleasure.

Chapter 62

A new name shall be a symbol of new character.

See 62:2; 62:4; 65:15 and Revelation 3:12.

Jehovah will adore his new people as a husband adores his wife.

Israel shall be a crown of glory to God just as a woman is to be the crown of glory to her husband in the New Testament.

The prophets as watchmen and the elders of the New Testament are to continue to warn and preach the Word.

There is to be a time of peace and plenty.

A highway is to exist for the passage of all who wish to move from the kingdom of darkness into the new Kingdom.

They shall be called "sought out" which sounds amazingly like the "called out" of the New Testament Church.

Chapter 63

Jehovah will trample his enemies in the winepress of his wrath. Compare Revelation 19:11-21.

Man will never be able by his own power to remove evil from his midst.

Only by the power of God will the final battle be won.

God had saved his people over and over again.

Since this is true there is hope that he will continue to bless his own.

Isaiah longs for God to act since it is only by his power that deliverance may come from the captivity.

Chapter 64

There is a continuation of the plea for God to act both with respect to the righteous and the wicked.

God has done so many impressive things in the past.

Now man can only wait and hope for action in the future.

Israel now recognizes her sins are responsible for her troubles.

They call upon God and try to show a penitent heart.

All of Jerusalem and Mount Zion are in trouble.

Will God act?

Chapter 65

God will be found by the Gentiles.

His own people of Israel had been deaf to his voice.

Their afflictions were of their own making.

They stand by themselves in a "Holier than thou" attitude.

They sting God's nostrils like smoke.

Jehovah will not remain silent—the answer will come.

A small remnant like a cluster of grapes after harvest will be spared.

God's servants will eat.

The unfaithful will become spiritually hungry.

The new creation will include the redeemed only.

The new Jerusalem will not be confined to a specific geographical location.

There shall be blessings of every kind, peace, joy, many offspring and genuine happiness.

Chapter 66

There will now be no need for an earthly temple.

Animal sacrifices will be abolished. See Romans 12:2.

A new birth will bring children to Zion.

God has watched pregnant Israel for some time.

Now the new Creation is to be born.

Zion will be bountifully blessed by Jehovah.

The enemies of Jehovah are warned.

God's people shall be gathered from all nations.

His enemies shall be burned as chaff.

His own people shall be in continual worship.

6. *Important lessons from the book of Isaiah*

A. Men become conscious of their own unworthiness when they catch a vision of the glory of God.
B. God will replace a corrupt earthly Israel with a new creation.
C. A Redeemer will come to deliver God's people from captivity.
D. Out of ancient Israel there should be a small remnant preserved to bring God's plans and promises to bless the world into practice.
E. In the new creation both Jew and Gentile shall be united in one flock with one Shepherd.

KINGS OF ISRAEL AND JUDAH

KINGS OF ISRAEL

NAME	REIGN	CHARACTER	PROPHETS
Jeroboam	22 years	Evil	
Nadab	2 years	Evil	
Baasha	24 years	Evil	
Elah	2 years	Evil	
Zimri	7 days	Evil	
Omri	12 years	Evil	
Ahab	22 years	Evil	Elijah
Ahaziah	2 years	Evil	Elijah
Jehoram	12 years	Evil	Elisha
Jehu	28 years	Evil	Elisha
Jehoahaz	17 years	Evil	Elisha
Joash	16 years	Evil	Elisha
Jeroboam II	41 years	Evil	Jonah, Hosea, Amos
Zachariah	6 months	Evil	
Shallum	1 month	Evil	
Menahem	10 years	Evil	
Pekahiah	2 years	Evil	
Pekah	20 years	Evil	
Hoshea	9 years	Evil	

KINGS OF JUDAH

NAME	REIGN	CHARACTER	PROPHETS
Rehoboam	17 years	Evil	
Abijam	3 years	Evil	
Asa	41 years	Good	
Jehoshaphat	25 years	Good	
Jehoram	8 years	Evil	Obadiah
Ahaziah	1 year	Evil	
Joash	40 years	Good	Joel
Amaziah	25 years	Good	
Uzziah	52 years	Good	Isaiah
Jotham	16 years	Good	Isaiah, Micah
Ahaz	16 years	Evil	Isaiah, Micah
Hezekiah	29 years	Good	Isaiah, Micah, Nahum
Manasseh	55 years	Evil	
Amon	2 years	Evil	
Josiah	31 years	Good	Jeremiah, Zephaniah
Jehoahaz	3 months	Evil	Jeremiah
Jehoiakim	11 years	Evil	Jeremiah, Ezekiel, Daniel
Jehoiachin	3 months	Evil	Jeremiah, Habakkuk, Ezekiel, Daniel
Zedekiah	11 years	Evil	Jeremiah, Ezekiel, Daniel

BABYLONIAN CAPTIVITY
Jeremiah, Ezekiel, Daniel

RETURN FROM CAPTIVITY
Haggai, Zechariah, Malachi

NAHUM
(Consolation)

1. *Background for the book of Nahum*
   A. Assyria is at the very height of her power.
   B. The Assyrian kings are as follows:
      1. Tiglath-Pileser—747-727
      2. Shalmaneser V—727-722
      3. Sargon II—722-705
      4. Sennacherib—705-681
      5. Esarhaddon—681-668
      6. Assurbanipal—668-625
      7. Asuritililani—625-620
      8. Esarhaddon II—620-612—Destroyed in Nineveh's fall
   C. Nahum speaks to the time of Esarhaddon II.
   D. Opression and injustice reign.
      1. Captured enemies were inhumanly treated.
      2. Nineveh seduces the world with her glory.
      3. The bloody city is full of lies and robbery.

2. *The man, Nahum*
   A. Nahum is contemporary with Jeremiah, Zephaniah and Habakkuk.
   B. He is a native of Elkosh. (Location uncertain)
      1. Some say a short distance from Nineveh.
      2. Others say from Capernaum (village of Nahum) Galilee.
      3. Still others believe him to be of Judah.
   C. He is a single-minded poet. (Nineveh must fall)
   D. His name infers a message of consolation to Judah that their tormentor will meet an end.

3. *The nature of the book of Nahum*
   A. Date of the book.
      1. After the fall of No-amon which occurred 663 B.C.
      2. Before the fall of Nineveh which occurred 612 B.C.
      3. Probably about 620 shortly before Nineveh's fall.
   B. The theme of the book is the doom of Nineveh.
   C. The book is vivid in description.

D. Nineveh becomes the symbol of all God's enemies.

E. Outline of the book.

  1. God is judge of Nineveh.

    a. He is severe and powerful toward the wicked.

    b. He is a refuge to the righteous.

  2. Sentence is pronounced.

    a. God will arise against Nineveh.

    b. She will be utterly cut off.

  3. Her punishment is described.

    a. Her power shall be removed.

    b. Her riches shall be plundered.

    c. She will be laid waste like No-amon of Egypt.

  4. Her sickness cannot be healed.

  5. Her tributary nations will rejoice at her downfall.

NOTE: For a good description of the inhumanity of Nineveh see Farrar, *Minor Prophets*, pp. 147-148.

4. *Comments on the text of Nahum*

Chapter 1

Nineveh was located on the Tigris River.

Long ago Jonah had reluctantly preached to them.

Jehovah is mentioned five times in verses two and three.

Several characteristics of Jehovah are listed: he is jealous; he is furious; he will not acquit the wicked; all nature trembles at his presence; nothing can stand before his wrath.

Yet he provides a stronghold in time of trouble for those who obey him.

God will bring Assyria to a complete and utter end.

When he is finished they shall not rise up again.

They had become drunken upon their own power.

The yoke of Assyrian oppression shall be broken.

God himself will dig their grave.

He did such a good job it was not found until the 19th century.

The feet of those who carry such good news are most beautiful to God's people.

Chapter 2

God had turned away from his people and allowed them to be emptied by the Assyrians.

Now Assyria itself will be plundered.

The battle shall rage in the streets.

The Assyrians shall hasten to the walls to defend.

The cry to STAND shall be met by panic.

The enemy will empty Assyria of her ill-gotten riches of silver and gold.

The place where the fierce lionlike soldiers have made their headquarters will see faint hearts and knocking knees.

Her armies shall be destroyed.

Her boldest warriors shall be killed.

She shall no longer feast on other nations.

Other nations shall no longer fear her demanding messengers.

I AM AGAINST HER!

Chapter 3

Nineveh has been a city ruling by bloodshed and lies.

The battle continues to rage.

Corpses lie in piles in the street.

Her immorality and false religion have brought severe consequences.

Nineveh shall be exposed for the vile thing she is.

She shall be made a laughing stock before the nations.

Nineveh is no more secure than the Egyptian city of No which was plundered and taken captive.

Nineveh shall reel as a drunken man before God.

All the defenses shall fall like ripened figs.

God will open the gates of the city to her enemies.

The rulers and princes shall flee away in fear as grasshoppers.

The people of the city shall be scattered and never reassembled.

Nineveh suffers from a terminal illness and thus must die.

Those who hear of the calamity will rejoice in her annihilation.

The wickedness Nineveh has spread over the earth shall cease.

5. *Important lessons from the book of Nahum*

   A. God is a righteous judge, being both good and severe at once.

   B. There is no strength or glory of men which will stand before the Lord.

   C. Lying and injustice are an abomination to Jehovah.

   D. There shall come a time when the righteous will rejoice for their patient endurance.

   E. Oppression of others is not the best way to win friends.

ZEPHANIAH
(Jehovah Hides)

1. *Background for the book of Zephaniah*
   A. Political background
      1. Good king Hezekiah was succeeded by his evil son Manasseh.
      2. Manasseh repented of his evil leadership while captive in Babylon.
      3. His later efforts to undo the harm were useless.
      4. Manasseh's son was named Amon.
      5. The son of Amon was the good king Josiah.
      6. Josiah turned to the Lord early and began to institute reforms by the age of twenty.
      7. During repair of the temple a copy of the law was found and Josiah sent for Huldah the prophetess to inquire for advice.
      8. Zephaniah does not emphasize Josiah's reforms, perhaps because he knew they were doomed to failure because of the shallow hearts of the people.
      9. Assyria had been queen of the nations for a century.
      10. In 626 B.C. Babylon declared their independence.
      11. By 612 Nebuchadnezzar conquered Nineveh with the aid of the Medes.
      12. Pharaoh-Necho decided to march through Palestine to aid Assyria and Josiah intervened only to lose his life. (At Megiddo)
      13. Nabopolassar died and Nebuchadnezzar hurried back to become king, carrying Daniel, and others with him.
   B. Moral and religious background
      1. Josiah's reforms did not change the hearts of the people.
      2. Among their sins were:
         a. Corruption, b. Injustice, c. Luxury, d. Extravagance, e. Baal worship.
      3. The leaders were evil:
         a. People unteachable, b. Prophets were traitors, c. Courts were merciless and warped, d. Priests were profane, e. The Princes were preying on the people.
      4. It was time for judgment!!

95

2. *The man, Zephaniah*
   A. His name means Jehovah hides.
   B. He is a direct descendant of Hezekiah.
   C. He lived in the Southern Kingdom.
   D. It is probable that he inspired Josiah's reforms.
   E. He along with others of the prophets would have been considered a fanatic today.

3. *The nature of the book of Zephaniah*
   A. The theme is the nearness of the Day of Jehovah.
   B. This great day will bring purification.
   C. It will be followed with a Messianic salvation.
   D. Earlier prophets spoke of the Day of the Lord.
   E. Zephaniah makes it his major theme.
   F. Use of the phraseology of earlier prophets is not copywork as is shown by the progressive unfolding of God's scheme of redemption.
   G. Outline of the book
      1. A Judgement day of the Lord is at hand.
         a. Upon Jerusalem and Judah. b. Also upon the nations.
      2. This is a day of Salvation.
         a. In the midst of Judah's sinfulness God is Holy. b. This will bring about salvation and restoration.

4. *Comments on the text of Zephaniah*
   Chapter 1
   Zephaniah is a direct descendant of Hezekiah and he reigns in the time of good king Josiah.
   God will come in judgment sweeping all before him.
   Baal and his priests will be punished along with the unfaithful priests of Jehovah.
   God is preparing a feast in which the guests shall be presented as sacrifices.
   Several classes shall be destroyed.
      The persons who traffic with heathen.
      The robbers who steal to fill their masters' houses.
      Those that settle back on their haunches in confidence that God is inactive in men's affairs.
   The cry of alarm shall sound.
   The plunderers and idlers shall see their own possessions removed and useless.

The Day of the Lord will be awesome:
1. Darkness.
2. Wrath.
3. Trouble.
4. Distress.
5. Desolation.
6. Men shall stumble as blind.
7. Their flesh and blood shall be considered as less valuable than dust and manure.

No silver or gold will be sufficient to deliver them.

The object will be purification.

Chapter 2

One translation gives verse 1 as "O nation with no shame."

Any nation whether Jew or heathen which is filled with the kind of things described previously is not desired by Jehovah.

The remedy is in seeking God.

The prophet then draws a circle around Judah.

Woe unto the Philistines to the west.

Woe unto the Ammonites on the east.

Woe unto the Ethiopians on the south.

Woe unto the Assyrians on the north.

Jehovah will remove all the sacrifices upon which the false gods feed.

Notice that God has forecast the power of Babylon while she was still an infant, and now he tells of the destruction of Assyria while she reigns supreme.

Nineveh the capital shall be pastures and desolation.

She has cried out I AM and there is none beside *me—*.

This statement is the exclusive prerogative of God.

Chapter 3

Jerusalem is the rebellious and polluted city.

She is the very opposite of that which God requires.

Her princes are preying lions.

Her priests are profane and worldly.

Her judges are greedy bribe takers.

Her prophets are twisters of the law.

What a terrible contrast they make with the Holy God who stands within their midst.

God has provided instruction for them.

But they were so anxious to do evil that they rose up early to get started.

God will therefore gather the nations in order that he may devour the evil as a consuming fire.

He will provide a language unconfused with the pride of human wisdom.

Those who understand it and heed will call upon the name of Jehovah.

Sacrifices shall be his from the distant parts of the earth.

Shame shall be removed along with all pride and haughtiness from his Holy Mountain—the Church.

The remnant which is left after the judgment and purification will be pure in both word and deed.

They shall be surrounded by the protection of God's wall of salvation.

Their hands shall not hang loosely in despair for the God of Heaven will support them in his power.

His people may be in shame and dispersion, but the time to come will see them released from bondage in a Gospel dispensation, praised and known throughout the earth.

5. *Practical lessons from the book of Zephaniah*

    A. The God we worship will shape us in his likeness whether it be false gods or the true and living God.

    B. A Day of accounting will inevitably come.

    C. The impure will be burned away, with the pure remaining.

    D. The meek shall inherit the earth.

HABAKKUK
(Embrace)

1. *Background for the book of Habakkuk*

   A. Babylonia was a very ancient nation, known in 1,000 B.C.

   B. Sennacherib of Assyria destroyed it.

   C. It was restored in 681-669 by Esarhaddon.

   D. King Ashurbanipal died in 633 B.C. and Nabopolassar began his reign.

   E. Nebuchadnezzar was a Babylonian general under Nabopolassar when Nineveh, the Assyrian capital fell in 612 B.C.

   F. Egypt under Pharaoh-Necho marched through Palestine to meet the Babylonians and Josiah died in an attempt to intervene.

   G. The Babylonians or Chaldeans then marched through Palestine taking Jerusalem and carrying away captives. (Daniel, etc.)

   H. Josiah's son Jehoahaz was made king by the Jews but reigned only three months.

   I. His brother Eliakim replaced him, appointed by Pharaoh-Necho with Eliakim's name now Jehoiachin.

   J. Jehoiakim revolted and was killed and replaced by his son, Jehoiachin.

   K. When Jehoiachin was carried away to Babylon Zedekiah became king.

   L. Zedekiah reigned for ten years and revolted, at which time Babylonia besieged and destroyed Jerusalem.

   M. The conditions of Judah are abominable and include:
      1. Tyranny.
      2. Strife and violence.
      3. Lawlessness.
      4. Idolatry.

2. *The man, Habakkuk*

   A. There is little about Habakkuk that is not strained with mythology.

   B. What we learn must be gained through his own writing.

99

C. He is an honest doubter.

D. The sin of God's people is completely abhorrent to him.

E. His name means "embrace" perhaps describing the way he would take up his nation as a sick child to cure it with the aid of Jehovah.

3. *The book of Habakkuk*

A. This is the study of age-old questions:
   1. Why is evil allowed to continue?
   2. When will God bring the scales of justice to balance?

B. Outline of the book
   1. The first perplexity.
      a. Why is wickedness allowed to exist among God's people? b. God is preparing the Chaldeans to punish them.
   2. The second perplexity.
      a. How could God use such a wicked nation? b. They will also be punished after God uses them.
   3. Habakkuk's psalm of praise to Jehovah
      a. Jehovah has continued to work throughout the ages. b. If he has acted in the past there is confidence that he will do so now and in the future.

C. The date of the book
   1. The Chaldeans seem to be strong on the world scene. See 1:6-11.
   2. But the invasion appears to still be future. See 3:16.
   3. Thus it is dated as just before the first captives are taken to Babylon, between 612 and 606 B.C.

4. *Comments on the text of Habakkuk*

Chapter 1

The prophet wonders why God has not answered his cry for judgment in the midst of wickedness.

Upon every side he sees evil and unrighteousness:
1. There is violence.
2. There is strife.
3. There is contention.
4. The law is disregarded.

The righteous are overwhelmed by the wicked.

God then returns an answer.

He is raising up the Chaldeans as a punishing rod.

They shall be an ominous force.

They shall march through the land.

They are compared to wolves, leopards and eagles.

Kings and strongholds shall fall before them.
The Chaldean worships his own power as a god.
But the prophet now has another question.
How can a Holy God look with favor upon such a vicious nation?
This nation catches other nations as fish in a net.
They worship their net of oppression.
Will they be allowed to continue filling and emptying the nets?

Chapter 2

The prophet decided to simply take a wait-and-see position as from a watchtower.
The Lord then reveals a vision for him to write down.
It is to be written so that others may be inspired to proper behavior before Jehovah.
The fulfilment of the vision may take a while, but it will be accomplished.
The bold and pride-filled will be brought down, but the just shall act in such manner that their lives shall be preserved.
Paul quotes Habakkuk 2:4 in Romans 1:17.
God now provides an answer to the matter of association with the wicked Chaldean nation.
He will bring punishment upon them as a nation of evil-doers, after he has used them for his purpose.
A series of woes is pronounced upon them.
Woe unto them that live by lust of conquest.
Woe unto them that build an empire by blood and cruelty.
Woe unto them that use other men to accomplish their ends while ignoring their misery.
Woe unto those who become intoxicated with their own power.
As the Chaldean has brought others down he shall be caused to fall naked and exposed in shame.
Even nature itself has been devastated before this shameless nation.
Woe unto those who revel in idolatry and materialism.
Two kinds of images are included here.
The graven image—engraved from wood.
The molten image—molded from metal.
God speaks of both as "nothing."

Chapter 3

Habakkuk now begins a prayer of memory of God's workings in the past.

The Lord is asked to continue the wondrous works of the past.
He had used pestilence as a tool.
He had driven the nations before him.
The very mountains had trembled with his power.
When God bared his bow nothing stood before it.
All this was accomplished in preparation for God's anointed, the Messiah.
The word "Selah" is used three times in this prayer.
As the prophet heard of the wonders of God's providential action of the past and considers the future invasion of the Chaldeans he trembles within but realizes he may rest in peace.
Nothing shall disturb his confidence in his God now.
Though the fields refuse to produce.
Though the flocks and herds fail.
Though every means of livelihood be cut off—
He shall climb like the deer and walk the high places above the troubled seas of the unbelievers.

5. *Lessons from the book of Habakkuk*

   A. The wicked will be judged.
   B. The faith of the just will provide security.
   C. Evil will destroy itself.
   D. Suffering is disciplinary.
   E. One may move from honest doubt to the most sublime faith.

JEREMIAH
(Jehovah Appoints)

1. *Background for the book of Jeremiah*
   A. Historical background
      1. Good king Hezekiah had begun constructive reform.
      2. When he died in 698 B.C. evil Manasseh, his son replaced him.
      3. He introduced idolatry and persecuted true worshippers.
      4. Amon, his son continued his wicked ways.
      5. After three years he was murdered and Josiah was placed upon the throne.
      6. At an early age Josiah began religious reform.
      7. Josiah began his reign in 641 B.C.
      8. Nineveh of Assyria fell in 612 B.C.
      9. Nebuchadnezzar became king of Babylon in 605 B.C.
      10. When Pharaoh-Necho marched through Palestine Josiah lost his life attempting to stop him.
      11. Jehoahaz was put in his place by Pharaoh but reigned only three months before being taken to Egypt by Pharaoh.
      12. His brother Jehoiakim was crowned by Pharaoh.
      13. When Nebuchadnezzar pushed through from the north Jehoiakim changed his allegiance.
      14. Jehoiakim reigned eleven years before rebelling against Nebuchadnezzar and losing his throne.
      15. Jehoiakim's son Jehoiachin (Coniah) followed reigning for three months.
      16. He was then taken to Babylon and kept for years.
      17. The Babylonians appointed Zedekiah as a puppet king.
      18. When Zedekiah conspired with Egypt Nebuchadnezzar besieged Jerusalem.
      19. Zedekiah was blinded and carried to Babylon.
      20. Gedaliah was appointed as governor but was soon murdered.
      21. At this point the Jews who were left took Jeremiah into Egypt where his life concluded.
      22. The list of kings of Judah were then: a. Josiah, b. Jehoahaz, c. Jehoiakim, c. Jehoiachin, e. Zedekiah, f. Gedaliah. (governor).

B. Social background
1. The rich and powerful are completely unscrupulous.
2. The poor are bound into slavery without compassion.
3. Greed swallows up all within its sight.
4. Deceit and lying are prevalent.
5. Robbery and murder take men's lives and possessions.
C. Religious background
1. Syncretism is the order of the day with a blend of many kinds of false religion.
2. Formalism has paralyzed true religion.
3. Sensualism and degeneracy dominate the thinking.
4. Josiah made every effort to alter the conditions but was unable to change more than the outward appearances.

2. *The man, Jeremiah*
A. He was raised in Anathoth, a priestly village.
B. The son of Hilkiah.
C. His life spanned the reign of five kings.
D. He preached from the call in the thirteenth year of Josiah until the fall of Jerusalem in 586 B.C.
E. His task was to pluck up, but also to build.
F. Jeremiah and Josiah may have known each other as young boys.
G. He was naturally timid but God had called and would give him support.
H. He is forbidden to marry or to be present at feasting or mourning.
I. He is hated, isolated and shunned.
J. He is opposed by priests and prophets.
K. He is from the upper class:
1. Owns property.
2. Has a secretary.
3. Is acquainted with literature and history.
L. He is a rebel:
1. Against formalized religion.
2. Blasting kings and princes.
3. Proposing surrender to Babylon.
M. He is a statesman looking beyond the present to a new and better age.
N. He has a rare sensitivity to the magnitude and consequences of sin.

O. There are a number of similarities between Jeremiah and Christ:
   1. The simplicity of his teaching.
   2. Opposition to formalism.
   3. Wept much over the people.
3. *Nature of the book of Jeremiah*
   A. Difficult to follow systematically.
   B. Dictated by Jeremiah to Baruch.
   C. Discrepancy between the Septuagint and the Hebrew.
   D. Tells of a time of chaos and decline.
   E. A wicked and shameless people will face punishment.
   F. Later a new covenant and a new age shall come into existence.
   G. Outline of the book
      1. The Call, Chapter 1.
      2. Condemnation of Judah.
         a. Denunciation and warning, Chapters 2-20. b. Charge against the rulers, Chapters 21-24. c. The sentence described, Chapters 25-29.
      3. Promise of restoration, Chapters 30-33.
      4. The Penalty inflicted.
         a. Last years of the kingdom, Chapters 34-38. b. Destruction of Jerusalem, Chapter 39. c. The Wretched Remnant, Chapters 40-45.
      5. Judgment of the nations, Chapters 46-51.
      6. Captivity and release
   H. Some great texts: 1:5-10; 1:17-19; 2:2-7; 2:11-13; 2:28; 5:31; 6:30; 7:8-11; 7:23; 9:2; 9:23; 10:3-15; 12:5; 18:3-6; 23:30-32; 29:13; 31:31-34; 32:37-41.
4. *Comments on the text of Jeremiah*
   Chapter 1
   Jeremiah receives a call from Jehovah in the thirteenth year of the reign of Josiah.
   God had chosen him to preach to Judah.
   The call is most definite in that God had:
   1. Sanctified him from the womb.
   2. Ordained him a prophet.
   There is no difficulty here with freedom of will since God is able to look from beginning to end and was able to know of Jeremiah's faithfulness before he was born.
   Jeremiah is timid and objects that he cannot speak.

God will not accept his objection: "Be not afraid; I will be with thee."

God touches his mouth and places words in it.

Jeremiah is commanded to pluck up, to pull down, to destroy —but also to build and to plant.

He is given a vision to assure him:

1. An almond tree indicating that God's word will be hastened in fulfilment.

2. A seething pot indicating the Chaldean army ready to boil over from the north.

Jeremiah must stand firm against both rulers of politics and rulers of religion.

He will be opposed but he must prevail for God supports him.

Chapter 2

Jehovah recalls the ardent devotion of Israel during the days after they were taken from Egypt.

At this time God was jealous of her and blessed her bountifully.

He asks what offense he had committed that Israel could justify her abandonment of him.

After having made Israel healthy with a good land she had gone after:

1. Unfaithful priests.

2. Shepherds who scattered.

3. Prophets who go after Baal.

They are to look around and see if any such example can be found among the heathen who do not forsake their gods.

They have turned away from the fountain of life and accepted broken cisterns which contain nothing.

He had planted them as a noble vine but their fruit had been strange and unpleasant.

She is like a wild ass who follows her own ways but offers herself to the male when she is ready without discrimination.

Israel has indicated by her actions that her stick and stone idols have brough her into existence.

If this is true let her call upon her idol gods when the Babylonian invasion takes place.

How is it possible that a bride like Israel could forget her bridal dress or the husband of her youth?

With her sin in plain view she denies it, compounding the sin.

She will come to realize that her gadding around with Egypt and Assyria will bring shame.

Chapter 3

Jehovah has been more lenient than a human husband would be with a wife who had played harlot with many lovers.

She has acted like a spoiled child and will suffer shame and loss of natural blessings.

The entire land is brought into disgrace.

After watching Israel Judah should have learned.

Instead she followed the same foolish path.

Jeremiah then mentions the remnant; when Israel is destroyed there will be a trace left.

Compare Nehemiah 8:7-8 with verse 15 here.

The ark of the covenant will be forgotten.

Jerusalem will be the source of the law rather than Mount Sinai.

Jew and Gentile shall be united and walk together.

They will confess the sins and be ashamed and thus God will respond.

Chapter 4

Judgment is predicted for Judah.

The fallow fields which should have been growing fruit for God must be cultivated. Their souls are choked with thorns and thistles and must be cleansed.

Sound the alarm for Babylonia is coming.

Everything shall be laid waste.

Kings, princes and prophets shall quake before the invader.

The entire land shall be surrounded and helpless before the Lord's outstretched hand.

Jeremiah cries out, unable to contain himself at the vision of destruction.

Has God forgotten his promise to Israel?

No, it is because of the foolishness of the people who act as spoiled children.

The picture is so serious it resembles the very reversal of the original creation:
1. Cosmos becomes chaos.
2. Light turns into darkness.
3. The men and birds disappear.
4. The fruitful place becomes a wilderness.

Though Jerusalem deck herself in her brightest ornaments she shall be forsaken by her pagan lovers.

The Daughter of Zion (Jerusalem and her people) shall cry out in pain as a woman bearing her first child.

The murdering invaders will be absolutely merciless.

Now the false prophets who cried peace, peace, when there are only war on the horizon will be demonstrated for the liars that they were.

Chapter 5

God calls for a righteous man to be found in Jerusalem—if so he will spare it.

They cry out that God exists but the confession is strictly outward.

These can be described as the truly poor and foolish.

The important men among the people will have to face Jehovah for their broken yoke.

The enemy is called upon them but is told not to make a full end—a remnant is to be left.

The people have made the Lord out as a liar by refusing to believe his prophets who tell of danger.

It shall become evidence that their false prophets are spouting hot air.

The strange nation of the Babylonians will be sent upon them speaking a strange language and devouring everything as a fire.

They shall question God for his reasons.

His answer shall be that they have failed to see and hear his message and have not respected his will.

Since they have desired to take up with strangers God will send them into a strange land to serve as slaves.

The waves of the sea respect the Lord's command and remain within the limits set.

But Israel trespasses and flees from his wishes.

They stand to lose many blessings:
1. Natural blessings such as the latter rain.
2. Communion with the Lord as his people.

Their sins are many:
1. They excuse the sins of the wicked.
2. They misuse the courts.
3. The needy are ignored.
4. The prophets and priests are perverted.
5. The people love to have it this way.

Chapter 6

Trumpets and fires are to signal the coming invasion.

The beautiful daughter of Zion will be attacked.

Even the remnant will be gleaned and carried away.

God's fury will no longer be held back.

Young and old, wives and possessions, all shall be taken away.
The prophets have attempted to cure the illness by saying all
will be well when it will not.
"Peace, peace, when there is no peace."
God's people had gotten beyond the ability to blush.
They are invited to walk in the holy paths of old.
They refuse.
Sacrifices from far countries and burnt offerings are only an
abomination when offered in hypocrisy.
God shall send the Babylonians as a stumblingblock to slow
down their headlong rush toward wickedness.
Jeremiah is to act as a watchman in warning them.
But they are so corrupt that only dross remains after the re-
finer's fire.

Chapter 7

Since the temple has been abused Jeremiah is told to stand at
the gate of the temple and preach.
They cannot continue in the ways they now follow.
There are a number of conditional *ifs* which must be observed
for them to remain in the land:
1. If they amend their ways.
2. If they execute true judgments.
3. If they oppress not the widow and the fatherless.
4. If they cease their lying words.
Their sins are manifold: stealing, murder, adultery, idolatry,
lying.
Then they proceed to enter the house of the Lord and worship.
They make the house of God a den for robbers.
They should look northward to the plight of the place of wor-
ship at Shiloh.
As Shiloh had tumbled with the captivity of the worshippers so
will Jerusalem's temple.
Jeremiah is told not to pray for such a people.
Such prayer is useless for God will not hear it. Compare 1
John 5:16.
The entire family dedicates their efforts to the false gods: Chil-
dren gather wood; fathers kindle the fire; mothers prepare
the meat and drink offerings.
God's unquenchable fury will be poured out upon them.
They were just as stiff-necked as their forefathers whom he had
brought out of Egypt.
The truth has died among them.
They are to prepare to lament for their condition.

It has gone so far that they even sacrifice their children in the valley of Hinnom.

When God is finished there will be no more room for bodies in the valley for it shall be filled as the Babylonian armies stack carcasses together.

Jerusalem shall see the removal of all happiness and laughter.

Chapter 8

The rulers shall be humiliated by having their bones scattered before the sun, moon and stars before whom they have worshipped.

They shall not be cherished but shall be as manure.

Conditions shall be so bad that men shall choose to die rather than to live.

God listened for a penitent voice but it was in vain.

The animals obey the Lord through instincts which are ingrained in them.

But it is not so with Judah—they know not the judgment of the Lord.

The wise men who are supposed to know the law of Jehovah have ignored it.

From the priest to the prophet they deceive and lie.

What is more they have no sense of shame and cannot blush.

All of the good things which God has given shall be removed.

In addition pestilence and plague will be sent upon them.

Jeremiah grieves that:

The harvest is past—Summer is ended—The people are not saved.

He is overwhelmed with grief.

There is medicine for the people to use but they act as if it were not even there.

Chapter 9

Jeremiah wishes he could cry a river of tears for his people. (The weeping prophet.)

He even wishes that he could remove himself from among them because of their sinful condition.

Again he recounts a list of their sins.

Because of this God will try and purify them as he sends the invading army to capture them.

Instead of feeding them with milk and honey they shall now be fed wormwood and offered gall to drink.

They shall weep and be in a state of confusion.

Glory in wisdom, in riches or in might are sadly misplaced.

The duty of man is to know and understand the God of Heaven, and to glorify him. See Rev. 4:11.

Man is to exercise lovingkindness, judgment and righteousness.

There will be no consolation to the circumcised in the day of God's visitation for those who have rebelled among his own people shall be as if they had never been a part of his own.

The most important circumcision is a circumcision of the heart. See Romans 2:28-29.

Chapter 10

His people were guilty of three kinds of false worship:
1. Natural worship—stars, animals.
2. Artificial worship—graven and molten images.
3. Imaginary worship—serving invisible gods.

All such worship is utter foolishness.

They have been much impressed by unusual occurrences within the heavens.

This is a mark of heathenism.

How silly to worship the work of a man's hands.

Gods made out of trees and stones must be carried about from place to place and served by men.
But see Acts 17:25.

The true and living God has created the very materials out of which the false gods have been carved and molded.

Worship of such false gods lowers man to a brutish and animal level.

The true God has three characteristics which all false gods gods lack: power, wisdom, and discretion.

Following such gods can only lead to massive confusion.

Worshippers of false gods have nothing to look forward to.

On the other hand Judah has an inheritance which is promised by one who is able to deliver.

How sad the future is because of Judah's unwillingness to obey.

The prophet recognizes the seriousness of the future but knows he must face up to it.

The place of worship will be removed.

The spiritual leaders shall be cut down.

The people will be scattered to the land of Babylon.

The noise of the approaching army indicates how futile it is for men to direct their own steps.
See Psalms 37:23 and 16:1.

Jeremiah pleads that the punishment to come will be diluted with mercy.

Chapter 11

Judah has failed to honor the covenant delivered by Moses.

They are rebellious as were their forefathers.

Their cries when in trouble will fall upon the deaf ears of their idols and God's ear will be turned away.

Jeremiah is again told not to pray for a people so obstinate.

The people of Judah no longer belong in the House of God because they have polluted their holiness with a host of sins.

They are like an olive tree which is in need of pruning.

Because of his condemnation of the priests of Anathoth Jeremiah's life is placed in danger.

Their evil lives have brought about a promise from God that they shall be utterly cut off.

There will be a remnant of Israel saved, but the ruling class shall be completely snuffed out.

Chapter 12

Jeremiah now wonders about the prosperity of the wicked.

How long shall both man, beast and the land itself groan under their evil ways?

They have already brought wearisome problems upon themselves, but in comparison the invasion of the future will be worse.

God will make them like a chicken pecked by others because of its difference from the rest of the flock.

While the land groans they care nothing about it.

The harvest of their foolish actions will be an unexpected crop of thorns, not valuable wheat.

Both an invading army and God's own people will be plucked up as God works in their affairs.

After they have been chastised return is possible.

They must turn from Baal to Jehovah.

If not the nation may be removed forever.

Chapter 13

Jeremiah is told to go find a linen girdle which would ordinarily be worn with pride.

He is then told to go hide it in a hole in the rock near the Euphrates River.

God's own people were going to be hidden beyond the Euphrates.

When Jeremiah went back many days later the fine girdle was ruined.

In just such manner God's people would have their pride marred since they had failed to glorify him.

For their foolishness they shall find priest, prophet, and prince drunken and confused in friction against one another.

In this condition their enemies shall find it easy to overcome them.

They are as tied to their evil ways as a leopard to his spots or a black man to his skin.

Chapter 14

The land shall fail to give nourishment to man or beast.

Thirst, hunger and shortness of breath abound.

Their condition is such that Jeremiah is told not to pray for them. Compare 1 John 1:9.

In spite of their evil the false prophets have prophesied good days.

The prophets themselves will die by the same sword and famine which they have said will not come.

Compare: Jeremiah 5:31 "the people love it so"; Matthew 15:14 "the blind lead the blind"; Romans 1:32 "pleased at the evil in others."

Jeremiah weeps copiously as a representative of God's grief over Judah.

Some few cry out in penitence, but too late to save the entire nation from captivity.

Among the penitent few there is realization that God is creator and sustainer and that false gods of the heathen are void of power.

Chapter 15

As Jeremiah pleads with God for Israel because of Jeremiah's own righteous life God returns answer.

The punishment is not because of any lack in Jeremiah's life.

Neither Moses nor Samuel could have intervened.

They will be divided up by their separate reactions to the Babylonian invaders.

Judah will be scattered throughout the entire dominion of Babylonia.

They will be blown around like chaff before the fan.

There shall be rapid increase of widows as the men fall before the violence.

Judah's sun will go down in the middle of the day.

She shall suffer a national sunset.

The sword of the Babylonian will break the iron of Judah.

113

Jeremiah had consumed God's word as a nourishing food.

The people should now heed the teachings of the prophet.

They must return to *him*—he dare not be conformed to *them* and their ways.

The people will resist his teachings and attack him.

But God will protect the prophet.

Chapter 16

Jeremiah is told not to marry or produce children.

The punishment which is coming would cause children to be a source of sorrow rather than a blessing.

Jeremiah is not to pity them or mourn with them for their distress since they are not worthy of it.

The people will ask what sin they have done.

Jeremiah is to accuse them of forsaking Jehovah.

Since they have loved strange gods they shall be cast into a strange land and serve other gods.

The release from this new captivity shall overshadow the release from Egyptian captivity in importance.

There shall be no place for Judah to hide from the coming Babylonian army which will hunt them out.

Under the affliction of the Babylonians they shall come to know that idolatry is a profitless lie.

Chapter 17

The record of Judah's sin of idolatry is engraven boldly in their hearts and through their worship.

God's anger is so hot that they will be removed from the promised land.

The man who trusts in human wisdom and ability will be withered as a plant in a parched desert.

The man who trusts in the Lord will be as a tree planted by rivers of water.

The man who follows his heart's desire performs all his sins under the searching eye of Jehovah.

Jeremiah declares that he has faithfully proclaimed God's word and expresses his confidence that God will terrorize only the wicked.

He was to warn the leaders of the people to observe the Sabbath.

If they had listened the city of Jerusalem would have been safe.

Instead they ignored the warning and the destroying fire of God's wrath would leave Jerusalem in ashes.

Chapter 18

Jeremiah is told to go and watch the potter work.

The potter ruined one vessel and so made a new and more pleasing one.

God indicates that the same can be done with Judah.

If they will turn and please God he will not discard them.

They affirm that they will walk only after their own desires.

They have shown their back to God, now he will do the same and scatter them abroad.

The people decide to conspire against Jeremiah for these severe words.

Jeremiah calls upon God to see that justice is done.

Chapter 19

Jeremiah is told to get a potter's vessel and go to the gate of the city.

He is to accuse them of idolatry within sight of the valley of Hinnom.

They had allowed their sons and daughters to pass through the fire to Molech.

God will allow such calamity to come upon them that they will eat the flesh of their children if they care no more for them.

Jeremiah is to break the potter's vessel before them.

God will break Judah in like manner. See Rom. 9:22.

The entire city of Jerusalem will be turned into a Tophet-like slaughterhouse.

Chapter 20

Pashur, the governor of the Lord's house is angered by the boldness of Jeremiah's prophecy.

Jeremiah is placed in the stocks but is released the next day.

Jeremiah predicts the slaughter of Pashur's friends before his eyes.

He also predicts everything worthwhile in Jerusalem shall be carried away to Babylon.

Because his lot is so distasteful Jeremiah decides to prophesy no more.

He cannot carry out his plan because the Word of God became like fire in his bones.

He realizes that God is willing to protect him and praises him for this.

Yet his condition is very unpleasant and he wishes he had never been born.

NOTE: *How many preachers under somewhat similar circumstances have felt like feelings?*

115

Jeremiah's feelings here are similar to those of two other great men of God: Job in the hands of Satan, and Ezekiel as he eats the roll which becomes bitter.

The writer of the Revelation also found prophesying difficult.

Chapter 21

The events of this chapter occur very late in the history of Judah under its last king, Zedekiah.

Zedekiah sends Pashur (not likely the same Pashur who put Jeremiah in the stocks in the reign of Jehoiakim) to get advice from Jeremiah.

What are the prospects of defending themselves from Nebuchadnezzar whose army is upon them?

Pashur is told to advise Zedekiah that God will act in favor of the Babylonians rather than Judah.

Those who live through the famine and pestilence will be captured by Nebuchadnezzar including king Zedekiah.

Some few will remain in the city but it would be better to have been captured.

God's fire of fury will not be quenched until the evil of Judah has been punished.

Chapter 22

Jeremiah is given a message for the king of Judah.

He is to promote justice, righteousness and mercy throughout the land.

This would insure the perpetuation of the throne of David.

If he does not do this the house of David will become desolated.

The surrounding nations will be amazed at the punishment visited upon the city of Jerusalem.

When asked the reason they shall be told that Judah forsook Jehovah for other gods.

They had wept sorely for Josiah but there was more reason to weep for his son Shallum who would see Jerusalem no more.

But they are not to weep even for Shallum (Jehoiakim) because he built his throne upon covetousness.

By the loss of its leaders the beautiful land will be brought down to shame.

If Coniah who is also called Jeconiah or Jehoiakim were the most valuable possession Jehovah had he would still be cast away.

Jeconiah and his seed will be sent into a strange land.

As far as Jeconiah's sons sitting on the throne of David and ruling in Judah there would be none.

NOTE: *Though Jesus Christ was a descendant of Coniah and now reigns on the throne of David he does not rule in Judah.*
This chapter simply indicates the line of wicked kings which has ruled just before the captivity from Shallum to Jehoiakim to Coniah.

Chapter 23

Jeremiah once again declares the responsibilities of the leaders of Israel for their sad condition.

These leaders will be punished and then his sheep will be brought back to his fold.

New and more faithful shepherds will be set up over the sheep.

A righteous descendant of David will be raised up to execute judgment.

Under this righteous king both Judah and Israel will be shepherded in safety.

Since he shall be called THE LORD OUR RIGHTEOUSNESS it seems obvious the king is Jesus the Saviour.

Under this king the remnant will be brought out of the land of captivity and into their own land.

Jeremiah's heart is broken because of the sins of his people.

Even the priests and the prophets bring darkness and folly to the people.

The prophets of Jehovah are no better than the prophets of Baal.

The people must not listen to such lying prophets.

They are acting as if they could hide from the God who fills both heaven and earth.

The prophets are to distinguish between their own fanciful dreams and the revealed visions of Jehovah.

Because they have not distinguished, God will cease to reveal his will through them.

The prophets had cried out peace when the people were filled with sin and violence was about to be visited upon them.

Since they do not wish to cling to God's Word they shall find it removed from them.

God will send them to Babylon and act as if they were not in his presence.

Chapter 24

Jeremiah is shown two baskets of figs, one very good and the other very bad.

God explains that the good figs are like the choice Jews who are carried captive into Babylon.

The bad figs are those who are left behind, who find their way

117

to Egypt and are finally scattered to every nation of the earth
to be mocked and taunted.

The good figs will be taught to respect Jehovah and then will
be returned to his good grace.

Chapter 25

This chapter occurs during the first year of Nebuchadnezzar,
the year in which he invaded the promised land.

Jeremiah warns the people that he and the other prophets had
been sent with God's Word in plenty of time.

They had not listened for these many years and therefore the
Lord is prepared to punish them.

The land shall be made a desolation and the people shall serve
in Babylon for seventy years.

At the end of that time Babylon and its king shall be punished
and their land shall become a desolation.

Not only shall Babylon be punished but so also shall be those
nations which have enslaved Israel and Judah.

This will include Egypt, Uz, Philistia, Ashkelon, Azah, Ekron,
Ashdod, Edom, Moab, Ammon, Tyre, Zidon, Isles beyond the
sea, Dedan, Tema, Buz, Arabia, the people of the desert,
Zimri, Elam, Media and so on to every kingdom of the world
upon the face of the earth.

They may not wish to drink of God's cup of wrath, but they
shall do so anyway.

All the earth has sinned and all the earth shall be punished, beginning with God's chosen people.

Compare here 1 Peter 4:17-18.

It is not well to get into a controversy with the Lord since it
should be obvious that he will win.

Now the shepherds will be sorry they have led God's sheep as-
tray.

Their seeming security and peace shall melt away before the
whirlwind of the Lord.

Chapter 26

During Jehoiakim's reign Jeremiah is told to go to the court of
the Lord's house and prophesy.

The worshippers are told to repent of their evil ways.

If they will repent, God will not punish them.

If they will not repent they shall meet the same end as did the
place of worship in Shiloh in the Northern Kingdom.

This prophecy that Jerusalem may become like Shiloh angers
the people and they turn against Jeremiah.

Jeremiah unafraid repeats his exhortation to repentance and says that he is in their hands to do with as they please.

But if they kill him their blood will be payment for his.

Some of the elders recall that Micah prophesied such dire things previously and he was not put to death.

If they put Jeremiah to death they may bring evil upon themselves.

They had already killed Urijah who spoke as did Jeremiah and they had buried him without the honors due a prophet of Jehovah.

Ahikam persuades them not to kill Jeremiah for the prophecy which he has given.

Chapter 27

This chapter occurs during the reign of Jehoiakim.

Jeremiah is told to put a yoke upon his neck.

Messengers are then to be sent to a number of nations telling them Babylon will make them servants.

To resist service would be to resist God.

They are not to listen to prophets who tell them otherwise.

The nations who do not resist will be allowed to remain in their own lands to serve.

King Zedekiah of Judah is included in this warning.

The prophet who declares to Zedekiah that the vessels which have been taken from the Lord's house will soon be returned are doing a terrible disservice.

These prophets will not prevent removal of the remainder of the utensils of worship in the Lord's house.

The house of the Lord shall be completely stripped and carried away to Babylon.

They will stay there until God restores them.

Chapter 28

This occurs during the fourth year of Zedekiah.

A false prophet named Hananiah attempts to refute Jeremiah's yoke prophecy.

He speaks in the name of the Lord.

He declares that the vessels which had been carried away will be returned within two years.

Also that Jeconiah and the captives will be removed from the yoke of Nebuchadnezzar.

Jeremiah answers that he would like the Lord to do this thing.

Nevertheless he must contradict Hananiah.

He will only believe that the Lord brings peace when he sees it.

Hananiah then breaks the yoke from the neck of Jeremiah.
God speaks to Jeremiah and instructs him to take a message to Hananiah.
You have broken the yoke of wood—You have made them a yoke of iron.
Jeremiah accuses Hananiah of being a false prophet.
He predicts the death of Hananiah within the year.
Hananiah dies within a few months.

Chapter 29

Jeremiah writes a letter to the captives who were first taken along with Jeconiah.
It is sent by the hand of a messenger to the captives.
They are told to settle down for a long period building houses and planting vineyards.
They are told to bear children and increase their numbers while in captivity.
They are to seek peace for Babylon for this shall mean peace for them.
Not until seventy years have passed will they be returned in spite of the false prophets' lying promises.
By the end of seventy years they will have had a change of heart and turned to seek God's Word.
Those who remained in Palestine will be scattered as bad figs.
Those who had been taken into captivity in Babylon will speak of Zedekiah as being roasted by the king of Babylon.
Shemaiah, a false prophet in Babylonian captivity sends a letter to Zephaniah, a priest in Jerusalem.
He asks why Zephaniah has not rebuked Jeremiah for his prophecy of seventy long years' captivity.
When Shemaiah's letter is read to Jeremiah he receives word from God to send to Shemaiah that Shemaiah's seed shall be cut off and that Shemaiah shall not see the return from captivity.

Chapter 30

The instructions which Jeremiah is now to receive are to be collected in a book.
Both Israel and Judah are to be brought out of captivity and returned to their own land.
Deliverance from captivity shall not be easy for it is represented as a woman in labor pains.
Then the yoke of Babylon will be broken and God's people will serve the new King of Righteousness.

Note the following: Psalm 89:3; Isaiah 55:3; Ezekiel 34:23; 37:24; Luke 1:69; Acts 2:30; and Acts 13:23.

God will not destroy them completely but will leave his remnant which will be brought from bondage.

The nations which have enslaved Israel will be punished severely.

God will heal the wounds of Israel.

Jerusalem shall be built back.

The Temple shall be restored.

They shall multiply and be merry in thanksgiving to God.

Their rulers shall be from among themselves and not from Babylon.

The latter days of verse 24 is clear proof that the material preceding is speaking of more than simply the return of Ezra and Nehemiah although this physical return is most certainly involved.

Chapter 31

Upon Israel's deliverance God shall be their God, not the gods and idols they had before.

Now that they turn to the true God he will turn to them and they shall truly be his people.

Even while they were in the captivity God loved them with his everlasting love.

The promised land shall once again bring forth grapes.

Even Ephraim (the 10 northern tribes) shall turn to Zion and the Lord Jehovah.

God will be praised for his salvation of the remnant of Israel.

God himself will lead the lame and the blind and the penitent to rivers of waters.

There shall be wine, oil, herds and flocks, and the soul of the people shall no more sorrow at all.

The priest shall have abundance to sacrifice and the people will recognize the goodness of God.

Unlike Rachel who died in childbirth, Israel shall see new life as they are liberated in Zion.

The once backslidden virgin of Israel will conceive and bear a man. (Though it was specifically Mary who conceived Christ, yet she was of the remnant of the people of Israel.)

The contemplations of Jeremiah are very sweet in comparison with the dire predictions so often necessary.

In the captivity children suffered for the sins of their fathers. This shall not be true after the restoration.

A new covenant will be made with both Israel and Judah.

121

The new covenant will be different from the one which was delivered by Moses on Sinai.

It will be one of a much more spiritual nature as contrasted with the physical nature of the older covenant.

True Israel will then be those who have allowed the law of God to penetrate to their very heart and who serve him not because of the accidents of being born a descendant of Abraham, but because they truly love Jehovah.

The Word of God shall be so spread over the land that even the children shall know that Jehovah is the true and living God.

Under the new covenant God will forgive and remember their sin no more.

The God who makes these promises is the same who created and sustains the universe.

When he ceases to control the universe (which is never) Israel will cease to exist.

Not until the heavens can be measured and the foundations of the earth searched out will God abandon his chosen.

The earthly city of Jerusalem which was rebuilt in the time of Ezra and Nehemiah was later destroyed, but the spiritual city of Jerusalem will never be plucked up or thrown down.

Once again we see the importance of seeing the reality beyond the shadows.

Chapter 32

The prophecy of this chapter comes in the tenth year of Zedekiah.

At this time Jeremiah had been imprisoned for his prophesies which seemed to lend aid and comfort to the enemy.

At God's instruction Jeremiah tells Hanameel to go and buy a field for him in his native town.

The purchase is carefully sealed and witnessed.

The evidence of the purchase is carefully preserved.

This was a token of the confidence Jeremiah placed in God's promise to bring Judah back to Palestine.

Jeremiah prays to God admitting all the sin of the people.

God recounts the insolence with which the people have rejected his guidance.

In spite of this God indicates that the time will come in which he will bring them again into the land.

They shall serve only him and he will care for them.

A new and everlasting covenant will be enacted.

His people will not turn away from God, nor will he turn away from them.

As surely as they were to meet bondage for their sins they were to see deliverance and life upon their land.

The land which is overrun with Babylonians will return to the activities previous to their punishment.

Chapter 33

The prophecy of this chapter also occurs while Jeremiah is confined within prison.

The reason Judah fights with the Babylonians is that God may teach them a lesson about wickedness.

He will cure their desperate condition and then will return them to their land.

After their iniquities have been punished and pardoned they shall praise and honor God before all nations.

The desolate land will once more swarm with activity.

From the stock of Jesse, a BRANCH OF RIGHTEOUSNESS will grow up as a descendant of David to judge the land.

There shall be an abundance of priests.

If a man can break God's natural laws of night and day then this promise and covenant might be broken.

The everlasting throne of David will see a multiplication of its subjects as the stars of heaven or the sand of the sea.

It is true that God has for a time cast away his people of Ephraim and of Judah (the ten tribes and the two tribes), but as surely as the planets move in their orbits he will bring them from bondage and maintain a ruler from the descendants of David.

Chapter 34

During the siege of Jerusalem in the reign of Zedekiah.

Jeremiah is told by God to inform Zedekiah that Jerusalem will fall to Nebuchadnezzar and be burned.

Zedekiah will be captured, will speak with Nebuchadnezzar and will be taken to Babylon captive.

He will however not die by execution but with a natural death in honor.

Zedekiah declares that all the servants within Jerusalem shall be freed and no Jew shall serve another Jew.

At first they obey but apparently the siege conditions abate and they reconsider their actions, taking the servants bond again.

God reminds them that they were taken out of the land of bondage, also that after seven years no servant was to be held.

They had not listened to his instructions.

They had for the moment begun to obey and then they had regressed.

Since they would not proclaim liberty God will proclaim one for them.

His liberty shall be that of the sword, the pestilence and the famine as these are released upon them to act at will.

The idolatrous priests, princes and people will be made carcasses for the prey of scavengers.

The Babylonian army which had backed off will come back and will capture Zedekiah and desolate Jerusalem.

Chapter 35

This prophecy occurs during the reign of Jehoiakim.

Jeremiah is to make contact with the Rechabites who usually wander with their herds.

The Rechabites are to be taken to the house of the Lord and offered wine to drink.

They refuse to do so because Rechab, their ancestor fastened certain restrictions upon them:

1. They were not to build houses.
2. They were not to plant or own vineyards.
3. They were not to drink wine.
4. They were to dwell in tents.

Such instructions would prevent them from being corrupted by riotous city living.

When the prophet offers them wine they refuse to disobey their father Rechab.

They have only come into the city of Jerusalem now to escape the fury of the Babylonian army.

Jeremiah is told to rebuke the people of Judah by using the Rechabites as an example.

The Rechabites obey Rechab but Judah will not obey Jehovah.

Judah will be chastised for their disobedience.

The house of Rechab is established forever.

Chapter 36

This prophecy occurs in the fourth year of Jehoiakim.

Jeremiah is told to write the burdensome words which have been spoken against Judah and the nations in a book.

The book is to be read to the people to give them an opportunity to repent.

Since Jeremiah is in prison he sends for Baruch who writes what Jeremiah dictates.

The next year a day of fasting was proclaimed and Baruch read the book in the gate of the Lord's house.

When the princes of the people hear of this they call for Jeremiah to read it to them.

Somewhat shaken the princes tell Baruch to hide along with Jeremiah while they tell the king of the matter.

One of the king's servants obtains the book and begins to read it to the king.

After hearing a few pages the king cut the book apart and burned it in the fireplace.

The servants are commanded to go get Baruch and Jeremiah but God has hidden them.

Jeremiah is told by the Lord to prepare another book.

It shall include all of the first words plus many other things.

Among the new words will be that Jehoiakim will not have children who will reign in Judah.

NOTE: *Though Coniah was Jehoiakim's son his three months of reign was not considered significant.*

The body of Jehoiakim will be cast out into the heat of the day and the cold of the night.

"Penknife Religion" which supposedly eliminates the undesirable aspects of God's word ultimately leads to the destruction of the would-be mutilator.

Chapter 37

This prophecy occurs during the reign of Zedekiah.

After the very short rule of Coniah Zedekiah began his reign.

It is immediately apparent that he will not respect Jehovah.

Zedekiah commands Jeremiah to pray to God for the welfare of Judah.

At this time the Egyptian army has entered Palestine to fight against the Babylonians.

The Babylonians turn away from Jerusalem to meet the Egyptians.

Jeremiah informs Zedekiah that rather than favoring Judah, Jehovah will see the Babylonian army victorious and back again to burn the city of Jerusalem.

The king is told that even if the entire army of the Babylonians had been wounded they would still be able to destroy Jerusalem.

Jeremiah then hastened to leave Jerusalem but he is captured as he leaves through the city gates.

He is accused of leaving to join the Babylonian forces.

The princes then beat Jeremiah and place him in a very unpleasant dungeon.

After several days in the dungeon the king calls for him and asks if there is any news from Jehovah.

Jeremiah tells him there is word from the Lord.

The word is that the king shall be captured by Nebuchadnezzar.

The king is asked what crime Jeremiah is guilty of.

He also sarcastically asks where the false prophets are who
cried out "Peace, Peace."

The king is persuaded to relieve Jeremiah's conditions somewhat by removing him from the dungeon and allowing him
to wander in the courtyard of the prison with a daily ration
of bread.

Chapter 38

The princes are determined to keep Jeremiah in prison.

They do not appreciate his predictions that Jerusalem will be
burned and the temple sacked.

They claim that his words weaken the will of the army.

They request permission to punish him.

They receive that permission and place him in the dungeon.

He sinks into the mire.

Ebed-Melech intercedes for Jeremiah fearful that he will die of
hunger in the dungeon.

The king sends thirty men who drag Jeremiah from the dungeon with rags tied under his arms.

He is taken to the king who requests information.

Jeremiah says he will give the information but pleads for his
own life and the king's obedience.

Receiving the promise he tells the king he must surrender to
Nebuchadnezzar to save his own life and prevent the burning of Jerusalem.

Zedekiah is afraid that if he surrenders he will be ill-treated by
the Jews who have already been taken captive when he
meets them.

Jeremiah assures Zedekiah that surrender is the best course of
action.

Zedekiah instructs Jeremiah to reveal no more of the conversation they have had then is necessary.

This is done and the king allows Jeremiah to stay in the courtyard of the prison until the city falls.

Chapter 39

This prophecy occurs during the ninth year of Zedekiah.

For nearly two years Jerusalem had been under siege.

Finally the walls of the city are broken.

The princes of Babylon enter in and take over the important
positions in the city gates.

Zedekiah and his army attempt to flee from the city.

The Babylonian army pursues them and captures Zedekiah returning him to stand before Nebuchadnezzar.

Zedekiah's sons are slain before his eyes.

Zedekiah's eyes are put out.

The king's house is burned with fire and he is removed to Babylon.

Most of the people are carried away captive with the exception of the poor who owned no property.

Jeremiah is released from the courtyard of the prison and placed under the supervision of Gedaliah.

Jeremiah assures Ebed-melech that because of his trust in the Lord he shall not be harmed even though the city is to undergo much tribulation.

Chapter 40

Jeremiah is given the choice of going with the captives into Babylon or remaining in Jerusalem.

It is suggested that if he chooses to remain in Jerusalem he place himself under Gedaliah whom the King of Babylon has appointed as governor of Palestine.

Things begin to look more promising under the governorship of Gedaliah and the Jews who have scattered every direction move back into their land.

Some of the captains of his forces warn Gedaliah that the king of the Ammonites is planning to slay him but he refuses to believe them.

Johanan offers to kill Ishmael and protect both Gedaliah and the remnant of Judah but Gedaliah thinks the whole report to be false and is unconcerned.

Chapter 41

During the course of a meal with Gedaliah Ishmael succeeds in the assassination of the governor along with a number of the high soldiers.

Ishmael proceeds to take the Jews to the land of the Ammonites.

Johanan overtakes Ishmael and retrieves the Jews.

Since the Jews are afraid of the Babylonians' reaction to the murder of Gedaliah they decide to flee to Egypt.

Chapter 42

Johanan and the chief men of the Jews consult Jeremiah for the Word of the Lord.

They promise they will do whatever the Lord shall indicate.

God says he will protect them if they stay in the land of Palestine.

However he will see that they die by the sword, by famine and by pestilence if they flee to Egypt.

Jeremiah rebukes the people for asking for God's counsel and then deciding to ignore it.

Chapter 43

The Jews accuse Jeremiah of lying about God's advice.

They decide Jeremiah is working with Baruch to deliver them into the hands of the Babylonians.

All the Jews who had been left in Palestine go to Egypt.

Jeremiah is told by the Lord to bury stones in the shadow of Pharaoh's palace and then to indicate to the Jews that these will be the foundation for the Throne of Nebuchadnezzar when he conquers Egypt.

The Jews will not escape the purposes of Jehovah by being in Egypt.

Nebuchadnezzar will burn the gods of Egypt and carry away captives.

He shall put on the land of Egypt as easily as putting on a garment.

Chapter 44

Jeremiah continues to denounce the actions of the Jews in Egypt.

They know God's hatred of their idolatry in Palestine.

Yet they follow the same practice by worshipping the Egyptian gods.

These Jews who thought to escape in Egypt shall become a mockery to the land where they are found.

They shall never see their own land again.

The people rebel against Jeremiah and assign the reason for their troubles as being the cessation of their worship to the *queen of heaven.*

Jeremiah tells them that they are quite mistaken and that they shall see a sign that he is correct.

The Pharaoh of mighty Egypt will be given to the power of those who seek to kill him just as Zedekiah was taken.

The longsuffering of Jehovah was very nearly at an end with respect to these obstinate and foolish men.

Chapter 45

This prophecy occurs during the fourth year of Jehoiakim.

Jeremiah is giving consolation to Baruch who had written many of the prophecies of Jeremiah.

Baruch is suffering much mental anguish.

God will bring great disturbance unto the people and the land of Palestine.

But Baruch is not to expect these terrible things to happen to himself.

His life will be spared.

Chapter 46

Jeremiah prophesies against Egypt.

Egypt has moved across the land in splendid armor.

Jeremiah sees their defeat near the river Euphrates.

The sword shall drip with their blood and the wounds shall be incurable.

Though this happened earlier there shall be a further conquest by the Babylonians as they move down across Palestine and invade Egyptian territory.

It will be of no use for the Jews to hide in Egypt.

Egypt will be delivered into the hands of the Babylonian king Nebuchadnezzar.

This does not mean that God will completely destroy the descendants of Jacob.

They will be corrected and the remnant will be returned and blessed.

Chapter 47

This chapter is a prophecy against the Philistines.

The Babylonian army from the north will overwhelm the Philistines.

The defenders of Tyre and Sidon in Philistia will be rendered helpless.

The oppressors of Israel will be chastised by the sword of the Lord which in this case is the army of Nebuchadnezzar.

The sword will not be quieted until it has accomplished the purpose for which it was sent.

Chapter 48

This chapter is a prophecy against the Moabites.

The cities of Moab shall be cut down.

The praise formerly given to the land shall cease.

There shall be much lamentation and weeping among young and old.

He who swings the sword of the Lord is admonished to wield it efficiently.

Moab has known nothing but ease in the past.

Now he shall be disturbed and caused to wander.

Those who observe Moab's fate shall be shocked.

Moab shall be caused to wallow in his own vomit.

The gods of Moab shall be left without worshippers.

Proud Moab who flies like an eagle shall fall.

The eagle shall be snared because it has magnified itself in opposition to Jehovah.

The Moabites will not be annihilated but will be returned from bondage, probably through conversion to Christ.

God does not promise their massive national conversion but he does apparently hold out to them the possibility of freedom if they will individually accept the terms of salvation under Christ.

Chapter 49

This is a prophecy against a number of nations surrounding the land of Palestine.

The Ammonites are to be punished because they have taken the sons of Israel into their land.

Their king shall be taken captive and the people scattered abroad.

God will however bring them out of their wandering.

This seems to be the same promise as to the Moabite.

Edom is also threatened with invasion.

Their wise men shall fail them.

The invaders shall take everything.

There shall be absolutely no place to hide.

God holds out his cup of wrath to Edom and through they desire not to drink they shall do so.

Even the smallest nations will hear of Edom's weakness and shall come upon her.

When the invaders come, the courage of the mightiest men shall be no more than faint-hearted women.

Damascus of Syria shall be included in the general punishment visited upon the nations.

The soldiers shall fall in the streets and the palace of the king shall be burned.

Nebuchadnezzar shall take their animals and scatter the people.

Elam shall also feel the divine rod.

The bow of the Elamite warriors shall be broken.

The people of Elam shall be scattered to every nation.

A king whom God shall chose shall have his throne in Elam.

As in the case of Moab and Ammon, God will offer them freedom from bondage in the latter days of Jesus Christ.

Chapter 50

Now the sword of the Lord turns against mighty Babylon.

The idol gods of Babylon will be proven useless and broken down.

Babylon shall be desolated by a nation coming upon her from the north.

At that time the children of Israel shall have become penitent and will be seeking Jehovah.

They shall desire the perpetual covenant which the Lord is making ready.

Israel has been wandering like lost sheep scattered by their own shepherds.

It is understandable that their captors have found it so easy to captivate them since they have offended Jehovah.

Now it is time to come out of Babylon.

Babylon is to be attacked by many northern nations.

Those who would take Babylon for a prey shall be able to satisfy their appetite for spoil.

Babylon has destroyed the heritage of God but now she shall be made a target of mockery by those who pass by her.

The walls, the soldiers and the harvest shall all fail.

God will bring Israel forth out of bondage.

He will forgive their sins and pardon them.

Babylon will fall because God himself has striven against her.

When Babylon falls no one shall be able to lift it up.

The sword of God shall fall upon the Babylonians:
1. Upon their inhabitants.
2. Upon their princes.
3. Upon their wise men.
4. Upon their lying tongues.
5. Upon their horses and chariots.
6. Upon their treasures.

Babylon shall become a home for wild beasts rather than men.

It shall be overthrown as was Sodom and Gomorrah.

It shall never again be inhabited.

When the enemy comes the king of Babylon will be filled with anguish and as weak as a woman in labor.

When Babylon is taken the entire world shall be aware of it and be astonished.

Chapter 51

God will send those into Babylon who will fan out the useless chaff found there.

When Babylon is overthrown it will become clear that Jehovah did not forget his people while they were captive in that land.

Though Israel sinned grievously against him. God still had plans for his chosen people.

They are to flee out of Babylon when given the opportunity.

Babylon has given all the nations to drink themselves into a stupor which ruined their judgment and turned them against the Lord.

Now Babylon is fallen and cannot be healed.

The Medes are the people who polish their weapons to chastise the mighty Babylonian empire.

Even though protected, men shall come into Babylon like a swarm of grasshoppers consuming everything.

This is Jehovah Babylon faces, not their metal gods.

The Medes shall act as God's battle axe.

Nothing shall be able to stand before the power of Cyrus and his Medo-Persian army.

The evil deeds of Babylon shall be turned back upon them now that they have punished Israel.

Babylon shall be turned from a mountain of destroying power into a melted volcano from which not even a cornerstone may be taken.

The Medes, Ararat, Minni and Ashchenaz shall all combine their forces.

Messengers shall run to and fro spreading the news throughout the Babylonian empire.

The violence done by Babylon upon the people of God shall now be upon herself.

Babylon shall become so drunken that she shall sleep forever and never awake.

All the words that Jeremiah spoke against Babylon were recorded in a book.

Seraiah was told to read the book and then take a stone and tie it to the book and throw it into the Euprates River.

Just as the stone sinks into the Euphrates Babylon sinks never to rise again.

Chapter 52

This last chapter seems to be much earlier than the ones just previous to it.

It tells of the fall of Jerusalem.

Nebuchadnezzar besieged Jerusalem in the tenth and eleventh years of the reign of Zedekiah.

The Babylonians broke into the city.

132

Zedekiah fled but his army was scattered and he was taken.

His sons were slain before him.

His eyes were put out.

He was carried to Babylon where he remained in prison.

The Temple of God was burned as was the king's palace.

Many of the people were carried captive, but some of the poorer residue were left behind in Judah.

The furnishings of the Temple were confiscated.

And so Judah having not learned a lesson from the fall of Ephraim into the hand of the Assyrians now must weep beside the Rivers of Babylon.

LAMENTATIONS

Introduction

Much of the introductory material for the book of Jeremiah may be extended to this book. There is little doubt that Jeremiah is the author and that the book is written in grief over the fate of Israel, particularly that of the city of Jerusalem.

It is written in the form of poetry and each chapter except the last is an acrostic with each verse beginning with a succeeding letter of the Hebrew alphabet. Chapter 3 has 66 verses and is a triple acrostic. It becomes clear during the study of this book why Jeremiah is labeled the *weeping* prophet.

Chapter 1

Jerusalem which was once a reigning princess is now weeping as a widow.

Her former lovers have now become enemies and give no comfort.

The people are gone into captivity.

Feasting, worship and child-bearing have all ceased.

She now remembers the glory of the former times.

Her sin has become apparent to all who look.

The temple is desecrated by the presence of heathen unbelievers.

Jerusalem begs for comfort from someone.

It is admitted that rebellion against God's commandments is responsible for her plight.

Her enemies gloat over her tribulation.

She pleads that punishment come upon them as it has come upon her.

Chapter 2

Jerusalem, whose beauty has been as high as the heavens, is now cast down to sack cloth and ashes.

God has, in his wrath, cut off all the power of his chosen nation.

Instead of an ally and a supporter God has now become an enemy.

Both the worship and the place of worship have been rejected by Jehovah.

The gates of the city are destroyed and the walls are broken down.

The priests, the princes, the prophets and the people have in unison rejected God and now they find themselves without help.

Jeremiah weeps on the outside and groans on the inside for his beloved city.

Children die in the arms of their mothers.

Jeremiah would like to give comfort but he knows of nothing he can do.

When the enemies pass by and mock it is exactly as Jehovah declared it would be if they failed to heed.

The best advice Jeremiah can give is for Jerusalem to weep in penitence and wait for the Lord to respond.

Without exception God's children whom he has cared for so well are now to be punished.

Chapter 3

Jeremiah describes his own grief over the Jews:

1. He feels like an old man.
2. He feels as if bound with chains.
3. When he prays it seems God does not hear.
4. The path he treads seems crooked and long.
5. The very people he tried to teach have mocked.
6. His strength is being drained.
7. Yet he cannot forget his people deep in his soul.

If it were not for God's mercy the people would be completely destroyed.

It is good that the people bear the yoke of punishment that later things may be better.

God's actions are always planned for the benefit of his people.

Again he calls upon his people to repent and turn to the Lord.

Even when in a dungeon and placed there by his people Jeremiah wept for them.

The Babylonians have brought great sorrow to the prophet and the Jews.

Jeremiah pleads that God will bring upon those enemies the sorrow they deserve.

Chapter 4

What once was glorious is now dimmed out.

The princes of the people have turned from gold to earth.

The people care no more for their children than do ostriches.

Those who once had every comfort are now ready to feed from manure piles.

Unlike the quick punishment of Sodom, Israel suffers over a period of time.

The once clean and pure whiteness of the Nazarites has now turned to black skin cleaving to the bones.

Mothers have consumed their own children in the terrible siege.

Jerusalem has been brought down by the fire of God from great reputation to the despised level of the leper who cries out, "unclean, unclean."

She looks for help but no nations are found who are willing and able to aid.

The land of Edom shall also feel the cup of wrath.

Edom need not enjoy Jerusalem's difficulties since she is about to share them.

Chapter 5

This chapter seems to indicate a complete willingness to accept their miserable condition as a chastisement from Jehovah.

It is a summary of all the griefs described in the previous chapters.

But God reigns from heaven for ever and ever.

They beg that he will help them turn to him.

Yet they know well that he has reason to be angry and they . must simply wait and pray.

5. *Important lessons from Jeremiah and Lamentations.*

  A. God's message must be preached though people object.

  B. God will providentially care for his messengers.

  C. There comes a time when God's longsuffering ceases.

  D. The chastisement of God is meant for our development.

  E. When men reject God there will be much weeping.

EZEKIEL
(God Strengthens)

1. *Background for the book of Ezekiel*
   A. Historical background
      1. Jeremiah began his ministry about 627 B.C.
      2. Nineveh, capital of Assyria, fell in 612 B.C.
      3. Josiah died and a period of confusion began.
      4. Daniel was among the captives taken by the Babylonians in 605 B.C.
      5. Eight years later Ezekiel was taken captive along with king Jehoiakin. 597 B.C.
      6. Zedekiah became king but rebelled against Nebuchadnezzar to whom he was vassal.
      7. Eleven years later in 586 B.C. the Babylonians dealt a crushing blow to Jerusalem.
   B. Social background
      1. The cream of the people and the treasures were in Babylon.
      2. The land was fairly fertile but the wealth was gone.
      3. Injustice and pride are still much in evidence.
      4. The weak and dependent were left in Judah.
   C. Religious background
      1. A strong Egyptian party urged aid from Pharaoh.
      2. False prophets taught an early return to the promised land.
      3. God describes his people as hard-headed and impudent.
      4. They remember God's promises but they forget his conditions.

2. *The man, Ezekiel*
   A. Ezekiel is the son of Buzi of the line of Zadok.
   B. He is both prophet and priest.
   C. Though his people would not listen *then*, his influence has been enormous over the years.
   D. With the aid of the Spirit he has a vivid and powerful imagination.
   E. For five years he lived among the captives without prophesying.

F. When God finally calls he sits "where they sat" for seven days before given a message.

G. Then he speaks with all the authority of God in a most dramatic and powerful declaration.

3. *The nature of the book of Ezekiel*

A. The book is extremely orderly and organized.

B. It comes from the years between five and twenty-seven of Jehoiakin's captivity.

C. This then covers a period of twenty-two years.

D. The mission of Ezekiel is to:
   1. Destroy false hopes of an early return.
   2. Interpret the meaning and purpose of the exile.
   3. Preserve the teachings of Jehovah.

E. There are many symbolic pictures:
   1. The chariot.
   2. The dry bones.
   3. The scattered sheep.

F. Outline of the book
   1. Denouncement of Judah and fall of Jerusalem.
      a. The call. b. Destruction of Jerusalem. c. The cause of this destruction. d. The certainty of the destruction.
   2. Prophecies against the nations:
      a. Ammon, b .Moab, c. Edom, d. Philistia, e. Tyre, f. Sidon, g. Egypt.
   3. Prophecies of Future Hope for Israel.

G. Great passages. 2:1-3:15; 3:16-21; 11:19-20; 18:1-32; 33:11; 34:2-6; 34:11-16; 37:1-14; 48:1-12.

4. *Comments upon the text of Ezekiel*

Chapter 1

Ezekiel is among the captives by the River Chebar in Babylonia.

After five years of captivity he sees visions as the heavens are opened to him.

A storm cloud approaches him.

From the cloud come four living creatures:
   1. They have four wings.
   2. Four faces—man, ox, lion and eagle.
   3. Feet without joints like calves' feet.
   4. An appearance like coals of burning fire.

Each creature is associated with a wheel.

Each wheel has another wheel inside it.

Around the wheels are eyes.

When the four creatures move the wheels move.

Above the creatures is a firmament or platform.

Upon the platform is a throne.

Upon the throne is a man's likeness representing the Lord.

He is associated with fire and is surrounded by a bow like a rainbow.

Ezekiel is overwhelmed by the vision and falls to the ground upon his face.

He then hears a voice.

Chapter 2

The voice tells him to stand upon his feet.

The Lord addresses him as his son from among mankind.

He is told to stand upon his feet and the spirit provides strength for him to do so.

God says he is to speak to the rebellious children of Israel.

They are impudent and stiff-hearted but they must be given opportunity to hear and respond.

It will be unpleasant to perform this task but Ezekiel must not be afraid of their person or their words.

He is to be careful not to become as they are.

God provides him a book of lamentation and woe that he is to digest.

Chapter 3

Ezekiel consumes the book or roll and finds it to be as sweet as honey. See Revelation 10:9 also Psalm 19:10.

Then he is told to speak to the children of Israel.

Though strangers might hear and respond they will not.

He is then taken up by the Spirit and taken to the captives that he may speak to them.

That which was sweet as he consumed it now becomes bitter as it must be preached to a rebellious people.

Ezekiel sits among the captives for seven days before he is commanded to speak by the Lord.

He is to be a warning watchman.

If they take warning he will save both he and they.

If they do not he will save himself.

If he warns one who has turned from righteousness and the man take warning, both will be saved.

If that man does not take warning his previous righteousness will be counted for nothing.

He is told to move out into the plain country.

138

There the spirit strengthens him again and he is given further instructions.

He is to preach from his own house rather than to go out among the people.

God will make Ezekiel dumb or eloquent as he sees the children respond to the preaching.

Chapter 4

Ezekiel is to take a clay tile and draw the city of Jerusalem upon it.

This tile could be as much as 12 x 24 x 4 inches.

Miniature battering rams and enemy weapons are to be built around it.

An iron pan is then placed between Ezekiel and the model city and Ezekiel is to go through the actions of besieging it.

The meaning of the iron pan has left the commentators guessing. Perhaps it represents Jerusalem's hard heart.

Ezekiel is to show by this tile, etc. that Jerusalem is doomed and that they need not think about a return.

Ezekiel is to lie upon his left side for 390 days representing 390 years of Israel's iniquity.

He is then to lie upon his right side for 40 days representing 40 years of Judah's iniquity.

During this time he is to uncover his arm and prophesy against Jerusalem.

God's stretched-out arm will bring disaster to the city.

He is also to indicate the difficulties the people will suffer.

He is to make his bread not from wheat but from an undesirable conglomeration of materials.

Then he is to bake it with human manure.

Some believe the manure to be mixed with the bread.

Others believe it to have been fuel only.

Ezekiel objects that the food will then be polluted.

God allows him to substitute cow manure for human.

He shall have only twenty shekels a day. (About one half pound.)

Thus Jerusalem shall suffer severe want and actually be wasted away because of their sins.

Chapter 5

Now another picture is presented.

Ezekiel is to cut his beard with a sharp knife.

The hair is to be divided into three portions by the balance.

One third is to be burned on the tile inside the sketch of the city.

One third is to be chopped up with the knife into bits.

One third is to be thrown into the wind.

Just a few hairs are to be saved for a little while.

Then they are also to be thrown into the fire.

God explains that this is symbolic of Jerusalem itself.

The children of Israel have set themselves against him.

Therefore he will play along with the game and become their enemy.

His treatment of them will be worse than they have seen before or will see after.

They shall go so far as to eat or consume their own children and their own parents.

God will have no pity upon them.

They will die by famine and pestilence (one third).

They will die by the sword. (one third).

They will be scattered abroad to many nations.

They will be made a reproach to all that pass by them.

Chapter 6

Ezekiel is to direct his prophecy toward the mountains of Israel where idolatry was practiced on high places.

The living bodies bowed before idols will be replaced by their carcasses.

The objects of their false worship will be demolished.

There shall be a small remnant kept alive and scattered among the nations.

This remnant shall live to repent of their wickedness.

Ezekiel is told to use vigorous gestures with his speech.

They shall die by pestilence, sword and famine.

They shall know by these things that Jehovah is Lord.

Chapter 7

God has reached the end of his longsuffering.

Note the similarity to Revelation 10:6.

There will be absolutely no pity whatsoever.

Like an execution taking place at dawn the morning has come.

Pride has brought forth its fruit of violence.

The seller will not miss that which he has sold, nor the buyer enjoy what he has purchased because the upheaval will make all this meaningless.

Those who manage to escape will mourn like frightened doves.

Silver and gold which are able to buy off human beings will not placate the Lord.

God's ornament, the temple, will be turned over to strangers.

Violence shall fill the city of Jerusalem.

Then they shall seek peace in vain.

Then they shall seek a message from God but shall only receive the message of his fury.

Prince, priest and prophet shall all fail them.

And they shall know Jehovah is Lord.

Chapter 8

The person on the throne appears again to Ezekiel.

He is taken in vision to the city of Jerusalem.

At the north gate of the temple he observed an image which provoked Jehovah to jealousy.

God indicates that such provocation will cause his departure from the temple.

Ezekiel is shown into the secret parts of the temple where animal worship is being practiced.

The supposed wise men of the Jews have concluded that God no longer sees their actions.

We call such persons today deists.

Next women are seen weeping for Tammuz who may be the god Adonis.

Finally twenty-five men are seen turned away from the temple and worshipping the sun.

The branch to the nose is not explained satisfactorily by anyone we have found.

After such disgusting behavior they may cry loudly in God's ear without being heeded.

Chapter 9

Now seven angels are called into action.

Six of them have smashing tools in their hands.

Perhaps they come from the north because this is the direction from which Jerusalem's conquerors came.

One of the men or angels is prepared with an inkhorn.

He is told to move through the city and mark those who show they are true to God by their repulsion of the abominable worship going on.

Compare the marking of Revelation 7:2-4.

Of the ones who are not marked there shall be destruction without pity.

Ezekiel is concerned that all Israel may be destroyed.

God explains that the *wickedness* encompassses *nearly all.*

As they have sown, so shall they reap.

The angel with the inkhorn reports that he has marked God's servants.

Clearly the other six have performed their gruesome tasks also.

141

Chapter 10

The angel with the inkhorn is then told to get coals from the fire of the cherubim and throw them on Jerusalem. Compare Revelation 8:5.

The description of the glory of God is given again.

The glory of God begins to depart from the temple.

An interesting comment from one writer is that the great wheels of this vision represent the continually rolling providence of God.

Chapter 11

Twenty-five men are seen who should be giving wise counsel to the city.

Instead they devise mischief and provide foolish and wicked information.

The false information is that Jerusalem is safe and destruction is far off.

The caldron here does not seem to be undesirable by these false teachers. They see it as protection to the weakness of their flesh.

As a protective caldron however Jerusalem will not serve them.

God will bring them out of the midst of it and give them to strangers.

While Ezekiel was prophesying to these twenty-five men Pelatiah fell dead.

He may have been struck as Ananias and Sapphira were.

Again Ezekiel is fearful that God will bring a full and complete end upon Israel.

God then tells Ezekiel of a brighter day ahead.

He will be a place of refuge while they are scattered.

But he will assemble them again out of the various countries.

Their idolatry will be removed.

They will be renewed in heart and spirit.

They will be happy to keep the commandments of Jehovah.

They shall serve no other gods.

Consequently he will be glad to own them as his people.

Compare here Jeremiah 31:31-34. Also see Hebrews 8:8-12.

At this point the glory of God departed from the City.

The Spirit returned Ezekiel to the land of Babylon.

And Ezekiel conveys the things he has seen to the captive people.

Jerusalem is full of abominable rebellion.

God will destroy the city.

They must not look forward to an early return.

Chapter 12

The rebellious Israelites have shut their ears and eyes to spiritual things.

Ezekiel is told to provide a sign by moving out of his house.

He is to gather his possessions and move out during the day while he can be easily seen.

He is to dig an opening through the solid wall of his house.

He is to carry his possessions upon his shoulders and wear a blindfold so he cannot see the ground.

The Israelites will then ask him what he is doing.

He is to answer that this is a sign of things to come.

The prince of Jerusalem shall leave the city bearing a load upon his shoulder.

He shall find a way through the wall.

He shall not look at the ground.

He shall not escape from God's net but will be captured and taken to Babylon.

He shall not see that land though he shall die there.

The reason this could be true is that he was blinded.

See Jeremiah 52:9-11.

The king's defenders shall be overwhelmed.

The citizens of Jerusalem shall be scattered abroad.

Only a remnant should escape to tell of the abominations to the countries where they would be scattered.

Ezekiel is then told to eat and drink with trembling and shaking, to show the anxiety with which the people of Jerusalem would eat.

God asks about a saying that his prophets' visions are not being fulfilled.

He will cause that saying to cease through what shall happen.

The longsuffering is about to end.   See 2 Peter 3:4.

The prophecies of destruction will happen in their days.

God is not slack concerning his promises. . . .

Chapter 13

Ezekiel is now commanded to prophesy to the false prophets.

They are badly mistaken in following their own wisdom.

Like cunning foxes they take the people prey and hide when the enemy appears.

Instead of filling the weaknesses in the wall of salvation they promote such weakness.

They speak when God has not given them a message.

Their lying prophecies of peace for Jerusalem when the city was doomed set them against God.

The people think they are safe behind their wall of false teaching and the prophets provide them rotten mortar of lies.

God will bring the wall down with rain, wind and hail.

See Matthew 7 (The Two Builders) and Psalm 127:1.

The wall and the false prophets shall both be destroyed.

There are also false prophetesses.

These women use strange costumes to snatch souls from God.

They are willing to pollute God's people for material gain.

Their costumes will be ruined and the souls will be set free.

God's people will be carried off into Babylon where they will learn to avoid such liars.

Then Israel will know that Jehovah is God.

Chapter 14

The elders of the captivity gather at Ezekiel's house.

God is displeased that they inquire of him with idols in their heart and sin before their face.

They will not find the truth, but will receive an answer appropriate to their own wicked desires.

The inquirer of this type will be cut off from God's own.

In addition the prophet who pleases his itching ears will share in the same punishment.

Israel must be caused to realize that Jehovah is God and that only if they repent may they be his people.

He is prepared to send four judgments against them:
1. The sword of war.
2. Starvation and famine.
3. Wild animals.
4. Disease and pestilence.

But they have reached such a condition that even if Job, Noah and Daniel preached to them they would not listen.

Of the few who come through the destruction of Jerusalem there will be some who will come to Babylon.

Those few will show by their lives that God was just in his punishment of that wicked city.

Chapter 15

Israel is now compared to an unproductive vine.

A vine is not good for building construction.

A vine will not even provide a pin for hanging pots.

When it is thrown into the fire it quickly shrivels from both ends to the middle.

Israel is like a vine which produces no fruit.

God will continue his burning of Israel.

144

They have already been scorched at both ends by the Assyrians
and the Babylonians.

Now they shall be turned to ashes.

All this because they have sinned against Jehovah.

Chapter 16

Ezekiel is told to tell Jerusalem of her sins.

She is not acting like a descendant of Abraham but as if her
parents were wicked nations of Canaan.

As Israel came into existence she was like an abandoned child.

She would have died except for the strength of God.

Under God's care she grew into mature beauty.

When she reached maturity God made an agreement with her
as a man would a wife.

He provided for her until she was known among the nations for
her outstanding beauty.

But foolishly she began to depend upon her beauty.

She used the fine clothing God provided to attract other gods.

She used the treasures he made available to form idols.

She offered the food he provided as sacrifices to these idols.

The children who were born were even burned as sacrifices to
idols rather than raised as God's children.

Every high elevation was used as a place for false worship.

Israel was happy to embrace the false worship of the Assyrians
and depend upon them.

But they did not satisfy so she turned to the Babylonians.

Still looking for new loves she committed fornication with
Egypt.

She was worse than most harlots in that she ran after the lovers.

In addition she paid them from God's own provisions rather than
receiving payment from them for her favors.

God will gather all of her lovers at once and reveal to them just
how foolish Israel has been.

They shall combine to destroy her, removing all the wonderful
blessings which God had given.

Israel has shown that she is a spiritual descendant of the Hit-
tite and the Amorite.

And she has acted like a sister to Sodom and Samaria.

Neither of these places committed such terrible sins as did Israel.

In spite of her filthiness God will remember his agreement with
her as husband and wife.

A new and everlasting covenant will be established.

Heathen nations and people such as Sodom and Samaria will become God's children with Israel as his woman.

But it will not be because of Israel's faithfulness.

It will be because of God's longsuffering.

The time will come when Israel shall turn back to God and be ashamed of her actions, and then he shall receive her.

Chapter 17

Ezekiel is to present a riddle in the form of a parable to Israel.

Nebuchadnezzar swoops down into Lebanon as a great eagle.

He takes King Jehoiakin prisoner to Babylon with many people.

In Babylon the nation of Israel is kept low but spreads like a vine instead of a cedar.

Then King Zedekiah who reigns in Jerusalem as a vassal sends his roots of Israel toward Pharaoh-Necho of Egypt.

God considers this a break of both the agreement with Babylon and with himself. His people are never to depend upon Egypt which is the symbol of bondage.

God will allow Nebuchadnezzar to take Zedekiah and Zedekiah will die in Babylon.

But God will take things into his own hands and plant a tender twig from the nation of Israel.

It will be planted on Mount Zion.

It shall grow like the mustard seed and become a shelter for more than just eagles like Nebuchadnezzar and Pharaoh-Necho.

All the nations shall come to recognize that when God steps in, the mighty may be abased and the humble exalted.

Chapter 18

God is concerned about a strange saying going about in the people of Israel.

This saying is that they are suffering captivity because of the sins of their ancestors.

This is not true. They are suffering for their own sins.

If a person acts in a righteous manner he shall have life.

If that person's son acts wickedly he will not be protected by his father's righteousness but will die for his sins.

Compare here Deuteronomy 24:16 and Exodus 20:5.

If that wicked son have a child who does righteously he shall be saved in spite of his father's wickedness.

If a wicked man turns from his sins he may live.

But if a righteous man turns from his righteousness he will die.

Israel has accused God of being unjust and being a respecter of persons.

It is not God but Israel whose ways are crooked.

God calls upon them to repent, taking upon themselves both a new heart and a new spirit.

God takes absolutely no pleasure in seeing the wicked perish. Compare 2 Peter 3:9.

Chapter 19

This chapter deals with the princes of Israel.

Israel lives among lion-like nations and she has allowed her princes to take on these characteristics.

Jehoahaz is able to become a ruler by his devouring of other men.

But he reigned only three months before he was captured by Pharaoh-Necho and placed in chains.

There is disagreement as to whether the second lion who was taken to Babylon in chains was Jehoiakim or Jehoiakin. See 2 Chronicles 36:6 and 2 Kings 24:15.

There was a time when Israel had strong men to bear the ruling sceptre.

But because of her corruption fire broke out from the inside and consumed and withered her leadership.

She has been uprooted and no longer is able to bear strong rulers.

This is a sad description but it shall continue for some time.

Chapter 20

Once again the elders or wise men of Israel come to Ezekiel to get advice from Jehovah.

God refuses to consider their request.

Ezekiel is told to point out their errors.

Long ago God has chosen Israel of all the nations.

He had revealed his will to them for their direction.

He had reached out to them to bring them out of Egypt.

They had been brought to a land flowing with blessings.

Yet they rebelled and would not forsake the idols of Egypt.

As they wandered through the wilderness he gave them his law and Sabbaths to remind them of his covenant.

But they despised his law and polluted his Sabbaths.

They scorned walking in the ways of life and determined to walk in their own ways which lead to death.

Because they rejected his laws he allowed them to have laws which led to death.

Because of all these abominable sins God will not respond to their request for advice from Ezekiel.

Though they wish to be like the heathen countries God will not permit this to happen.

They will be scattered in the heathen countries.

But this will lead to their repentance.

The time shall come when they shall pollute his Holy name no more.

They will be brought out from among those heathen nations to the Mount of God (Zion).

This will not be because of their own righteousness.

It will be because God is longsuffering and desires that his name continue to be carried among men.

But without doubt a purifying fire shall descend upon Israel.

It shall burn away all the wickedness until all men see that God's will is to be done.

Ezekiel then expresses his fear that the people will simply mock him because he speaks in figures.

Chapter 21

Since Ezekiel has deplored the use of parables he will now hear some straight talk.

The sword of the Lord is to be brought against both Israel and Ammon.

Ezekiel is to sigh deeply to indicate the weakness which will appear when hearts fail before God's sword.

Ezekiel is to show by his vigorous gestures just how the wrath of Jehovah has been stirred up.

Ezekiel is to choose a place where he may demonstrate to the captives that Nebuchadnezzar is making up his mind whether to come against Jerusalem first, or against Ammon.

The Babylonian king is making use of three forms of divination to decide the question: shaking of arrows—see other translation than King James; consulting idols—perhaps the teraphim; use of an animal's liver—let it fall and observe the direction of the lobes.

Nebuchadnezzar will decide to come against Jerusalem.

But the people will not accept this truth.

They will consider it to be a mistaken prophecy.

The fact remains however that the king of Israel will fall.

The people will have no king until Christ takes his place at the right hand of God.

Amon has been misled into believing that they will escape the coming fury.

But the fire of God's wrath will extend into their land and extinguish them from the face of the earth.

Chapter 22

Jerusalem is guilty of the shedding of much blood.

She is also defiled by her idolatry.

She shall therefore become a nation reproached and mocked by those far and near.

The list of crimes which have been committed *in thee* is extensive.

She shall be scattered among the nations that her sins may be consumed.

Israel has become as the scum from the purification of precious metal.

The situation is most serious because all are involved:
1. The prophets eat up souls for material reward.
2. The priests make no difference between holy and unholy.
3. The princes shed blood to get gain.
4. The people rob and oppress one another.

There is no man found who is able to mend the broken city.

God's wrath is deserved.

Chapter 23

The two capital cities of the Northern Kingdom and the Southern Kingdom are compared to two harlots.

Even before they were well grown they had an affair with Egypt.

The older sister, Aholah, or Samaria became enamored with the Assyrian way of life.

She was therefore allowed to be taken captive by the Assyrians.

Her plight was well known among the other nations.

The younger sister, Aholibah, or Jerusalem saw but paid no attention.

She also flirted with the Assyrians.

Then she turned her attention to the Babylonians.

After defiling herself completely with them the infatuation turned to hatred.

But by this time God had been repulsed by her foolishness.

Now all her former lovers would be allowed to debase her to the very depths until she will desire to mutilate the breasts which once were attractive to them.

They have been willing to give their sons to pass through the fire and now their children shall be slain by the sword.

The other nations shall be taught by the absement of Israel.

They shall know after this that Jehovah is the Lord.

149

Chapter 24

Ezekiel is told to take note of the day for it is the day the king of Babylon begins siege of Jerusalem.

The captives are told to set a pot with water on the fire.

Pieces of meat are to be placed in the pot along with the bones.

There is to be rust on the inside of the pot.

The pieces of meat will be brought out after cooking but will not be eaten.

The scum will not be removed and will thus make the contents foul.

The pot is the city of Jerusalem.

The pieces of flesh are the inhabitants.

The scum is the filthiness of the sin-filled city.

Previously God had subjected the city to fires of purification.

Now the judgment shall be complete and he will not turn back.

Jehovah then informs Ezekiel that his wife shall be taken from him.

He is told not to go through any of the usual forms of mourning.

The people will ask him why he behaves in such manner.

He is to tell them that the temple will be taken away from them and their children will also be killed.

And they are not to mourn or weep because it is only their just dessert.

A messenger will come to the area where the captives are with news of the destruction of Jerusalem.

At that point Ezekiel will be allowed to speak for himself.

NOTE: *He had apparently been allowed to speak only when God told him exactly what to say from 3:15-17.*

Chapter 25

We now begin a series of prophecies against seven nations, Ammon, Moab, Edom, Philistia, Tyre, Sidon and Egypt.

These prophecies teach us as well as the ancients several lessons:

1. God will not permit corruption anywhere to go unpunished.

2. Jehovah is God of all the nations.

3. Judgment *begins* at the house of the Lord but it does not *stop* there. See 1 Peter 4:17-18.

It is well to remember through the entire book of Ezekiel that it is a highly figurative book.

Ammon was brought into existence through Noah's wicked drunkenness and it followed wicked ways as a tribe.

150

When Israel suffered persecution for defilement Ammon rejoiced.

Because of such rejoicing God would allow them to be overrun by invaders from the East. (Perhaps Nabatean Arabs.)

The tribe would perish and the country would become a desolation with the chief city only fit for camel pasture.

Then they would know that Jehovah is Lord.

Now Ezekiel's prophecies turn to Moab.

The origin of Moab is similar to that of Ammon.

Moab has sinned in classifying Israel no different from the heathen nations.

The same invaders from the east which overwhelm Ammon will take the land of Moab.

And Moab will also know that Jehovah is Lord.

The next nation to be attended to is Edom.

Edom descended from Esau and there had been steady envy between the two groups, Israel and Edom.

But Edom went farther than just to rejoice over Israel's misfortune, they helped to plunder it.

Edom also shall be made a desolate land.

But in addition, because they have taken vengeance upon God's people God shall cause them to fall by the sword.

Edom shall know the vengeance of Jehovah.

The Philistines are next in line.

They have hated God's people from the time of Joshua.

Their hatred has erupted in violence against Israel.

Therefore God would take vengeance upon this people of the seacoast.

And they also shall know that Jehovah is Lord.

Chapter 26

A lengthy prophecy is now directed against Tyre and its prince.

The time here given is the same year in which Jerusalem was taken.

Tyre viewed Jerusalem as having been broken and delivered into her hands.

Now that Jerusalem had been rendered ineffective Tyre expected to take over her trade.

But God would send nation after nation against Tyre until she was as barren as the top of a rock where fishing nets were laid to dry.

Nebuchadnezzar would be the first to batter the glorious seaport.

When mighty Tyre's fall was noised abroad even the islands far away would shudder at the calamity. Compare Revelation 18:9.

Her glory should be sunk into the depths of the sea and never return again.

(It took some time for this prophecy to be fulfilled but today we are not at all sure as to the exact location of this ancient city.)

Chapter 27

This chapter speaks of the great glory before destruction and the lamentation following it.

Tyre is described as a magnificent sailing ship.

This is reasonable since it was an island off the mainland.

Tyre had been built up by materials from the most important places known.

Lebanon, Egypt, Bashan, Senir, Tarshish and Persia as well as others had made their contributions to the ship of Tyre.

Those who traded for her merchandise included Damascus, Syria, Judah, Arabia, Sheba, etc.

Tyre was sailing gloriously and her praise was sung abroad.

But her oarsmen had failed to watch where she was headed.

She would be caught in Nebuchadnezzar's storm from the East and she would be sunk in the midst of the waves.

All who are connected with her shall sit in ashes, tear their hair, and weep in bitter sorrow.

The same merchants and kings who praised her before would later mock and hiss at her pathetic state.

Chapter 28

The prince of Tyre should go down in shame with his city.

The Bible clearly states that this is a man. *(Verse 2.)*

However one cannot help but be struck by the similarity in three cases:

1. The Prince of Tyre—Ezekiel 28.
2. The King of Babylon—Isaiah 14.
3. The King of Egypt—Ezekiel 29.

We might also add Daniel 4:29-34 with Nebuchadnezzar.

A similar attitude is forecast in the latter days by Paul. (2 Thess. 2:3-4.)

It is Satan's very nature to set himself up against the will of Jehovah.

Even Peter found that Christ detected Satan working in him. "Get thee behind me, Satan." (Matt. 16:23.)

This chapter then tells us much about a man, the prince of

Tyre, but it also tells us a great deal about Satan as he devours men with pride.

The following characteristics of the prince are listed:
1. He sees himself as God.
2. He has great wisdom and understanding.
3. He possesses great attractiveness.
4. He was surrounded by the beauty and blessings of the Garden of God.
5. He had been assigned special responsibilities.
6. He began by being sinless and living in the presence of the Almighty.

As often happens his beauty and his wisdom had caused him to lift up his heart against God in his pride.

Because of this the prince of Tyre would be:
1. Cast out of the Holy Mountain.
2. Cast to the earth and burned to ashes.
3. Made an astonishment and a lesson to men.

Again one cannot fail to be impressed with some related statements.
1. Revelation 12:9-10—Satan cast out of heaven to the earth.
2. John 12:31—Now shall the prince of this world be cast out.
3. 2 Peter 2:4—God spared not the angels that sinned, but cast them down—

IF WE WISH TO WALK ON GOD'S HOLY MOUNTAIN WE MUST AVOID THE MISTAKE OF THE PRINCE OF TYRE!

In the end of the chapter Ezekiel turns to the city of Sidon.

She has long been a brier and a thorn to Israel.

Now the sword shall come upon her and she shall *know* that Jehovah is Lord.

As in the book of Revelation God causes Ezekiel to flash back after such scenes of horror to the blessed future happiness of his marked remnant.

After their punishment they shall be separated from the nations.

They shall dwell in his own Kingdom.

The judgments shall be executed upon those who defiled and mocked them.

And both the heathen and the saints will *know* that Jehovah is Lord.

Chapter 29

Now Ezekiel is to give his attention to Egypt.

153

The dragon could have been translated crocodile.

This Pharaoh is Pharaoh-Hophra, grandson of Pharaoh-Necho.

He has exalted himself, but God will bring him down.

He shall not even be given the respect of proper burial.

When Israel leaned upon Egypt for support Egypt was like a fragile reed unable to hold Israel up and breaking under the weight.

The majesty of Egypt should dim to a mere shadow with a number of their people being taken to Babylon along with the Israelites.

Since that time Egypt has never regained her former glory.

Nebuchadnezzar had acted as a minister of vengeance for Jehovah against Tyre.

He had not taken any riches for his trouble there.

Now he would be allowed to invade Egypt and receive his wages from that source.

The horn of Israel's power will rise again providing evidence of Jehovah's position as ruler of all nations.

Chapter 30

Once again a day of the Lord approaches!

All those people associated with Egypt shall fall with her.

For the rivers of Egypt to become dry is a most serious promise for her health has always depended upon them.

The chief cities of that nation shall be destroyed.

No is the city mentioned by Nahum 3:8.

The strong right arm of Egypt will be broken and there shall be no way to make it heal.

When his arm is broken there will be no way to swing the sword.

Egypt shall groan before the King of Babylon like a wounded man.

Egypt shall come to realize that Jehovah is ruler of Egypt as well as of Palestine.

Chapter 31

The Egyptian Pharaoh is similar to the Assyrian in his desire to exalt himself.

Both had been allowed to grow to great power on earth.

Because they failed to appreciate blessings comparable to the Garden of Eden they shall find their way to the pit of Sheol. (The *hell* of verse 17 is from Sheol.)

All the trees of Eden are other proud nations who have lifted themselves up against God.

154

Chapter 32

Like a lion or a whale Pharaoh and Egypt have tried to dominate everything in sight.

God will remove him from dominion as a small fish is pulled from the water on a fishhook.

All Egypt's ruling bright stars shall go out and her greatest governmental luminaries will fade into darkness.

Both man and nature would turn against this once proud country.

Now we have a trip through Sheol.

Egypt shall sink into the very depths of the pit.

There she would find other wicked nations such as Asshur, Tubal and Meshech, Elam and Edom, the princes of the north and the Sidonians.

The only comfort that Pharaoh shall have is that he is not alone in his condition.

Adam Clarke believes that this chapter should be studied side by side with Isaiah 14.

There the King of Babylon is associated with Sheol.

Chapter 33

Ezekiel must once more be reminded of his duty as a watchman.

As in Chapter 18 God declares that he has no pleasure in the death of the wicked.

Jehovah's people must be warned in order that they turn from their unrighteousness if it be possible to turn them.

Those few who are righteous must be warned to remain so.

God's ways are impartial and perfectly just.

But now the messenger comes from Jerusalem telling of the conquest of that city in 586 B.C. by Nebuchadnezzar.

Ezekiel's tongue is now released whereas he had been unable to speak for himself.

God declares that not even those who may have fled to the caves or the mountains of Judah will escape his chastening.

One day Israel must know that Jehovah is serious.

As of this time all they do is praise Ezekiel's pretty voice and pay no attention to the meaning of his preaching.

One must here be reminded of James 1:22.

When the people of Israel see that all the things Ezekiel has been prophesying are happening they shall see the difference between him and the false shepherds who lie to them.

155

Chapter 34

Ezekiel, the true prophet is to speak against the false prophets, the evil princes and the priests who are called inadequate.

They should have: fed the flock; healed the sick; bound up the wounded; driven away the beasts; collected the strays.

Instead they: fed themselves from the flock; delivered them to the wild beasts; left them scattered over the face of the earth.

Therefore God must intervene and shepherd the flock himself.

God himself will: take his flock away from the false shepherds; search for them and collect them; feed them; strengthen them; bind the broken and heal the sick.

Compare here Psalm 23 and John 10:9-16.

All this shall be accomplished through David, a prince among them.

David, the king had long been dead by this time.

The one shepherd, David can only be the Messiah.

See Jeremiah 30:10; 33:5-6; Hosea 3:5; Isaiah 9:6-7.

Through this new Shepherd there would come a new era of peace.

Showers of blessing or times of refreshing should come from the presence of the Lord. See Acts 3:20.

The plant of *renown* to be raised up for the people is the same as the *root out of dry ground* or *tender plant* of Isaiah 53:2.

Through the *branch* or *root of Jesse* God's scattered sheep shall be comforted for they shall know him as their God and he shall claim them as his people.

Chapter 35

Again the prophet turns to prophesy against Edom or Mount Seir.

God's hand will be stretched out in fury against it.

Edom probably represents all those who have a perpetual animosity toward the people of God.

See Genesis 36:9; Numbers 20:14-17; Amos 1:11; Obadiah 9-14 and Ezekiel 25:12-14.

The jealousy over the birthright and being the chosen people of God continues.

Since Edom has had a love for blood she shall have blood.

Edom has had no mercy but looked upon Israel covetously.

As she has shown no mercy she shall have no mercy.

Through her judgment the nations shall learn that Jehovah is Lord.

Chapter 36

The mountains of Israel have been under the chastisement of God. (Ezek. 6:1-7.)

They will not forever be in desolation but shall be fruitful.

They will not become the prey of the Edomites who look upon them greedily.

By Israel's disobedience God had decided to drive them out among the nations.

This profaned his holy name because the nations thought he could not provide for his people.

There would come a restoration of God's people.

This would not be because they deserved it but would be because of God's concern for his name and its effects over the world.

The sprinkling of clean water is a reference to the ashes of the heifer. See Hebrews 9:13-14; 10:22; Zechariah 12:10; 13:1.

It is closer to the sprinkling of the blood of Christ upon the heart than to the burial in baptism of Christians.

Note that God says *I* will sprinkle them, not *men*.

The result of this will be clean hearts which are no longer hard as rock against the absorption of God's Word.

New Spirit and new life will result as men are pricked in heart and ask, "What must we do?"

When these things happen there will also be a penitent loathing of the former attitudes of rebellion.

The language of this chapter is clearly too exalted to apply only to the restoration under Ezra, etc.

It refers also to the Church of Jesus Christ.

Israel is in most serious straits at the time Ezekiel is speaking here: they have been driven from their *land;* they have lost their king; they have no national *status*.

God is now ready to promise them all three: the new land will be the *Kingdom of God;* the new King will be Christ, the *King of kings;* the new national status will be *spiritual* Jew.

Chapter 37

Israel has given up hope and God provides a vision of hope in this chapter.

It is true that Israel looks like a valley full of dry and lifeless bones.

This will not always be true for God will give new life.

This has particular application to the fleshly Jew, yet one must admit that the opening of the graves seems like the picture of the resurrection in Revelation 20.

Israel shall be brought from the graves (the countries where she has been scattered) and given new life though such may seem absolutely hopeless.

The stick of Ephraim is representative of the Northern Kingdom.

The stick of Judah is the Southern Kingdom.

After they have been restored to God's grace they shall be united as one nation under one king.

Israel never had a king after they returned under Ezra and others, nor did the Northern Kingdom find its way back to earthly Palestine.

It must be that this unity spoken of is unity in the Kingdom of God under Christ.

The letter of James is addressed to "the twelve tribes of Israel."

The tabernacle of God is with us as Christians today. See Revelation 21:3.

It is as if God were telling us in Revelation 21:3 that he has completed the promise given in Ezekiel 37:27-28.

God will establish them—*New King—New land—Secure status.*

Chapter 38

Many believe this to be one of the most difficult chapters in the Bible to understand.

This chapter and the next answer a very important question.

After the restoration promised previously, is it possible that another enemy may take all this away again?

God answers by showing a defeat to the biggest army one can imagine (as many as 300 million men).

The American Standard gives a more accurate translation in calling God the Prince of Rosh.

Some point out the similarity of this word to *Russia.*

They also compare:
1. Meschech with Moscow
2. Tubal with Tobolsk

Gomer, Tubal and Meschech were all sons of Japheth, the son of Noah who moved into the area which is now the Caucasus region of Russia. (Note also the connection of the Caucasian race.)

This giant army is then presumed by these persons to be primarily Russian and to be the same as that mentioned in Revelation 20:7-9.

But Ethiopia and Libya are actually south of Israel and they join this mighty horde.

We believe it to be *more than the Russians* and symbolic of *all the forces Satan can muster* to attempt severing God's people from his protecting hand.

There is no force in heaven or earth capable of tearing God's people away from him if they are not willing.

See Romans 8:35-39.

This vast army shall descend upon God's people thinking they are completely defenseless.

They shall seek to carry away much spoil and riches.

God had anticipated such an effort by Gog and predicted it through the prophets.

The invasion will be allowed to progress until the enemy is in the land of Israel.

Then God will intervene to protect his own and all shall know that Jehovah is Lord.

All nature shall quake in the presence of God's wrath. Earthquakes, fire, brimstone and hailstones shall come along with bloodshed and infighting within the army of Gog.

Chapter 39

Only one sixth of the forces will be left when God finishes.

The punishment shall not only be found in God's land which they have invaded, but shall extend to their homes even if it be the farthest parts of the earth.

God's people shall have a complete victory and they shall glory in his name no longer polluting it.

Instead of the army taking spoil from Israel, Israel shall take spoil from them after God has intervened.

Once again the day of the Lord has been described. (Verse 8.)

This is more than a real army as indicated by the time required to bury them.

Seven months with all the people of Israel burying and calling in help from the people traveling through.

The bodies shall even block passenger travel through the seacoast travel routes. (Noses is italicized in verse 11.)

Hamon-Gog means "the multitude of Gog,"

Thus the valley is named for the multitude buried there from the army of Gog.

God will also feed the beasts of the field and the fowls of the air, offering them a sacrifice from him.

They have refused God's sacrifices provided for them.

Now they shall be lowered to the level of a sacrifice to the beast world.

Compare the feast described here with that in Revelation 19:8-9.

Note that the birds are to eat the chariots in verse 20.

Therefore much of this is to be interpreted symbolically.

This entire occasion shall prove that God has been constantly behind the scenes in Israel's experiences:

He allowed them to be captivated for chastisement.

It was not that he could not protect them.

It is he who restores them from captivity.

And no force is capable of making them a prey against his will.

See here the repeated statements of security for the 144,000 who are sealed with the Spirit in Revelation.

All things have been done that Jehovah's name might be respected throughout the earth by both Jew and Gentile.

In God's Kingdom, as a Christian, ruled by Jesus as King, and blessed by the outpouring of his Spirit, none can make us afraid.

Chapter 40

Isaac Newton, the greatest scientific mind of all time wrestled mightily with the following chapters describing the temple.

He felt that there were spiritual truths involved which matched or exceeded the laws of physics for which he was praised so highly.

Your present writer believes that these chapters will only be fully appreciated when time has run its course and God's plan is completed.

Here we see two temples being described:
1. One is the temple built when Israel returned from Babylonian captivity.
2. The other temple is the Church. (1 Cor. 3:10-17.)

The mountain of verse 2 is the mountain of the Lord's house. (Isa. 2:2; Psa. 48:2; Psa. 132:14; Psa. 2.)

All things are to be measured:
1. Smaller things with the measuring reed.
2. Larger things with the line of flax.

But all are to be measured for separation to God. (Ezek. 42:20; 44:23; 48:15; Zech. 2:13 Rev. 21:15.)

Everything in this temple is to be by Divine dimension.

The Holy must be distinguished from the common.

After the restoration Israel must have a proper worship.

Chapter 41

In chapter 40 the courts were measured, now the temple.

Along with this description one should compare both:
1 Kings 6; 1 Chronicles 28.

The most holy place of the tabernacle was half the size of the one in Solomon's temple and Ezekiel's.

The sons of Zadok have a special place in this temple.

Ezekiel is of the line of Zadok.

While the temple of Solomon was resplendent with gold and silver this one has wood wainscoating.

The cherubim here have only the face of a man and a lion. Compare chapter 1:10-12.

Chapter 42

It is very difficult to be sure of the precise measurements because we are not sure of the cubit length.

Obviously these dimensions are large.

Adam Clarke believes the entire wall was some thirteen thousand paces around it.

Another commentator believes the whole territory described to be larger than Mount Moriah, leading either to the necessity of a change in the size of the literal mountain, or else a symbolic interpretation.

Chapter 43

The glory of God departed from the temple in Ezekiel's previous vision.

Now with the restored temple he envisions its return.

See Exodus 40:34-35 and 1 Kings 8:10-11.

Also Haggai 2:6-7 and Isaiah 4:5.

The east gate is reserved for Divine entrance as if the spiritual light of the world arises like the sun, from east to west.

When Jesus was asked about the end of the world he mixed the end of Jerusalem with the final judgment. (Matt. 24-25.)

The same mixing seems to be the case here between the temple of Ezra's time and the temple of the Church.

See 2 Corinthians 6:16; Acts 7:47-50; Ephesians 2; 1 Peter 2; Revelation 21:3.

Premillennialists see the sacrifices here as literal and being offered in the future.

They suppose them to look back toward the cross in thanksgiving just as those of the Old Testament looked forward in anticipation of Christ's blood.

This runs counter to the book of Hebrews.

1. Here we have bulls, goats and sheep—But Hebrews 10:4;
2. Here we have sin offerings—But, Hebrews 10:9-10.

The tenth verse of this chapter is very important.

If this verse is for the Babylonian captives alone it serves as a lesson for us similar to Noah's gopherwood.

If it is pointed directly toward the Church temple we may have much to learn about Divine patterns.

How inadequate one lifetime is to fathom God's unsearchable riches!

Chapter 44

Who is THE PRINCE of this chapter?

The commentators have avoided this person since there are characteristics which present difficulties to all three major positions.

We believe him to be the same as David, the prince, mentioned in Ezekiel 37:24-25.

And this David, the prince is clearly the one of Psalm 16:8-10 and Acts 2:22-36.

It seems that this prince has a Divine nature for when he enters by the east gate it is shut and no other may enter by that way.

He is also described as a prince among priests which is what Jesus Christ was.

We must frankly admit that the fact that he has sons is a difficulty since Jesus had no one to declare his generation.

Yet Paul addressed Timothy as "my son" when the begettal was through the gospel.

With Christ as the husband of the Church thousands have been begotten.

The sons of Zadok become official priests in the restored temple while the rest of the Levites are housekeepers.

This is because only the house of Zadok remained faithful when the previous temple was defiled. (Verse 15.)

They are commanded not to drink wine before they offer sacrifices.

This must apply to we who are a royal priesthood presenting ourselves as continual living sacrifices.

It is the duty of a priest to show others the difference between the clean and the unclean.

The priests shall have no possessions to call their own except that which belongs to the Lord.

Chapter 45

When the land is divided again a large portion is to be dedicated to the Lord.

The dimensions are to be 25,000 reeds x 10,000 reeds.

Within this area there shall be portions for: the temple; the priests; the prince; the holy city.

The rest of the land shall be given according to the tribes.

The prince shall oversee the government and the sacrifices making sure that all is acceptable to Jehovah.

Purity and justice must reign in this restored temple forever.

Chapter 46

The prince is now the dominant figure as a host of sacrifices similar to the ones of the Law of Moses are offered.

Let us remember that we are dealing with a book which has been highly symbolic throughout.

Which part of this is Palestine and which Kingdom of God?

Chapter 47

Now the symbolism becomes so overwhelming to the premillennialist that he proposes the entire order of nature must be shaken up, with new natural laws in effect.

This is the same kind of living water which is described in Revelation.

1. Trees of life line the banks.
2. The water itself provides life and healing.

It is not a literal river for it grows larger without any source other than the throne of God.

It is the Divine healing influence which would even heal and bring life to the Dead Sea toward which it is shown as flowing.

Sadly there are some places where its waters are rejected and not allowed to heal.—But this is no fault of Jehovah.

Other scriptures which should be considered here are:

Isaiah 35:7; 43:19-20; Joel 3:18; Zechariah 14:8-9; Revelation 22:1.

The captives are promised that they shall have certain generous boundaries when they are returned to the inheritance.

Though the inheritance was first given to the twelve tribes they must be prepared to share it with the Gentiles who accept Jehovah as Lord.

Chapter 48

One should compare Numbers 34:7-12 with the allotment of the land here.

Each of the portions here strangely runs from east to west across the land of Palestine.

See the accompanying sketch of the division of the land and note that the lion's share is an oblation to the Lord.

The city of God shall be within his oblation and shall be four thousand measures on each side, foursquare.

There shall be three gates on each side amounting to twelve in all—one for each of the twelve tribes.

163

Ezekiel and John saw the same Holy City, New Jerusalem.
There is one major difference: John saw no temple.
John explains why—The Lord and the Lamb are the temple of it.
Ezekiel agrees. "The name of the city from that day shall be THE LORD IS THERE."
By the banks of the River Chebar Ezekiel has looked for restored glory for the children of God.—In the process he has caught a vision of the Christian dispensation and the final victory of the saints through the Church and the New Jerusalem.

5. *Practical lessons from the book of Ezekiel.*
    A. God knows better than we how our chastisement should occur.
    B. Every man must bear the responsibility for his own sins.
    C. If the watchman does not warn he shall die for his neglect.
    D. Impure lives and worship can lead to bondage.
    E. Those who scatter God's flock will suffer his wrath.
    F. History is ever moving toward a final victory for God, and the gathering of his children around him in the Holy City.

ALLOTMENT OF THE RESTORED LAND

DAN
ASHER
NAPHTALI
MANASSEH
EPHRAIM
REUBEN
JUDAH

POSSESSION OF THE PRINCE	LEVITES		POSSESSION OF THE PRINCE
	PRIESTS	T	PRIESTS	
		C	

BENJAMIN
SIMEON
ISSACHAR
ZEBULUN
GAD

T—THE TEMPLE   C—THE CITY

164

DANIEL
(God Is Judge)

1. *Background for the book of Daniel*
   A. Historical background.
      1. The rulership of Israel became very corrupt after the reign of Hezekiah.
      2. Josiah made attempts at reform but the people remained wicked at heart.
      3. When Josiah died in a battle between the Egyptians and the Babylonians chaos ruled.
      4. The Jews accepted Jehoahaz, the son of Josiah as king.
      5. But Pharaoh-Necho had sufficient power to replace him with Jehoiakim.
      6. When Nebuchadnezzar defeated Necho Jehoiakim became the vassal of Nebuchadnezzar.
      7. This lasted for only a few years when Jehoiakim rebelled.
      8. It was when Nebuchadnezzar defeated Necho that he marched through Palestine and took Daniel along with a number of other choice captives—605 B.C.
      9. When Jehoiakim rebelled, the Babylonians marched in again and he lost his life.
      10. Jehoiakin, his son, then ruled for only three months, before he was taken captive to Babylon with Ezekiel in 597 B.C.
      11. Zedekiah was then ruler until 586 B.C. when the Chaldeans came upon Jerusalem to demolish it.
      12. Only a pitiful few were left in Judah while the most of the Jews began a 70-year stay in Babylonia.
      13. It was at the end of this period of captivity that we find Daniel writing his book.
   B. Social background.
      1. There was little room for glee. See Psalm 137.
      2. The once proud nation of Israel had been humbled.
      3. Some had intermarried with the Babylonians.
   C. Religious background.
      1. There had been years of hope for return at first.
      2. These had turned to hopelessness when Jerusalem fell.
      3. God's purposes were being completed.
         a. Israel was to be chastised until penitent. b. The Gen-

165

tiles were being prepared for inclusion as part of God's chosen in the latter days.

2. *The man, Daniel*

   A. He is apparently of noble birth in Judah. (Dan. 1:3.)
   B. He is endowed with the gift of interpretation of dreams and visions through the Spirit.
   C. He is a man of tremendous faith, courage and conviction.
   D. Like others of God's prophets he feels great concern for the plight of his brethren.
   E. It is thought that after having entered Babylonia as a youth and spending the seventy years of captivity he may have died there without returning.

3. *The book of Daniel*

   A. This is sometimes called the apocalypse of the Old Testament because of its many mysteries.
   B. The purpose of the book.
      1. This is a book of comfort to the captives.
      2. It is also to inform Gentiles of their ultimate subordination to God's Kingdom.
         a. It was written in a Gentile country. b. And it was written partly in Aramaic.
   C. The style of the book.
      1. It is not chronological in order.
      2. It resembles Revelation in its symbolism.
      3. It is written in very specific form as compared to the more general prophecy of the other Old Testament prophets.
      4. The book contains many evidences of familiarity with the lands east of the Euphrates.
   D. The date of the book.
      1. There are two contrary views.
         a. The critical school sets the date at 167 B.C. b. Fundamentalists set it at about 536 B.C.
      2. The critical school presents three basic arguments.
         a. Linguistic. Greek and Persian words indicate a time after Greek domination. b. Historical. The Jews placed it among the Hagiographa or Holy Writings rather than among the prophets. c. Theological. Predictive prophecy is highly suspect and it must have been written after the events which it describes.
      3. The fundamentalists answer as follows.
         a. Greek influence was strong enough in 536 B.C. to have

introduced the words mentioned. b. Daniel was considered first a statesman instead of a prophet. c. To deny the predictive element in the prophets is a serious mistake.

4. Fundamentalists point out also that:
   a. All of the writings did not come later than the prophets. b. The specific nature of Daniel's reference to the Messiah may have caused concern among the later Jews who denied Christ was the Messiah. c. Daniel gives information which allows calculation of the 536 B.C. date. (Dan. 9:2.)

E. Author of the book
   1. The book itself claims Daniel as author. (Dan. 9:2.)
   2. Christ speaks of Daniel as a prophet. (Matt. 24:15.)
   3. Ezekiel was familiar with his abilities. (Ezek. 28:3; 14:14, 20.)

F. Outline of the book.
   1. Introduction.
   2. Nebuchadnezzar's dream of the image.
   3. The golden image and the fiery furnace.
   4. Nebuchadnezzar's dream of the great tree.
   5. Belshazzar's feast and handwriting on the wall.
   6. Daniel in the lion's den.
   7. The four beasts and the ancient of days.
   8. The vision of the ram and the he-goat.
   9. The prophecy of the seventy weeks.
   10. Jewish destiny in the latter days.

4. *Comments on the text of Daniel*

Chapter 1

1:1-2—Jeremiah 25:1 says the fourth year, but this may be the difference in accession year versus first full year.

To give Jehoiakim into Nebuchadnezzar's hand was to permit his capture.

These vessels mentioned are the ones Belshazzar was using later in his drunken feast.

1:3-7—It is possible that Daniel was a eunuch.

See Isaiah 39:7 and 2 Kings 20:18.

The king would surround himself with the most superior servants possible.

It is clear that the Chaldeans mentioned here are more than Babylonians and are a special class of wise men. See 2:2.

Often kings offered the men of their court the luxurious leftovers from their own table.

The names of the Hebrews are changed from connection with Jehovah to connection with false gods.

Belteshazzar—Treasury of Bel

Abed-nego—Servant of Nego

Masters named their slaves over to show their authority over them. (We take the name Christian.)

The food Daniel refused may have been too luxurious.

But it may also have been offered previously to idols.

1:8-16—The prince of the eunuchs fears that the Hebrew's refusal to eat will endanger his own life.

One never hurts others by their faith in Jehovah.

Daniel proposes a ten-day controlled experiment.

Daniel's diet of faith (vegetables and water) is more favorable to development than the king's food.

1:17-21—Now we find the source of Daniel's tremendous ability to interpret and reveal dreams.

The end of the days equals the end of the appointed time.

The king's men were depending upon human wisdom and human trickery.

Daniel and the other Hebrews were aided with wisdom from above.

The last verse of chapter 1 simply indicates that Daniel was still alive when Cyrus began his reign, since Daniel is reported alive in the third year of Cyrus. See 10:1.

Chapter 2

2:1-10—The dream so troubled Nebuchadnezzar that he could not return to sleep. (Compare Ahaseurus in Esther.)

At this time in history magic and superstition were not clearly separated from academic truth.

The wise men claim only the ability to interpret, and not to reveal.

It is in this section that the Aramaic language begins.

There are differences of opinion as to whether the king was lying when he claimed a bad memory here.

Could he have been suspicious of the wise men's ability and simply testing them?

Verse 5 may indicate that their houses would be made public toilets.

To gain the time was to squirm around long enough that

something about the situation might change and their lives be spared.

2:10-13—The wise men were exactly right—no MAN could do what the king asked.

Note the use of the plural as the wise men show their polytheistic beliefs; gods, not GOD.

Here are some men who need Jehovah badly, as many who are just as desperate need him today.

2:14-18—Daniel intercedes on behalf of the Chaldeans with power from on high.

But Daniel seeks the help of his fellow believers as they together request Jehovah's aid through prayer.

2:19-24—God answers his prayer with wisdom. Compare James 1:5.

Daniel does not then forget but continues his prayer.

Prayers of praise and thanksgiving like this one are all too seldom uttered.

All things are overseen and known by this God to whom both the light and the darkness are the same.

2:25-31—Daniel speaks with supreme confidence where the wise men fumbled as they depended upon human wisdom.

Arioch did not find Daniel—Daniel found him.

They have been speaking of many gods while Daniel now speaks of A GOD in heaven.

The latter days extend from Daniel's time even to the time of the Kingdom of Heaven.

Unlike Herod who was eaten by the worms Daniel gives God all the glory for both the revelation and the interpretation of the dream.

Too many of us would be tempted to take the glory.

2:31-35—The king has seen an image which was awesome in its brightness and its form.

The image is divided into four divisions by its composition: head—gold; breast and arms—silver; belly and thighs—brass; legs and feet—iron and clay.

A stone strikes the feet and the entire image turns to dust and blows entirely away.

The stone then replaces the image and fills the earth.

2:36-45—Daniel then gives the interpretation.

The entire image represents a series of powerful human kingdoms.

Each seems to have been far-reaching in influence.

Nebuchadnezzar and Babylonia are the first in order and are the head of gold.

To be quite honest the Bible does not specifically say what the other three kingdoms are.

The second kingdom is inferior to Babylonia, just as silver is inferior to gold.

A third kingdom will follow the second and will reach to all the known to be consequential earth.

Though the Orient and the new world were in existence here they made little difference to the king of Babylonia.

A fourth kingdom will arise which shall bruise and break, but it will be weak because it is corrupted by intermarriage and does not cling together in unity.

Note that this passage says absolutely nothing about *ten* toes.

The emphasis is on the *composition* of iron and clay rather than the state of subdivision.

It contains within itself the causes of its disintegration.

In the days of the last of these four kingdoms the Kingdom of God shall be set up.

As the Kingdom of God strikes the fourth kingdom the entire structure of human government will crumble and be replaced by Divine rule.

Compare Colossians 2:15 Triumph over principalities and powers through the cross. 1 Corinthians 15:20 The Kingdom reaches its culmination after destroying all rule and authority. Revelation 11:15, Kingdoms of this world become Kingdoms of our Lord.

Jesus Christ is the rock or stone.

See Isaiah 8:14; 28:16; 1 Peter 2:4, 6, 8; Psalm 118:22; Matthew 21:42; Mark 12:10; Luke 20:17; Acts 4:11; Isaiah 2:2.

There is no doubt that the Kingdom of Heaven was established in the days of the Roman empire. (Acts 2:34-35; Rev. 1:5-6; Eph. 1:20-23.)

Since Nebuchadnezzar was the first kingdom and the Kingdom of Heaven was established in the days of the Roman empire, making it the fourth kingdom, the other two kingdoms must have fallen between these two.

The two great empires in this time period are the Medo-Persian and the Greek and thus most students assign them as kingdoms two and three.

170

2:46-49—The king admits the power of Daniel's God but still calls him a God among gods rather than the ONE GOD.

Daniel was not made governor over the entire empire, but only the province of Babylon.

NOTE: The text does *not* say how suddenly the crushing of the image is to occur.

Chapter 3

3:1-7—This image may include a pedestal since the measurements are ten times as tall as wide.

It does not actually say the image is that of a man.

If the influential persons of the empire bow down the common people will follow.

This may well be the birth of a new god in Babylon.

If the image was of solid gold the amount of gold would rival that used in the Temple of Solomon.

The building of this image indicates Nebuchadnezzar's confession of 2:47 was woefully deficient.

This is the passage in which the musical instruments have Greek names taken by the critical school to indicate a late date for the book.

Nebuchadnezzar and the Babylonians could in good conscience worship this image and other gods.

The Hebrews were restricted to the worship of Jehovah.

Remember Jesus, "Render unto Caesar that which is Caesar's—and to God that which is God's."

It has never been a characteristic of the masses to think as highly of the commandments of God as they do those of economic and political powerholders.

3:8-12—Daniel had entered the administrative power jungle as had Joseph and Moses before him.

Now he is buffeted by the jealousies always found there.

It is better to face the fiery furnace of men's fury than to escape it and fall into the eternal furnace.

The Hebrews have no choice—they must serve Jehovah, and they must now do it in the presence of the entire public.

3:13-18—Nebuchadnezzar cannot believe it is true that any man would refuse such clear and simple orders.

He will prove his patience by giving them another chance.

To say they are not careful in their answer is to say they have no doubts or hesitations whatsoever.

Like Abraham in the sacrifice of Isaac they are certain God will find a way.

Seven times hotter is simply an indication of extreme heat.

Some wonder why Daniel was not with the Hebrews.

He may have been immune by his position, or he may have been occupied elsewhere with business matters.

3:19-25—Just as in the lion's den the men who persecute are destroyed while God's servants are protected.

Though the fourth person may have been Jesus, the Son of God, some believe it was only a protecting angel.

The literal translation here is "a son of the gods."

The objection is also raised that if this were Jesus it would take away from the signficance of his being incarnated later through the birth process.

3:26-30—Usually garments would burn first—not so here.

Nebuchadnezzar admits they have successfully ignored his command through the power of Jehovah.

He is willing to admit Jehovah's power—not his exclusiveness.

Chapter 4

4:1-7—How Nebuchadnezzar vacillates between recognition of Daniel's God and utter disrespect for him.

Now he declares Jehovah's wonders!

As many other oppressive men Nebuchadnezzar has difficulty sleeping with his guilt.

This time the king willingly tells the dream and they still have trouble interpreting it.

Again human wisdom fails where even the foolishness of God is victor.

4:8-18—It is not particularly shocking that Daniel was saved for last resort as he was a busy man.

He is recognized as master of the magicians in the same sense that Moses was master of the magicians of Egypt.

This dream is more specific in nature than was the one concerning the image.

The other spoke of the replacing of the kingdom.

This speaks of the replacement of Nebuchadnezzar.

The tree which reaches to heaven reminds us of the tower of Babel which was to do the same.

The mighty tree provides both food and protection.

The holy watcher here is probably an angel.

172

See Hebrews 1:14 and Matthew 18:10.

The holy watcher decides this mighty tree must be cut down.

Now those whom it afforded food and protection are ready to flee away.

The stump of the tree is to be left so it will not die.

The symbolism of the tree suddenly disappears as reference is made to a man.

"Let his portion be—"

"Let his heart be—"

And the man is to be cut down as a lesson to all of the living that Jehovah rules.

No man can remain in power against God's will and if God chooses he can rule the earth through a man who eats grass like a donkey.

Once again it is the spirit of the holy *gods* that Nebuchadnezzar recognizes, not Jehovah the one God.

4:19-27—Is it possible that Daniel's hesitation is due to respect for one who had bestowed high honors on him?

The dream favors the enemies of the king.

The tree is the king himself.

He is to be driven from among men to eat grass in the field.

The seven times may or may not be seven years.

It is sufficient for him to learn that Jehovah rules among men's affairs.

The king is urged to replace his sins with righteousness in order that the prediction might be postponed.

4:28-37—It took just twelve months for the king to forget.

No man ever built anything by his own power.

Like many men today every time Nebuchadnezzar accomplished something he felt less need for God.

Verse 31 reminds of the rich fool—"This night thy soul shall be required of thee."

Some report having seen men in mental institutions who behaved exactly as did Nebuchadnezzar.

What a contrast there is between man walking in sophisticated pride and man crawling in the resultant humiliation!

At the end of the days means when the matter had run its course.

We believe this was true penitence upon the king's part and that the restoration is evidence of such.

Verse 37 is the strongest confession yet made.

173

Chapter 5

5:1-4—Belshazzar is called the son of Nebuchadnezzar only in the sense of a descendant.

Until about one hundred years ago there was no extra Biblical proof that Belshazzar was the last king of Babylon.

At that time tablets were discovered with oaths taken in the name of both Nabonidus and Belshazzar.

The sin of Nebuchadnezzar had been pride—the sin of Belshazzar is insolence.

He proclaims a drunken feast.

Then he appropriates the vessels from the temple of Jehovah for drinking utensils.

It would be difficult to be more insulting than is Belshazzar.

5:5-9—It has been verified that palaces of this land had plaster walls.

Belshazzar shows every sign of terror with his pale face, weak back and trembling knees.

It is not unlikely that his terror was magnified by his guilt.

And here come the wise men again!

It seems that each king under which Daniel serves must learn the same lesson—his wisest men fail as Daniel interprets with the help of Jehovah.

5:10-16—Since the king's wives were already in the banquet hall (see verse 2) this may have been the widow of Nebuchadnezzar who remembers Daniel.

She is cognizant of the fact that Daniel has supernatural aid in the interpretation of secrets.

By the time of Belshazzar Daniel seems to have faded from his position of recognition under Nebuchadnezzar.

Belshazzar has *heard of him.*

Daniel is promised again a very exalted position if he can dissolve the king's doubts.

5:17-24—Daniel is more interested in the truth than in the reward.

Belshazzar has not learned from the example of his ancestor Nebuchadnezzar.

He has failed to glorify the God of Heaven and he has used the things which had been sanctified to Jehovah to praise other gods before him.

This will not be tolerated.

The three words written on the wall are:

MENE—numbered to its limit

TEKEL—weighed

PERES—Divided

The kingdom of Belshazzar has been allowed to reach its end.

It has been insufficient in service.

It will be given to new rulers.

Daniel is rewarded as promised even though the kingdom is doomed that very night.

5:30-31—Some commentators are concerned over the chapter division here.

It is felt that verse 31 may not have taken place immediately after the death of Belshazzar.

There is some confusion over the relationship between Darius the Mede and Cyrus.

It appears that they reigned jointly with Cyrus in the dominant role and that both of them were very likely present when Babylon was taken here.

Chapter 6

6:1-3—The one hundred twenty here is comparable to the one hundred twenty-seven of Esther 1:1.

Butler makes the point that Daniel's rise to the top was not through the help of the Holy Spirit alone.

He had the moral character required to yield himself as an instrument of God.

For a Jew to be prime minister was most distasteful to the natives.

Since there is no other available crime Daniel's holiness shall be portrayed as a fault.

This is parallel to the situation in which Christ found himself.

The technique will be to flatter the king and place him in the company of the gods.

He will then be persuaded to write a law which is irreversible and impossible for Daniel to obey.

6:10-17—When man's laws conflict with God's laws the choice is clear.

Daniel is not being insolent toward the king.

He simply prays just like he has been doing previously.

Any Jew outside the city of Jerusalem would turn his face toward the city to pray, and would turn his face toward the temple if he were in the city. (1 Kings 8:33.)

Now Darius is forced into the position of looking to Jehovah for help in retaining his most able president.

6:18-24—Daniel is protected by the same power which created all.

6:24-28—The Bible does not approve of the killing of the women and children; it records the event objectively.

The point is that the lions were healthy and hungry.

Darius now adds his confession of the true God to that of Nebuchadnezzar and Belshazzar.

Verse 28 is indication that Cyrus and Darius reigned over the Medo-Persian empire simultaneously.

Compare: 5:31—Darius the Mede; 6:28—Cyrus the Persian.

Chapter 7

7:1-8—Now we move into the solidly futuristic portion of the book.

Chronologically this chapter and chapter 8 occur before chapter 5 which records Belshazzar's death.

The dreams previously interpreted were others' dreams and were for the benefit of the Babylonians.

Now the dream is Daniel's and is primarily for the benefit of Israel.

The dream has such importance that Daniel writes it down and it becomes a part of the Holy Scripture.

The four winds of the heaven indicate divine providence is playing a part.

The great sea is the seething mass of the peoples of the nations. Compare Revelation 17:15.

The four beasts are four kings or kingdoms. See verse 17.

Though the Bible does not indicate such, they seem to be the same as the four kingdoms represented by the image in Nebuchadnezzar's dream.

In chapter 2 the first part of the image is Babylonia.

Both the lion and the eagle are symbols applied to Nebuchadnezzar by other prophets. (Jer. 48:40; 49:19; 49:22; 50:17; Ezek. 17:3, 12.)

The lion is king of the beasts.

The eagle is king of the birds.

The first beast's dominion is retarded as its wings are

176

plucked and its ferocious heart is tamed and made
human. Nebuchadnezzar's conversion fits here.

Persia was noted for the very large species of bear which
lived there.

While it is still finishing off the remains of one nation it
is persuaded to go after another.

The third beast, or leopard is thought by most students
to represent Greece under Alexander and his succes-
sors: Ptolemy—Egypt; Seleucus—Asia; Cassander—
Macedonia; Lysimachus—Thrace.

Note that it is *given* the kingdom, as is true of all rulers.

The fourth kingdom is important for its great strength.

This fourth kingdom may begin with Rome but likely extends throughout the Christian dispensation.

The beastly characteristics of godless human government
are still much alive today.

Verse 24 tells us that the ten horns are ten kings.

Note the following difficulty.

There are four beasts.

The four beasts are four *kings*. (Verse 17.)

Yet the fourth beast is also a *kingdom*. (Verse 23.)

And the fourth beast has ten horns which are ten kings.

We must then be extremely careful about dogmatism in
regard to whether the little horn of verse 8 is a single
individual or a rulership.

Whether it is a king or a kingdom it sees like a man with
limited vision yet speaks as if it were a god.

7:9-14—The ancient of days is he who is from everlasting unto
everlasting.

The white garments show his purity.

The white hair shows his wisdom.

He seems to be the same as the one sitting on the throne
above the wheels in Ezekiel, chapter 1.

He is ready to judge the beasts from the Divine records.

Daniel watches while the beast with the little horn is
slain.

His body is consigned to the fire.

When the fourth beast is slain the other three whose
lives had lingered are eliminated also.

With the destruction of the fourth beast comes the Kingdom of the Son of Man which shall never be destroyed.

Note the similarity with the stone which crushes the feet

177

of the image in chapter 2 at which time the entire image turns to dust while the stone fills the earth.

This Kingdom is clearly the same as that of chapter 2 and is the Kingdom of Heaven victorious.

7:15-28—Daniel is troubled and asks the meaning of the dream.

Though the four beasts are not specifically identified they are said to be four kings, or kingdoms.

After they have each fallen the Kingdom of God will be given to the saints and shall be everlasting.

When Daniel asks about the fourth beast which is different from the others he is informed that:

The fourth kingdom is more extensive than the others.

It shall include a plurality of kings within itself.

Finally a particularly rebellious king shall arise from this fourth kingdom to oppose God and his people.

This latter power source shall be allowed a period of time to persecute the saints.

He shall even try to take for himself the Divine rights of legislation and regulation.

Compare: The little horn—Daniel 7:8, 20, 25; The man of lawlessness—2 Thessalonians 2:3-10; The antichrist —1 John 4:3; 2:18; The second beast—Revelation 13.

Though the little horn is allowed great power it is limited in time.

He shall be allowed only a time, times and half a time.

This is the same as the:

Period of persecution of God's woman.

(1260 days of Revelation 11:3.)

Prophecy of the two witnesses.

(1260 days of Revelation 11:3.)

Treading of the Holy City.

(42 months of Revelation 11:2.)

It begins when the man child is caught up to the throne of God. (Rev. 11:6.)

And it ends with the proclamation of victory for Christ. (Rev. 11:15.)

While seven indicates completeness and perfection the three and one half is half of seven and indicates incompletion and termination.

All rule and power and authority must fall before the sceptre of the Son of God.

See Philippians 2:9-11; 1 Corinthians 15:24-28; Revelation 11:15.

What a message of hope this must have been for Daniel to deliver to the captive Israelites in Babylonia!

Chapter 8

8:1-12—This vision occurs two years after the vision of Belshazzar in chapter 7.

At this point the Hebrew language returns in the original as the thrust of the message is now toward the captives rather than the Babylonians.

Like chapter 7 this one expands upon chapter 2.

Esther's palace was also located in Shushan.

The Ulai River ran into the Tigris-Euphrates.

The ram is Medo-Persia—see verse 20.

Persia dominated the world under Cyrus and Darius the Mede.

The only direction it did not push was toward the Orient.

The rough he-goat is Greece under Alexander.—See verse 21.

He flew over the countryside so fast it seemed he did not even touch the ground.

The historians have a field day with the conflict between these two great powers.

Alexander succeeds in breaking the power of the Medes and Persians.

The power of Greece quickly waned when Alexander died at 32 or 33 years of age. The great horn was broken!

The four notable ones are thought by many to be the four generals who divided the empire between them when Alexander died.

The little horn which comes from one of these notable ones is considered to be Antiochus Epiphanes.

This must be deduced since the Bible does not identify them.

It might be wise to notice that the Bible is specific about the Babylonians, Medo-Persians and Greeks, but treats the Roman Empire and all that follows Alexander as though it is dealing with a hodgepodge beginning strong and ending in rebellious defiance of God, finally being destroyed by the Kingdom of God.

Antiochus Epiphanes fits here, but may also typify the rebellion which is to manifest itself in the last days as the antichrist. (1 John 2:18.)

179

The pleasant land seems to be Palestine.

The stars are God's own people who shine for him.

See Daniel 12:3; Jeremiah 33:22.

This horn like the dragon of Revelation 12:4 manages to sweep out the light of many of God's stars.

There is little comment upon the identity of the Prince of the Host!

Antiochus Epiphanes lived before Christ and must not have faced Christians.

But compare Revelation 12:7.

Perhaps Daniel like the other prophets has allowed us to see the war that rages in heaven while we see only the tip of the iceberg as we wear the Christian armor.

Not only does God have a heavenly Host, this little horn is allowed to gather a host to fight against God's own.

The little horn and his host oppose the daily sacrifice and walk all over the truth.

Compare Romans 12:1; Hebrews 10:29.

But the most serious part of it all is that such blasphemy appears to thrive and prosper.

8:13-27—Daniel hears one saint asking another how long this sort of action will be allowed to continue.

John heard a similar question in Revelation 6:9-11.

The answer is that it will cease in 2300 evenings and mornings.

Some say this is speaking of twice a day sacrifices and should thus be 2300 sacrifices or 1150 days.

But it is exactly the same type of language used in Genesis 1—and evening and morning were the first day.

In the 1800s Adam Clarke thought this period began in 334 B.C. and would end in A.D. 1966.

Perhaps verse 26 of this chapter gives us the interpretation of the 2300 days—the *many days* the prophecy would be sealed up until God's good time arrived.

The angel Gabriel is called to assist Daniel in understanding the dream which he has had.

Gabriel and Michael are the only angels named in the Bible. See Daniel 10:13; Luke 1:19, 26 and Jude 9.

When mortal men find themselves in the presence of sinless angels they become very uncomfortable as did Daniel here in the presence of Gabriel.

The time of indignation would seem primarily to refer to the indignation of the temple and worship of Jehovah.

180

But remember that Jesus spoke some confusing words about the time of the end in Matthew 24.

The end of the temple in Jerusalem and the end of the world are discussed simultaneously and may be a clue to understanding Daniel 8:19.

The apparent prosperity of the little horn is only because God allows it for a season.

The power of the little horn will be awesome and the destruction of the people of God will be tragic.

Compare Revelation 13:5-7.

Since Antiochus Epiphanes died before Christ reigned this must mean that if he is the power here described he actually embodies the spirit of the Devil himself in the long-lasting battle between him and Jehovah.

To be broken without hand is to be defeated without the use of human strength.

See the means of victory in Revelation 19:15-21.

Obviously here it is a sword from the mouth of Christ or the Word of God.

The list of those who try to fight against the Sword of God's Word is a pathetic list: Pharaoh: Nebuchadnezzar the King of Tyre; Belshazzar; the little horn; Antichrist.

The end of each is the same. They are broken and God invites the fowls and the beasts to feed upon their flesh, as he sacrifices them.

Now Daniel is told to shut or seal up the vision.

It will become meaningful in God's own appointed time.

Now one must compare Revelation 5:1-5 where a sealed book which no one has been able to open is to be opened by the Lamb of God as he takes his place at God's right hand.

With the coming of Jesus Christ as King comes the end of the Old Testament World with: a new King; a new priesthood; new Law; a new spiritual kingdom; a new and perfect sacrifice; a new temple.

The arrogant Satan is dealt a crushing blow and will thrash and writhe as the Kingdom of God casts him down to his inevitable torment in the fires of Hell.

Daniel like many since his time is made sick by the portion of the dream which he does understand.

He seems to say to us that even he himself does not comprehend its great mystery which would only be unrolled many days later.

181

Chapter 9

9:1-2—It was Darius the Mede who succeeded Belshazzar.
He is the son of Ahasuerus who reigned in the time of
Esther.—Several points seem to verify this.
His palace was Shushan—(Dan. 8:2).
The unchangeable laws agree.
The book of Esther is thus dated close to the latter part
of the Babylonian captivity.
Some liberals would like to identify the books Daniel was
studying here with the completed Old Testament.
Only the book of Jeremiah and one other is needed.
The passage in Jeremiah Daniel was studying was Jere-
miah 25:9-11 and 29:10.
How often the number 70 is important in the Bible.
The years of a man's life—(Psa. 90:10).
The years of captivity—See above.
The number of sevens to bring in righteousness.
Daniel 9:24 as well as verse 2 here.
Jerusalem has remained in desolation caused by her
abomination in the eyes of Jehovah for seventy years.
To better understand the use of the word *desolate* here
compare Jeremiah 25:9-11 with 2 Chronicles 36:21-23.
Notice that Daniel's concern here is not primarily with
the mystery of the seventy sevens, but with the par-
don of his people.

9:3-15—The sackcloth and ashes indicate the deep state of
penitence which Daniel will express in his prayer.
It was precisely this condition which God had stated
was necessary to return them from captivity.
See 1 Kings 8:46-48.
Here is the admission that God's ways had been correct
and Israel's ways incorrect.
Long ago the prophets had accused Israel of every sin
which Daniel now confesses.—But see Isaiah 26:9.
It is of interest to notice that both Judah and Israel are
included in the prayer of Daniel—verse 7.
He admits in verse 13 that if they had been penitent be-
fore this they would have been released.

9:16-19—Daniel readily admits that the desolation is because
of the iniquity of *both* them and their fathers.
His question is, "Is it not time that the desolation of the
city and the reproach of the people be forgiven?"

9:20-27—Such fervent prayers are always heard. Compare
Acts 10:2-4.

God knew and answered Daniel's prayer before he finished asking. See Ephesians 3:20.

Once again Gabriel is the angel sent to bring understanding. See 8:16.

The mention of the vision in both verses 21 and 23 are likely an indication that the statements of Jeremiah are to be made more meaningful.

The word translated *weeks* in verse 24 is literally sevens, and this can make considerable difference in the application of the interpretation.

During these seventy sevens a number of things are to take place: transgression will cease; sin will be removed; God and man will be reconciled; men may become perfectly righteous; there shall be no more need for vision and prophecy; a Holy Thing shall be anointed.

Verse 25 seems to mean that the Holy Thing is the Messiah.

In this period not only Daniel's little question shall be answered, but God will bring about the end of all the desolation and abomination through Jesus Christ and the judgment.

The writer believes that once again a prophet has been allowed to speak to his own people while at the same time speaking to all mankind in the Christian age.

The going forth of the commandment to build Jerusalem is made difficult by the fact that there were decrees by:
Cyrus in 539 B.C.
Artaxerxes Longimanus in 458 B.C.
Artaxerxes again in 445 B.C.

Some believe the seventy sevens should begin with Cyrus.
He was the first to state the decree.
He is called an anointed of God to rebuild Jerusalem. See Isaiah 44:28-45:1.

But there are also reasons for beginning with Artaxerxes' decree of 457-8.
Cyrus' decree did not set up formal government in Palestine, while Artaxerxes' decree did.
The seventy sevens can be considered weeks of years and the arithmetic becomes astoundingly revealing.

May it not be possible that the decree is considered by God to be Cyrus' decree, becoming effective only at the insistence of Artaxerxes Longimanus?

183

The Bible itself *does not* specify in the text of Daniel
that these sevens are seven years.

But—49 years after the year 457 B.C. the City of Jerusalem was rebuilt. See verse 25.

And—483 years later brings us to the beginning of Jesus'
public ministry. See verse 26.

And—Jesus was crucified and cut off after about 3½
years of public teaching. See verse 27.

The Jews did have sabbatical years. See Leviticus 25:8.

Adam Clarke provides a quote from this time that men
are not sent into battle after the sixth week because
age tends to prevent their effectiveness in battle.

Though we do not feel that in all cases where it has
been applied that the year-day theory is justified, it
does seem that circumstances indicate its use here.

There are then three periods of time.

The first seven sevens or 49 years—City rebuilt.

The next sixty-two sevens—until the Messiah.

The last seven during which several things occur: the
covenant is confirmed; the Messiah is cut off in the
midst of the week; the City and the Sanctuary are to
be destroyed; the sacrifices and oblations are to
cease; desolation shall last until a great war is over;
finally the abomination and desolation shall both
cease as the Messiah brings judgment.

One point still needs consideration—What is the identity
of the last half of the seventieth week?

Note that the Messiah is cut off in the *midst* of the
seventieth week.

This means it has already begun, contrary to those
who say it is a millennial age with Christ on earth.

But the covenant is going to be confirmed by the Messiah for the whole week.

We believe the book of Revelation cooperates with the
book of Daniel in identifying the last half of the last
week, or *seven.*

There is a 3½ year period mentioned several times in
both Daniel and Revelation.

Daniel 7:24-27—in the latter days a power shall arise
speaking against God and wearing out the saints for
time, times, and the dividing of a time.—But judgment sits on him.

Revelation 11:2—The Gentiles shall tread the Holy

184

City underfoot for 42 months. (The Gentile here is most likely anyone who is not a *spiritual* Jew.)

Revelation 11:3—During this same time period God's two witnesses shall prophesy. (We believe this to be the law and the prophets which testify of Jesus.)

Revelation 12:6—God's woman is driven into the wilderness for 1260 days where God nourishes her and protects her life. (We believe this to be the people of God after Christ ascended to the right hand of God.)

In each of these cases it appears that we are talking about the entire Christian dispensation.

The Christian dispensation begins with the ascension of Jesus after his crucifixion and ends with his coming in judgment.

This is precisely what the seventieth week (last half) of Daniel embraced.

We conclude that the 42 months = 1260 days = times, time, and half a time = 3½ years = ½ week of years = the last half of the seventieth week of Daniel 9.

It is not part of a millennium but is a difficult period of time during which abomination and desolation result from the influence of Satan and antichristian power.

And it will be concluded with the second coming of Jesus Christ in judgment.

Chapter 10

10:1-9—Some are convinced the third year of Cyrus was the first year of Darius. See chapter 11:1.

Thus this verse could be the result of the vision of chapter 9.

The truth is not always pleasant as evidenced here.

The anointing spoken of was a bathing process and Daniel's lack of it is a part of his mourning.

The great war which he saw in the vision would bring about such grief.

The end of the ninth chapter should perhaps come after verse 3.

The River Hiddekel is another name for the Tigris.

Daniel now sees a man very similar to the one seen by John in Revelation 1:13-15.

Some see this person as the pre-incarnated Christ.

Others believe it to be Gabriel as before.

See verse 12 and compare 9:21-22.

Among the characteristics of this person are: beauty, energy, perception, intelligence.

Daniel, like Saul of Tarsus, saw the vision while his companions did not. See Acts 9:7.

They were however highly impressed in some way since they fled to hide.

Some speak of visions of angels lightly, but this was not the case with:

Daniel—Jacob—Saul—Peter—Jeremiah—Isaiah

What Daniel had seen in himself as desirable before now seemed rotten.

He had actually fallen on his face unconscious.

10:10-21—Was this the hand of the person—or the hand of God?

Daniel will again receive divine understanding which he passes down through the ages to us.

There are those who believe the prince of the kingdom of Persia was the man Cyrus.

But could a human withstand an angel for 21 days when one angel destroyed 185,000 Assyrians in one night?

It seems more likely that spiritual powers were opposing one another over the actions of the Medo-Persian Empire.

This could be done by influencing Cyrus, king of the empire.

The passage sounds like the dispute mentioned in Jude 9 over the body of Moses. (Was Moses *alive* at the time?)

This may give us a glimpse of the eternal spiritual war which has lasted from the Garden of Eden to the Judgment.

See Ephesians 3:10 and 6:11-18; Colossians 2:15.

Daniel's prayer changed the course of angels' actions.

This passage tells us that angels are not omnipresent.

The vision is, according to the angel, to cover many days.

Only after Daniel had been strengthened was he able to converse with the angel at all.

Between the sorrow brought on by the vision of extended war, and the majesty of the angel Daniel wonders how he can possibly converse.

After having been strengthened by the angel, Daniel now feels ready to hear more about the terrible conflict.

186

The angel has urgent business, and must return to fight other spiritual powers such as the one influencing the kingdom of Persia.

Then the spiritual influence of the Greek Empire will arise to be contended with.

But before these matters are taken up, Daniel will be shown more about the momentous battles to come.

THE BOOK OF DANIEL AND THE BOOK OF REVELATION BOTH TALK ABOUT THE LONG-LASTING WAR IN HEAVEN WHICH CHRIST WILL WIN THROUGH THE WORD!

It is apparent that there are differences in the talents of the angels, and Michael has deep understandings of the truth of scripture.

Michael as our prince, along with his angels, opposes the Devil and his angels. (Rev. 12:7.)

Chapter 11

11:1-4—The *I* of verse 1 is probably the angel Gabriel.

He had been said several times to have strengthened Daniel. If this is as many think, the angel Gabriel, there are at least two suggestions as to the identity of the one he strengthened.

1. He strengthened Michael as he worked with Darius.
2. He strengthened Darius directly.

In either case one sees God's hand working through angels in the background of the visible wars on earth.

Verse 1 here may be the last verse of the previous chapter.

Verse 2 indicates that Gabriel will aid Daniel in understanding the truth of the scripture as of 10:21.

There is strong unanimity among commentators that the material from here to the 35th verse describes in detail the intertestamental period of power struggle around the east end of the Mediterranean Sea.

This is no doubt true, but it goes beyond that to embrace the victory of the stone which crushes all of the governmental systems based upon Satan's methods.

The eleventh and twelfth chapters follow each other perfectly and continuously.

There were to be yet three Persian kings after Darius.

See verse 2.

After these three another, the fourth, would rise.

The first three are: Cambyses, Smerdis, and Darius
Hystaspis.

The fourth very rich and powerful is Xerxes—the Ahasuerus of Ezra 4:6 and Esther.

Xerxes was famous for the riches of his kingdom.

The mighty king of verse 3 is Alexander.

His rule was extended and complete.

He died at 32 or 33 and his kingdom crumbled.

His son and his wife were killed, leaving the kingdom
to be ruled by those outside his posterity.

The four rulers succeeding Alexander were:

1. Ptolemy I (Soter)—ruling Egypt, *King of the South.*
The prince who overshadows him is Seleucus I
(Nicator)—who later rules Syria, *King of the North.*

2. Antigonus.

3. Cassander.

4. Lysimachus.

Antigonus became too ambitious and died on the battlefield as the others turned against him.

Seleucus I was then assigned the area of Syria.

AND NOW THE BATTLE RAGES BETWEEN THE
KING OF THE NORTH—OR THE DESCENDANTS OF SELEUCUS I, AND THE KING OF
THE SOUTH—REPRESENTED BY THE DESCENDANTS OF PTOLEMY I.

But in view of verse 1 of this chapter the angels must
also be involved behind the scenes.

Michael and his angels promoting God's cause.

Satan and his angels in opposition.

Though the commentators are agreed in assigning this
information to the rivalry between the Ptolemies and
the Seleucids the specifics as to identity do not always
agree.

Clearly Syria and Egypt make a number of excursions
into each other's territory.

And very important to Daniel, Palestine was caught in
the middle.

Could anything more aptly describe the condition of the
Christian today amid governmental power struggles?

The raiser of taxes was probably Antiochus the Great,
(not Antiochus Epiphanes) who was forced to pay
much tribute to Rome after a humiliating defeat.

See verse 20.

At this point enters Antiochus Epiphanes, called the *illustrious* by men, but a VILE MAN by Jehovah.

He obtained his rulership by flattery and treachery.

By deceitful treaties and powerful armies he will become more successful than the previous Seleucids.

He attacked God's covenant and God's people.

And for awhile he was permitted to punish Israel.

Antiochus Epiphanes made numerous attempts to conquer Egypt and the King of the South.

Finally when it appeared he might take all of Egypt, the Roman ships from Chittim, or Cyprus, brought Roman legions in.

He was told by a Roman officer to retreat.

He said he would think about it.

The Roman drew a circle around him and told him to finish his thinking before he stepped out of the circle.

He decided to retreat but took out his fury upon the city of Jerusalem.

He prohibited the use of the temple for Jewish worship.

He robbed the temple of its treasures.

He dedicated the temple to the worship of Zeus.

Some report that swine's flesh was offered on the altar of Jehovah.

It is interesting that Jesus spoke of the abomination of desolation spoken of by Daniel as though the event were still in the future. (Matt. 24:15.)

It may then be wise to think of several abominations of desolation.

1. One brought about by Antiochus Epiphanes.
2. Another brought about by the Romans in their conquest of Jerusalem, A.D. 70—
3. One brought about by the inroads of the antichristian filth into the Church, the Temple of God today.
4. Numerous abominations of desolation as God allows individual Christians (Temples of God) to contaminate themselves to the point where he gives them up to their own delusions. See Romans 1:24.

During such hideous times God's people make their faith evident, even to the point of martyrdom.

This is always a period of purification for the followers of Jehovah, as the fainthearted fall and do not endure to the end.

Would it not be appropriate here to look carefully at Revelation, chapter 6:1-10—*How long?, How Long?*

Verses 36-45 provide much dissension among Bible students.

Verse 35 has hinted at the Christian dispensation in the matter of purging and purification.

Yet some believe the mighty king of verse 36 continues the discussion of Antiochus Epiphanes after his contamination of the temple at Jerusalem.

If the king of the north is Antiochus Epiphanes this mighty king is not, he, since verse 40 would then have Antiochus Epiphanes pushing at himself!

The author believes this mighty king to be Roman power.

Notice the similarity of this king to:
1. The man of lawlessness—2 Thessalonians 2:1-4.
2. The king of Babylon—Isaiah 14:12-14.
3. The beasts—Revelation 13.

Rome allowed the worship of many gods, but the real god was the god of force.

The riches of Rome in gold, silver and precious stones is undisputed.

No forces brought against Rome by descendants of either the Egyptians or the Syrians could prevail.

Rome did enter into the *glorious land* of Palestine and overthrow many countries.

The spiritual descendants of Rome have planted great cathedrals among the people who dwell on God's Holy Mountain today as the Church.

But Daniel's story has now come to that consistent stopping place—the victory of the Stone which was cut out of the mountain without hands.

Again it strikes during the time of the Roman kings which time seems to last to the scene pictured in Revelation 19:11-21.

The situation shall be absolutely hopeless for all who have associated themselves with Satan.

Chapter 12

12:1-4—Just when it looks the most dreary for God's own, Michael will demonstrate the complete folly of opposing God's will.

The spiritual conflict will be furious and undoubtedly many of the saints will die.

190

But it was in Christ's death that true victory came.

Death for the Christian is merely the gate to life.

Death is the last enemy; Satan's final shudder.

Not a single person whose name is found written in the book of life shall die.

The picture is identical with the repeated reminder in Revelation that the 144,000, sealed with the mark of God, are safe.

Nothing can separate God's follower from his protecting arm. (Rom. 8:35-39.)

It is possible that verse 2 can be applied to the victories of the Jews under Judas Maccabeus.

But we believe everlasting life must follow judgment.

The thought of verse 2 is identical with that of Matthew 25:46—everlasting punishment vs. everlasting life.

The righteous illuminate the world now, but then the new spiritual body shall shine with a higher glory. See 1 Corinthians 15:40-44; 1 John 3:2.

The sealing of the book is a prelude to the scene of the slain Lamb opening it again in Revelation 5:1-10.

This will happen in the fulness of God's own time.

A number of things must happen and a number of things be taught before the unsealing of the mystery of God. (Rev. 10:7.)

12:5-13—Those by the river are probably angels who hold conversation with Gabriel.

Verses 6 and 7 give the boundaries for the final events.

This time of trouble beginning when Michael stands up (verse 1) shall last for a time, times and a half a time —3⅓ years—1260 days—forty-two months as Christ, Michael, God's faithful angels and the Church spread the power of the two-edged sword through all nations.

Those who see the scattering of the power of the holy people as the destruction of the Jewish system have missed the point here—the scattering speaks of victory, not defeat!!

Daniel pleads for more information in verse 8, but the answer is that he must wait for the time of the unsealing.

There must be adequate time for the purification process to take place with opportunity for the righteous to demonstrate their faith, and for the wicked to test the longsuffering of God in stubbornly walking the way to death.

191

The writer thinks it unwise to make specific historical interpretation of the 30 days difference between the 1260 and 1290 days.

It is referred to by Jesus Christ as future in his statement of Matthew 24:15.

The extra 30 days seems to carry us beyond the time of the seventy sevens and into a period which God has not seen fit to further describe at this place.

If one can remain faithful there will be a conquest over the abomination of desolation.

And if we patiently put on our white robes of righteousness we shall become more than conquerors, as with Daniel we inherit the new and glorious body and the mansion which Jesus has been preparing for us.

The 1335 days bring us past tribulation, past the memories of sin and death and into the rest which remains for the people of God. (Heb. 4:9-11.)

NOTE: How can it be possible that critics fail to see the touch of the Divine in the manner in which this book of Daniel slips into its niche in the unfolding of the plan of salvation?

5. *Practical lessons from the book of Daniel*

A. Refusal to contaminate oneself brings the approval and assistance of Jehovah.

B. God deserves all the glory, honor and power, thus self-glorification will bring certain abasement.

C. All authority based upon human wisdom, force or other devices of Satan will be finally crushed into powder and blown away.

D. God holds the affairs of men within his hands, permitting freedom of choice, yet guiding all things toward the victory of Christ and his Church.

E. A tremendous war is going on between spiritual forces in heavenly places.

F. Angels are vitally interested in the decisions made by rulers of earthly governments.

G. Patience by God's people through the trials brought on by abomination and its resulting punishments will be rewarded by glorification and blessedness when time shall be no more.

HAGGAI
(Festival)

1. *Background for the book of Haggai*
   A. Historical background
      1. Daniel had been taken captive in 605 B.C.
      2. Ezekiel was taken captive in 597 B.C.
      3. Nebuchadnezzar demolished Jerusalem and the temple in 586 B.C.
      4. Cyrus issued the first decree to rebuild in 538 B.C.
      5. The exiles returned and the foundation was laid in 536 B.C.
      6. Opposition developed from the Samaritans and Cyrus revoked his decree.
      7. The Jews turned to their own houses and let the temple go neglected for 16 years.
      8. In 520 B.C. Haggai and Zechariah appeared and urged them to build God's Temple.
   B. Social background
      1. The people were poor from unproductive crops.
      2. Much effort was being expended with amazingly low results.
      3. Zerubbabel was governor under Darius Hystaspis of Persia, and Joshua was high priest.
   C. Religious background
      1. Faith had reached a low ebb because of disappointment.
      2. There was nostalgic recollection of the glory of days gone by and worship in Solomon's Temple.

2. *The man, Haggai*
   A. He is the first of the post-exilic prophets.
   B. He is a man of strong conviction.
   C. He produces no majestic flights of figurative language as many other prophets do.
   D. He is blunt, plain and straightforward.
   E. He is a man who sees a work that needs to be done and challenges men to do it.

F. His name has been connected with certain of the Psalms though perhaps only in arranging them to music.

3. *The nature of the Book of Haggai*

A. The shortest book of the Old Testament except for Obadiah.

B. "Thus saith the Lord" or some like phrase 26 times within 38 verses.

C. The one overriding theme is BUILD GOD'S TEMPLE!

D. Outline of the book of Haggai.

   1. A rebuke and a call to action
   2. A challenge to courage in the face of disappointment.
   3. An explanation of the difficulties of the past few years and hinging upon their unclean condition.
   4. As Temple builder Zerubbabel will herald a new era of authority.

4. *Comments on the text of Haggai*

Chapter 1

1:1-2—This is Darius Hystaspis who reigned several years after Darius the Mede, of Daniel.

Cambyses who preceded Darius had stayed with the revocation of the decree which Cyrus had revoked through opposition by the Samaritans.

The reader should read the book of Ezra in conjunction with this book.

Some had perhaps decided that the seventy years had not been fulfilled since it had only been fifty years from the destruction in 586 B.C. to 536 B.C. when the foundations were laid.

Even in 520 B.C. when Haggai speaks they would count only sixty-six years.

But from Daniel's captivity to the laying of the foundation of this temple *is* seventy years.

The real reason for their neglect is selfishness.

1:3-4—God has kept silence long enough and he will now speak through Haggai.

A ceiled house was one finished nicely on the inside.

It is never time to live in houses of luxury if God's work lies neglected because of it.

1:5-6—God calls for a careful consideration of their ways of life.

Everything they try to do comes out wrong: when they sow they do not reap; when they eat they remain hungry; their clothing does not keep them warm; and their wages waste away mysteriously.

1:7-11—A better way is to first build God's Temple.
This will glorify him.
And he will be pleased.
As it is now they spend much time to bring home very little.
Then when they get it home God blows it all away: their crops suffered drought; their animals were unproductive; every labor they performed came to nothing.

1:12-15—God had spoken by Haggai first to the leaders.
When the leaders grasped the vision, the people followed.
Not only do they give mental assent to Haggai's words, they become stirred up in spirit.
Here is mention of the remnant, typifying the Church, and spoken of by almost every one of the prophets.
In exactly twenty-four days, or 3½ weeks Haggai stirred a people to action after 16 years of neglect.
This is the real proof of preaching.

Chapter 2

2:1-3—About one month after beginning, God finds need to speak a word of encouragement.
Some of them can still remember the glory of the Temple of Solomon.
Ezra 3:12 tells us they wept at the difference in the former temple and this one.
Some believe this is indication that Haggai was one of these, but there is no proof.
God admits this temple is nothing in comparison.
But there is one very good reason for summoning strength to continue.
Jehovah will be with them!

2:4-9—With Jehovah present among them, the world will be turned upside down beginning with this remnant and their pitiful-looking temple.
The entire earth will feel the repercussions.
The lack of gold and silver matters not at all for God owns it all anyway.
That which is truly precious to all nations will come and fill this new temple with his glory.
The *peace* which Jesus Christ brings to all the earth will

move from the temple to Jerusalem, to Judea, to Samaria and to the uttermost parts of the earth.

And when that temple is gone it will have been replaced by the temple not made with hands, the Church of Jesus Christ.

2:10-14—Three months after beginning work the people are told to ask the priests a question.

Does a holy thing make an unholy thing clean by touching it?—The answer is NO!

Does an unholy thing make a holy thing unclean by touching it?—The answer is YES!

In the past this has been Israel's problem.

Being unclean they have rendered all their offerings unclean.

2:15-17—For three months they had been proving themselves before Jehovah.

Even during this time blessings had been withheld.

2:18-19—To this very day things had gone wrong.

Beginning however with this day God would bless them.

2:20-23—Now Zerubbabel leads a people who place God first.

God will in return bless them as his people.

Authority which depends upon chariots and horses can never stand before the onslaught of this remnant of Jehovah.

As a builder of the temple of God Zerubbabel will be backed by the authority of God and will initiate the coming of a far more glorious one.

THE TEMPLE OF GOD AND OF THE LAMB—(Rev. 21:22.)

5. *Practical lessons from the book of Haggai*
   A. It is never wise to leave God's work unattended while attending one's own.
   B. Plain preaching can bring results.
   C. A plain temple in which God lives is better than a most elegant one which he has deserted.
   D. An unholy man cannot offer a pure worship.
   E. Authority which depends upon chariots, horses and instruments of violence is useless before Jehovah.

ZECHARIAH
(Jehovah Remembers)

1. *Background for the book of Zechariah*
   A. Historical background
      1. Two months after the time of Haggai.
      2. Conditions are parallel to those of Haggai.
         a. Crops have failed. b. The ruins of Palestine surrounded them. c. Persecution was most serious from the Samaritans.
   B. Social background
      1. A discouraged people.
      2. Again parallel to Haggai.
   C. Religious background
      1. Memories of past splendor.
      2. Lagging faith.

2. *The man Zechariah*
   A. He is the son of Berechiah who is son of Iddo. See Ezra 5:1 and 6:14; Nehemiah 12:16.
   B. In 2:4 he is described as a young man.
   C. While Haggai urged men to do mundane labor, Zechariah was providing visions of future glory.
   D. While Haggai was blunt and plain, Zechariah was preaching in figures and symbolism.
   E. His last recorded prophecy is two years after the last of Haggai.
   F. He looks beyond the immediate temple made with hands to the Messiah's spiritual Temple.

3. *The nature of the book of Zechariah*
   A. The date is between 520-516 B.C.
   B. This is the most difficult of the minor prophets.
   C. There is considerable difference in the first and last parts of the book.
      1. Chapters 1-8 deal with the nation.
      2. Chapters 9-14 deal with the coming Kingdom of the Messiah.

D. Angels are important.

E. A King rises from a wounded slave to victory over all opposition.

F. Outline of the book
   1. A Call to Repentance.
   2. Eight night visions:
      a. The angel of Jehovah and the Horsemen; b. four horns and four craftsmen; c. the man with the measuring line; d. the trial of the High Priest; e. the lampstand and the olive trees; f. the flying roll; g. the woman in the ephah; h. the four chariots.
   3. The Problem of Fasting:
      a. There is a need for sincerity. b. Fasting will turn to feasting.
   4. Prophecies of Future Blessing:
      a. Israel's deliverance; b. heathen kingdoms fall; c. God's Kingdom to be established and supreme.

4. *Comments on the text of Zechariah*
   Chapter 1
      1:1-7—Haggai had begun in the sixth month of this year.
      Zechariah addresses his remarks to those that needed further admonition beyond what Haggai had done.
      As with many of the prophets "Thus saith the Lord" is repeatedly emphasized.
      Compare 2 Chronicles 24:20—"Because ye have forsaken Jehovah, he hath forsaken you."
      Now the statement is—"Turn unto me and I will turn unto you."
      The prophets who spoke to the fathers are long dead.
      The people who heard them prophesy are in their graves.
      But the prophecies themselves stand confirmed.
      Other things are voided but God's Word endureth forever.
      Experience and history are good teachers if students listen.
      All too often as in the case of these Jews the pupils are dull.
      1:7-11—Now we come to the first of eight night visions.
      Dreams occur while asleep.
      Visions occur while awake.
      There is no sure way of interpreting the meaning of the horses' colors.

198

The difficulties of determing how many persons are involved can best be solved by assuming that the man in verses 8 and 10 is the same as the angel in verse 9.

He is an angel of the Lord in the form of a man.

Apparently the various colored horses have riders who answer the angel of the Lord who speaks with Zechariah.

The Lord had sent these riders to be guardians of the earth.

Compare this with the "Holy Watcher" of Daniel 4:13.

It is quite clear that God has subordinates who watch over human activities.

They report that the earth rests and the shakings promised by Haggai (2:6-7) have not yet taken place.

1:12-17—The angel of the Lord inquires as to how long the persecution by the heathen will hinder the work of building the temple and the city of Jerusalem.

Verse 12 may indicate the manner in which God calculates the seventy years of bondage.

The indication here is that it was from 586-516, or the period from the destruction of the temple until it was rebuilt.

Even though God used the heathen nations to chastise Israel he was always displeased with them.

Now their cruelty and opposition to rebuilding the city has stirred his further wrath.

The work shall not be stopped.

The territory will be measured.

The temple will be finished.

The city will grow because Jehovah has chosen it.

1:18-21—We come now to the second of the eight visions.

The four horns are worldly powers.

Verse 21 indicates they are Gentile.

The interpreting role of the angel here causes one to suspect that it is Michael or Gabriel.

Four carpenters are then seen and are explained as agents to dehorn these Gentile powers.

The word interpreted as carpenters is sometimes translated as craftsmen and sometimes as smiths.

The blacksmiths of many lands are those who dehorn the cattle.

For every horn which would push at God's people he will raise up a carpenter or smith to cut it off.

Chapter 2

2:1-5—The line stretched upon Jerusalem prepares for its building and growth.

A wall of protection is to be built around her.

Verses 4 and 5 show that this Jerusalem is more than just the immediate physical city.

No common physical wall will be needed in this city.

God himself will be a wall of salvation around her.

The city will be illuminated by his glory.

2:6-9—The land of the north is Babylon.

The people have already escaped from physical Babylon at this time.

But for centuries God's people have had to be reminded to separate themselves from spiritual Babylon.

See Revelation 18:4.

After the glory is not speaking of a time—after the glory.

The nations who persecuted Israel were refusing to give God his proper glory.

The angelic Lord of hosts was sent to obtain the glory God was due.

This would be done by shaking God's hand over them to shake them severely.

Those who once were masters should become slaves and vice versa when God shook them.

2:10-13—The people of God's holy Mount Zion will propser because God will be with them.

People from many nations will come into the Kingdom of the Lord.

The territory of the coming King will be extended from sea to sea and to the very ends of the earth. See Zechariah 9:10.

Verse 11 is interesting in that the Lord of hosts is said to send the Lord to this strange Jerusalem without walls.

This sounds very much like Lord Jesus sent by his Father in heaven.

All carnal and fleshly opposition to God had better cease their foolish racket for they have aroused Jehovah who dwells in the heaven of heavens.

And those Jews who have been discouraged in building the earthly temple must lift their eyes to the heavens.

Chapter 3

3:1-3—Joshua stands on trial as High Priest representing both the priesthood as well as his people.

200

As in the case of Job Satan stands ready to accuse him and prevent his service to Jehovah. (Job. 1:1-6.)

The angel of the Lord may be Jesus Christ himself.

It is true that both people and priesthood had been guilty.

Failed to distinguish between clean and unclean.

Taught for hire. See Ezekiel 22:26 and Micah 3:11.

But Satan was dead wrong!!

The mind of Satan just does not comprehend the possibility of forgiveness.

God had not abandoned his people and now they were snatched out of the fire.

The filthy garments will be taken off them.

The iniquity will pass away and new robes of righteousness will be provided.

The mitre was the bonnet worn by the High Priest.

Thus it is determined that Satan cannot prevent the rebuilding of the temple and installation of presiding priests.

Joshua is given two charges: He is to keep himself pure —he is to perform the duties of his office.

He is assured that this will allow him to: Judge God's people; retain the priestly office; keep company with the angelic host of heaven, immune from Satan's most vicious efforts.

Some believe the branch here to be Zerubbabel.

Is so he stands as a type of the Messiah.

See Isaiah 4:2; 11:1-10; Jeremiah 23:5; 33:15; Haggai 2:23.

The seven eyes assure God's providential care.

The Stone is Jesus. (Isa. 28:16.)

But let us remember also that the Church is the body of Christ and the conqueror of World Empires. (Dan. 2.)

The iniquity of the land was removed in that one day of the crucifixion.

Satan cannot prevent the peace which Jesus left with us.

For other mention of the vine and the fig tree see 1 Kings 4:24-25 and Micah 4:4.

Chapter 4

4:1-4—It seems that the angel came repeatedly on the same night to Zechariah.

Now he sees a new vision of a lampstand.

Upon the main stem there is a bowl.

From this bowl arise seven branches ending in an opening for burning the olive oil.

There are two olive trees, or containers for feeding oil to the openings.

From the two olive trees there are seven tubes or pipes, one running to each of the seven openings.

Zechariah sees them and knows what they are but he wishes to understand the meaning of them.

4:5-10—The angel seems somewhat surprised that he does not know the meaning.

This lampstand indicates the means by which the people will finish building the temple.

It will not be by their own might or power.

It shall be through the aid of God's own illuminating Spirit. See Revelation 1:4, 20.

There will be no obstacle which can stand before Zerubbabel as he directs the building. (Just as in the case of Christ's Temple.) (Matt. 16:18.)

Zerubbabel laid the foundation stone and he will lay the finishing capstone.

Putting verses 8 and 9 together the Lord of Hosts sent the Word of the Lord to them.

This sounds like the relationship between the Father and his Son.

Previously some of the older men had felt this new temple to be a small thing.

But God's face was turned toward it and his approving eye kept guard.

The two olive trees are the King and the Priest who serve Jehovah.

Primary meaning—Zerubbabel and Joshua

Spiritual application—Jesus Christ who combined the office of Priest, Prophet and King.

Chapter 5

5:1-4—This flying roll is really a scroll which flies because it must cover the entire country.

The dimensions are unusual unless it is rolled up when measured.

God's land is going to be cleansed.

On one side of the roll is a curse against those who steal.

On the other side is a curse against those who lie in the face of God.

No man in either class will be allowed to remain in the congregation of the righteous.

Both he and his household shall be removed.

5:5-11—The ephah which Zechariah now sees is related to the previous vision.

It is a large container.

The cover is made of heavy lead.

Inside there is a woman who represents wickedness.

All the spiritual harlotry will be removed from God's land. See Isaiah 1:21; Hosea 2:5; Ezekiel 23.

Wickedness will be deported to Shinar where Nimrod originated his rebellious government. (Gen. 10:10.)

Wickedness is at home in Babylon or Shinar, but GOD'S PROMISED LAND MUST BE KEPT CLEAN!

Chapter 6

6:1-8—The four chariots ride out from the presence of God to bring about his will upon the earth.

Chariots and cherubim are associated in Ezekiel. (Ezek. 10.)

The colors of the horses here is somewhat similar to those of Revelation 6.

Some believe these four indicate four world empires.

It is more likely that they represent the plagues of God such as War, Famine, Pestilence and Wild Beasts.

The angel explains them as four spirits.

Spirits are forces able to accomplish God's will.

Two of these move into the north country where Babylon is located.

The grisled or varicolored go into the south where Egypt has given much trouble.

The bay or red horses cover the rest of the world.

Do not take the chance of grieving God's Spirit.

On this occasion it seems to be quieted by sending judgments upon those who have grieved it.

6:9-15—Apparently the three men mentioned in verse 10 had come from Babylon carrying precious metals.

Zechariah is to take silver and gold from them and make a compound crown to set upon Joshua, the high priest's head.

As a high priest with a crown he then represents the BRANCH, or Christ, who combines the offices of King, Prophet and Priest.

It is of interest that even the name of this high priest means "saviour."

The comment here is not limited to Joshua of that day because it was Zerubbabel who built the temple.

But certainly the BRANCH, or Jesus Christ fits the description here perfectly:

1. He builds the spiritual temple today.
2. He bears the entire glory of God.
3. He rules upon his throne.
4. He serves as our high priest.
5. He provides the counsel of peace.

The gold and silver crowns are placed in the temple to remind men that the BRANCH will cause men to come from far and near to aid in building his Temple.

When these words come to pass men shall know that the prediction and message of Zechariah was inspired.

Chapter 7

7:1-3—Chapters 7 and 8 deal with the question of fasting which began when the temple was destroyed.

This was two years after the building of the temple had been reactivated by Haggai and Zechariah's preaching.

Representatives of the people are sent to the priests in the temple.

They are to find out if the people should now cease their sorrowing and fasting.

The fasting of the fifth month was particularly connected with the temple itself.

However they were also fasting in the fourth, the seventh and the tenth months.

God answers that their feasts and their fasts had both been matters of selfishness—not his command.

They were fasting because of their punishment—not because of their penitence.

In this case the "former prophets" indicates those who cried out for Jerusalem to repent before she perished.

7:8-14—God desires the obedience of men above their formal sacrifices. See Isaiah 1.

He had informed the Israelites what needed to be done:

1. Execute true judgment.
2. Show mercy and compassion.
3. Oppress not the unfortunate.
4. Eliminate malice and hatred from the heart.

They had turned a deaf ear, a cold shoulder and a hard heart toward him.

Since they would not listen to Jehovah he had also turned away from them.

If they had not acted in such a foolish manner they would not have been fasting over loss of the temple.

Chapter 8

8:1-8—As chapter 7 looks back to the reason for the fasting, chapter 8 looks forward to a change from fasting to feasting, joy and peace.

It was because of God's concern for Jerusalem that he allowed her to be punished.

Her spiritual unfaithfulness had provoked him to chastise her.

But now he was returning to Mount Zion and the Holy City.

Men and women should live to ripe old ages in peace.

Children should romp with joy in the streets.

Though all this might seem incredible in the eyes of men it was not so in God's Eyes.

From all parts of the world he would bring men to be built into his living Temple. See Matthew 8:5f.

They should be faithful to him and in turn he would protect and care for them.

8:9-15—The Jews of Zechariah's day are to be strong and continue the building which was begun again at the urging of Haggai and Zechariah.

They are reminded that when they failed to build there was friction between the people themselves.

Now that things have changed Jehovah will be with them.

Their spiritual faithfulness will cause resulting material prosperity.

How similar to the promise of inheriting the earth is the latter part of verse 12.

Rather than being a mocking and a hissing in lands where they are strangers they shall bless other nations from their own land.

Again the words are undoubtedly applicable to the Christian today who has been translated from the kingdom of darkness to that of God's own Son.

As God's purpose of punishing an unfaithful nation had

been fulfilled, so would his purpose of blessing them when faithful.

8:16-23—God gives four conditions for his continued blessings:
1. Speak the truth.
2. Be fair in treatment.
3. Keep malice out of your heart.
4. Respect God's name.

If this is done there will be far less need for fasting in the fourth, fifth, seventh and tenth months.

Not only will these Jews be a happy and blessed people, they will cause others to seek the Lord's way.

From all languages and all nations men would come to God's Holy City and his Holy Mountain as they see the desirable life lived by God's people.

They will walk together in Christ, no longer Jew and Gentile, but one people.

AND ONCE AGAIN A PHOPHET WITNESSES TO JESUS CHRIST AND THE VICTORY OF THE STONE CUT OUT WITHOUT HANDS!

Chapter 9

9:1-8—This chapter speaks of the fall of God's enemies and the coming of the King of Zion.

The translation of the American Standard is better here when it says the eyes of Jehovah are on man.

Men shall not stand if his eye perceives their rebellion beyond his longsuffering.

The description of the fall of the enemies moves down from Phoenicia to Philistia to Jerusalem itself.

No army with weapons can succeed against God's own for he will be with them.

9:9-11—Daughter of Zion is God's own beloved and cherished offspring.

He is sending a King (Jesus Christ) to lead her in battle.

He will be a strange lowly king, bringing salvation and riding on an ass colt rather than a white stallion.

His army will studiously avoid the use of weapons of carnal warfare such as chariots, horses, bows and arrows.

He shall cry for peace, not war!

He shall extend his rulership to every part of the earth.

The description of the event predicted in verse 9 is given in all four of the Gospel writers.

(Matt. 21:1-11; Mark 11:1-10 ; Luke 19:29-38; John 12:13.)

Through the blood of a new covenant the ones held captive for the pit of hell shall be sent forth.

9:12-17—These released prisoners are to man a stronghold.

God will lead in a ferocious battle.

The people who are faithful will be his weapons.

Some believe that Greece mentioned here indicates this prophecy referred to the Maccabean victories over the Macedonians.

If so it carries an overriding reference to the conquest of the Messiah.

The corners of the altar were filled with the blood of the sacrifices, thus the enemies of God and his people will become a sacrifice. See Revelation 19.

God's people will be lifted up as jewels in a crown or as a flying banner.

God's own beauty shall be demonstrated through the rejoicing of Zion in great happiness.

Chapter 10

10:1-4—The invitation comes to ask Jehovah for guidance and blessings.

The latter rain is that which is needed to fill the kernels as the grain matures.

Turning to any other source of guidance is foolishness.

Three classes of false leaders have misled them:

1. Idols who cannot speak.
2. Diviners who lie to them.
3. False dreamers.

God is angry that these have fed off his flock.

The misused flock shall suddenly become weapons in the hand of God.

His people shall be horses, cornerstones, battlebows and nails for building.

Those who depend upon horses and chariots for power shall be confused and defeated.

God's remnant shall be redeemed and shall multiply as he sows them like seed in all the nations.

He shall take his harvest from Assyria to Egypt as men move from bondage to freedom under the Messiah.

His people shall walk proudly for the meek shall inherit the earth.

Chapter 11

11:1-9—Throughout the land of Palestine the false shepherds and stiff-hearted Jews would be cut down.

Among them shall be men who are like great cedars.

Also those giant oaks will tumble.

The poor of God's flock shall no longer be persecuted and slaughtered.

God had provided Beauty (Grace) and Bands (Unity) for his own.

False shepherds were cut off quickly.

These had broken their covenant with God and so he feels no obligation toward them.

The poor remnant will be delivered but these evil ones would have Grace and Unity removed from them.

The picture here is rejection of God's leadership.

11:10-14—The people are asked to evaluate the true shepherd.

They declare his price to be thirty pieces of silver.

In disgust God declares that they are to be cast to the potter. See Matthew 27:1-7.

The position of earthly Israel is demolished because of their rejection of the Shepherd.

11:15-17—Foolish Israel will be allowed to follow the false leadership which they find attractive until they are starved and torn to pieces.

The leadership shall be shown to be what it is truly is— Blind and Powerless!

Chapter 12

12:1-2—Israel and Jerusalem will become a burden to those who oppose their well-being.

The danger lies in opposing Jehovah who created the universe and made life possible.

Those who try to swallow up Jerusalem will find that they have bitten off more than they can chew.

12:3-5—Like carrying a heavy jagged rock those who carry the burden of fighting Jerusalem will bleed from the bruises.

As God looks with favor upon his people he will make the horses and weapons of enemies useless.

The people and the governors shall unite in their efforts.

With the help of the people the leaders of Jerusalem would consume opposers like a roaring fire.

12:6-9—The glory of Judah shall be used in favor of the God of Heaven rather than hindering his cause.

With God's strength even the weakest of his people should have the strength of David against Goliath.

David's descendants shall lead God's people as if they were an angel of the Lord.

12:10-14—Judgment will come upon those who fight against God.

But grace will pour out upon those who turn to him.

God's people shall first pierce him and then shall mourn in repentance as deeply as one who has lost a firstborn child.

This would be similar to the mourning over Josiah's death in the valley of Megiddon. (2 Chron. 35:20-25.)

The grieving will not be a national grieving but families and individuals will be deeply sorrowful that the pierced Son had to die.

Chapter 13

13:1-6—With the piercing of Christ a fountain of blood poured forth to wash away sin and uncleanness.

One possibility for the meaning of verse 2 is that the age of prophecy would pass, along with the control of men by unclean spirits.

Those who take this stand would cite 1 Corinthians 13:8.

The present writer thinks it speaks of *false* prophets since it accompanies cessation of idolatry, and unclean spirits.

It also seems to be the result of the penitent attitude rather than a completion of the prophetic tasks.

This undesirable prophet is even condemned by his own parents as men's hearts turn toward God.

The prophet will find it expedient to leave his deceptive lying and proclaim himself a farmer.

When asked about the wounds he had inflicted upon himself he will lie about how he received them.

For the possible source of these wounds see 1 Kings 18:28.

13:7-9—God now calls for punishment to be visited upon the Good Shepherd. See John 10.

This action was taken by the determinate foreknowledge of Jehovah. (Acts 2:23.)

First the Shepherd (Jesus Christ) was to be smitten. (Isa. 53.)

Then his sheep would be scattered through persecution.

Even the tiny lambs would feel the bite of the oppressor.

209

Large numbers of the disciples would be killed as a result of their convictions.

Others who remained alive would have their faith tried
as by fire. (1 Pet. 1:6-7.)

But as a result they shall call upon Jehovah as their God,
and he shall claim them as his people.

Chapter 14

14:1-3—Rather than making spoil of Jerusalem the enemies of
the Holy City will find that their possessions have
been turned over to God's children.

A tremendous attack shall be made against the City of
God by men of every nation.

Much damage shall be done to the citizens.

But as always God will save his remnant.

Just as God led the armies of Old Testament times to
victories like that of Gideon he will now take his stand
before his precious City to defend it.

A way of escape from the horrors of oppression shall be
provided for the saints of Jehovah.

The darkness shall flee away as day and night pass away
before the continuous illumination of the Sun of Righteousness. See Malachi 4:2.

Under God's protecting hand the saints who flee from
earthly Jerusalem will carry the living water to all
parts of the world in every season.

Christ shall become known to people of every land.

All opposition must melt before the power of the Sword
which proceeds from his mouth.

His name will be exalted above every other name. (Phil.
2:9-11.)

A New Jerusalem will be inhabited and will tower above
all its surroundings as if they were a plain.

This new Jerusalem shall no longer be in danger of destruction as in past days.

All its enemies will be consumed.

The bodies which fought shall rot away.

The eyes which searched for spoil shall go blind.

The blaspheming tongues will be quieted.

The enemies of God's people will devour themselves.

God's people, Judah, shall fight in their own God-ap-
proved manner.

And they shall have the wealth of the heathen divided
among them as spoil. (Matt. 5:5.)

The possessions of God's enemies shall be removed through his intervention. (As did Egypt of old.)

Only those who are willing to accept Jehovah as God shall survive to worship him in thanksgiving.

The feast of the tabernacles memorialized the arrival in the promised land after much wandering and it followed the atonement.

God's blessings shall be rained down upon those who turn to him and the Holy City.

But for those who refuse there shall be only drought and plague.

All those who ally themselves with Egypt and her destiny of bondage shall share in her fate.

14:20-21—With this new order the people shall no longer employ horses for war. See Isaiah 2:2-4.

Every item found in the New Jerusalem will be pure and Holy.

The unclean heathen shall be cut off.

See Revelation 21:22-27.

5. *Practical lessons from the book of Zechariah*

1. Nothing can stand against the Lord's plan to build his temple.

2. The Kingdom of God will provide a haven for men from every nation.

3. God will provide the power to accomplish his purposes if we will offer ourselves.

4. God's priests, his land and his temple must be kept pure.

5. Worship must be for the purpose of pleasing God, not men.

6. Those who depend upon physical weapons of war shall be confused and defeated while the meek inherit the earth.

7. The Good Shepherd and Prince of Peace will reign victorious and deliver God's sheep.

8. The Lord will protect Jerusalem, and from it will flow fountains of living water.

9. For those who reject Jehovah there remain only plagues and curses.

10. For those who accept him there shall be showers of blessing in the New Jerusalem.

211

MALACHI
(My Messenger)

1. *Background for the book of Malachi*
   A. Historical background
      1. This is over one hundred years after the return.
      2. The temple had been rebuilt in 520 B.C.
      3. Ezra had returned in 458 B.C.
      4. Artaxerxes had allowed Nehemiah to return and build the walls of the city about 444 B.C.
      5. Greek culture had begun to really bloom in 480 B.C.
      6. Europe was beginning to succeed Asia as an intellectual center.
   B. Social background
      1. There was serious economic depression in Palestine.
      2. Social order had seriously broken down with failing marriages and injustice on every side.
   C. Religious background
      1. The people had lost faith in God's promises through Haggai and Zechariah of future glory and blessing.
      2. Idolatry had moved from outward idols to those obstructions of the heart such as materialistic covetousness and selfishness.
      3. The priesthood was misleading the people.
      4. The people were holding back offerings which should have been given to Jehovah.
      5. The ritualistic empty worship they offered was backed by cast-off wives and heathen entanglements.

2. *The man, Malachi*
   A. The name means "My Messenger."
   B. There is some dispute over whether Malachi was a real person or just the term used to designate an anonymous writer.
   C. Some have even said the book was written by an angel since the word messenger is also the word angel.
   D. No other prophet wrote anonymously and thus it is not likely that this one did either.
   E. He has the courage to attack such problems as divorce.

F. He has vision to see four hundred years in the future in talking about the coming of John the Baptist.

G. He is God's spokesman as the Jews are provided one last challenge to keep the covenant given on Sinai.

3. *The book of Malachi*

A. Constantly reinforces itself by using "Thus saith the Lord" and similar phrases over 25 times in 4 chapters.

B. A list of charges is brought against the people of God.

C. A unique method of presentation is used.

   1. A charge is made.

   2. The people then reply to the charge. ("But ye say.")

   3. The prophet then provides the details of the charge.

   See 1:2-3; 2:6-7; 2:10-16; 2:17; 3:7; 3:8; 3:13-14.

D. There are only three chapters in the Hebrew Old Testament.

E. Outline of the book of Malachi

   1. God has loved Israel.

   2. Israel has failed to respond.

   3. A Messenger will herald a new day of righteousness.

   4. The unrighteousness shall be turned to ashes.

4. *Comments on the text of Malachi*

Chapter 1

1:1-5—The word of God always leaves men with a burden to carry.

If they obey, the burden becomes pleasant.

If they rebel, the burden will be horrible.

The word Malachi in verse 1 is the word *My Messenger.*

The people are wondering "Where is the promised glory? Does God really love us?"

God knew from the womb that Esau and his descendant Edomites would provoke his hatred.

They had been taken by Nebuchadnezzar just as had Israel.

But Edom had not been allowed to return. See Jeremiah 49:7; 25:9, 21.

Edom had tried only to be driven away again by the Nabatean Arabs and the Romans.

This should be proof even in the future that Jehovah is Lord.

1:6-11—A father is due certain respect.

An employer or supervisor also commands honor.

213

But Israel has failed to show honor to God who is both Father and Master.

The offerings which the priests offer offend God because they have treated him with contempt.

Why should he be pleased with less than an earthly ruler would accept?

After taking the best for themselves they have offered God the blemished and undesirable.

Two widely different interpretations have been given for verse 10.

1. The priests will not even shut the temple doors or light the sacrificial fires without payment.
2. God looks for a man who will shut the doors of the temple and put out the fires which only offend him now.

The time will come when the heathen Gentiles will put these Jewish priests to shame as they honor God's name with pure sacrifices.

1:12-14—Their worship had become a weariness to them.

It was even a worse weariness to Jehovah.

They have turned up their noses at his plan for their approach to his throne.

He will not accept their blemished sacrifices, and his curse will rest upon them for their attempted deceit. See Acts 5:5-11.

Chapter 2

2:1-10—Failing to give God the glory due him is a most serious offense.

Balaam's curses were made blessings. (Num. 23:19-20.)

The exact reverse will happen to these priests.

They have offered offensive and foul sacrifices to God.

He now considers them no better than the manure which was to be carted away.

God had made a covenant with Levi for life and peace and Levi was true to it.

The priesthood was to guard the truth and lead men to it.

These priests had misled men and broken the covenant.

Because the priests had considered God with contempt he would see that the people viewed them with contempt.

The Jewish people were brethren with God as their Father, yet the priests applied the law with respect of persons.

214

2:11-13—The men of Israel had also broken the covenant by
their marriages with women of idolatry.
This was forbidden. See Exodus 34:16.
Both the one who married these wives and the one who
taught that it was alright would be cut off.
The tears which have resulted from casting off their Jewish wives would quench the fires of the sacrificial altar
and God would not accept their offerings.
God is witness of their original marriage and he considers
their actions a breach of promise both to the cast-off
wife and to him.
God desired the production of faithful Godly children,
but this will prevent such. See Ezra 9:1-2; Deuteronomy 7:3-4.
The phrase *covereth violence with his garment* is rendered *covereth his garment with violence* in the American Standard.
Rather than wearing white robes of righteousness these
men's garments are filthy with violent sin.

2:17—God is tired of listening to their rebellious sayings.
They seem to have drawn some erroneous conclusions:
1. The wicked are blessed.
2. There is no justice.
3. Righteousness is a waste of time. (1 Pet. 3.)

Chapter 3
3:1-6—And so God provides an answer to their questions.
He will send a messenger who will prepare the way for
a new covenant.
Then the Messiah will come to his temple.
The messenger is John the Baptist.
See all four Gospel records: Matthew 3:3; Mark 1:3;
Luke 3:4; John 1:2-3. Also: Luke 1:17; Matthew
11:10-14; 17:12; Isaiah 40:3-5; Malachi 4:5.
The coming of the Messiah will usher in a time of purifi-
cation and purging.
This refining and purifying is taking place today as
Christ supervises the process.
Under this new covenant the offering of God's people
shall once again be satisfying to him.
The purifying process will finally eliminate every sin and
every sinner.
It is because of God's promise to Abraham to bless the
world that he continues to allow the wicked to live.

215

But he is not slack, and his promises will be kept when the time is right. (2 Pet. 3:9-10.)

3:7—Throughout the ages the Jews had turned away.

When God asks them to return they deny knowledge of the nature of their sins.

3:8-12—His explanation is that they have robbed him.

A thief *steals* when the owner is not looking.

Men must *rob* God for he is always aware of their actions.

Even our free will offerings are due to God.

Therefore withholding our sacrifices is truly robbery in his case.

Their withholding from God has resulted in his withholding from them.

If they will open up their storehouses to him he will open the windows of heaven's storehouse to them.

And God's storehouses are much bigger than ours!!

Not only will he increase fertility, he will destroy the enemies such as insects and disease.

It shall be obvious ultimately that God's way of life is a blessed and satisfying path.

3:13-15—Again God returns to their faithless questions.

1. Is it not vain to serve God?
2. Are not the proud the happy ones?
3. Are not the blasphemers safe and secure?

The answer is that there is a book of remembrance. See also Exodus 32:32; Psalms 56:8; 69:28; 139:16; Ezekiel 13:9; Daniel 7:10; 12:1; Philippians 4:3; Revelation 20:12.

God's remnant shall never be forgotten.

These righteous are being polished as precious jewels that God will cherish like his own son.

When the Christian age is over there will be no difficulty in discerning righteous from wicked.

The righteous will be jewels collected by Jehovah.

The wicked will be as ashes under foot. See Matthew 3:10-12.

Chapter 4

4:1—There are three possible applications of verse 1.

1. The entire Christian dispensation.
2. The destruction of the Jewish system in the first century.
3. The final day of judgment.

4:2-3—Though the wicked be destroyed the righteous will thrive and frolic like calves in the bright glory of his righteousness.

Blessed are the meek for they shall inherit the earth!

4:4—In the meantime as they wait for the Messiah they are to keep the Law of Moses.

4:5-6—It will be possible to recognize the coming of the day of separation under Christ for Elijah will be sent to usher it in.

John the Baptist denied that he was Elijah in the body. (John 1:21.)

But Jesus affirmed that he was Elijah in the spirit. (Matt. 11:14.)

If the Jews of Jesus' day would compare the teachings of John the Baptist with that of their fathers they would recognize him as the Messiah.

If not they would bring a curse upon themselves.

5. *Practical lessons from the book of Malachi*

A. Our respect for Jehovah must be greater than for either an earthly father or a governor.

B. Sacrifices offered to God must be of the highest quality and given willingly.

C. Corrupt leaders will soon bring contempt upon themselves.

D. Withhold from God and he will withhold from you, but give to God and he will give to you.

E. God expects marriage to produce children faithful to him.

F. God will never forget his faithful ones.

G. There will finally come victory for the righteous and destruction for the wicked.

H. He that endureth unto the end shall be saved.

NOTE: THE WORDS OF MALACHI CLOSE ABOUT 1,000 YEARS OF TUTORING FOR THE COMING OF THE LORD. NOW THERE WILL BE 400 YEARS OF SILENCE BEFORE JOHN THE BAPTIST INTRODUCES THE LAMB OF GOD.

NOTES ON REVELATION

INTRODUCTION

The following set of notes is presented in hope that those individuals who come into contact with the material may be saved many hours of time. There is already a flood of books and pamphlets available. In his personal study the compiler has found it necessary to examine a number of commentators with a variety of viewpoints and schemes of interpretation. By bringing the results of these labors into a concise outline form the student should be enabled to more easily compare and evaluate for himself.

Although at times it may appear that a single view is emerging there will be other times when a number of interpretations will be laid out side by side. It will be the responsibility of any person using the notes to treat them primarily as resource material. After having examined the included ideas and having run the cross references, plus doing any additional investigation which time permits, the prospective teacher should be able to prepare his own outline and lesson plans in a more effective manner.

It saddens one to realize there are persons who lightly dismiss this wonderful Revelation of Jesus Christ with such comments as "It was not meant to be understood," or "I don't think it belongs with the rest of the Bible." Even a child is able to wonder at the dragon, the horses, the beast from the sea and the streets of gold. As maturity grows the one who really hungers for the truth will come to the realization that this book is properly placed at the end of the Holy Scriptures. We say this because its riches can best be mined after one has come to an appreciation of the Law, the Prophets, the Psalms, the Gospels and the epistles. The treasure is truly there but it must be earned by diligent study in a spirit of humility. May God bless your efforts toward that end.

The books listed below have been either read completely or considered carefully in this study. The fact that they are included in this list does not indicate agreement with the ideas expressed within them. They were selected for study because they represented a complete range of views. The approach taken by the book is indicated in a number of cases for the reader's convenience.

Barclay, Wm., *The Revelation of John*
Boles, H. Leo and Boll, R. H., *Unfulfilled Prophecy*

Clarke, Adam, *Commentary on Revelation*

Hinds, J. T., *A Commentary on the Book of Revelation*, (Continuous Historical Method)

Jehovah's Witnesses, *Then Is Finished the Mystery of God*

Johnson, Ashley, *Opening the Book of the Seven Seals*, (Postmillennial)

Johnson, B.W., *The People's New Testament with Notes*

Hendrickson, W., *More Than Conquerors*, (Progressive Parallel Method)

Lenski, R.C.H., *Interpretation of St. John's Revelation*

Murray, George L., *Millennial Studies*, (A Millennial View)

Rice, John R., *The Coming Kingdom of Christ*, (Premillennial View) (Futuristic Method)

Wallace, Foy, *The Book of Revelation*, (Praeterist Method)

Additional references are suggested in the bibliography.

In addition to these works the student should make readily available a good map of Asia Minor, and he should not be satisfied with his studies unless he has spent some time in running the many cross references suggested in his Bible. It would be of real value to compare cross references from two or three Bibles by different publishers as the references vary from one to another.

It will assist in the clarification of thoughts if the entire book of Revelation is read through over and over during the course of study.

An Introduction

1. *Revelation is a valid topic of study.*
   A. There are those who believe such a study can only lead to confusion.
   B. The book *is* a part of the Bible and must have a reason for providential protection.
   C. We are told to read, hear and keep the words of this prophecy. (1:3.)

2. *The Revelation is both prophetic and apocalyptic.*
   A. The word "apocalupsis" which is translated "revelation" carries the meaning of unveiling or disclosing a mystery.
   B. It deals with things which must *shortly* come to pass.
      1. It is likely that this means from John's point of view.
      2. It is also possible that this should be compared with the term quickly as found in "Behold, I come *quickly*." (22:20.)
   C. The book is typical of many apocalyptic writings.

219

1. Messages of hope similar to this were written in times of persecution.
2. Other apocalyptic writings include: a. The Assumptions of Moses; b. Baruch; c. Psalms of Solomon.
3. These books were often signed with names of famous persons who did not write them in hope of calling attention.
4. They were often symbolic in nature.
5. A general pattern was apparent.
   a. The present age was filled with evil. b. A deliverer or Messiah was to appear. c. There would be a "Day of the Lord"; a time of judgment and destruction. d. There would be a resurrection of the dead. e. A new and blessed age would begin.
   (1) There would be great fertility.
   (2) There would be no more war between men.
   (3) There would be peace between man and beast.
   (4) There would be no more pain.
   (5) Men would be completely righteous.

D. The student is invited to investigate and compare for himself in order to see the gap between the quality of Revelation and the other apocalyptic literature.

3. *Who was the author of Revelation?*
   A. The book does not say which John is the author.
   B. There is some disagreement among early Christian writers but the following are in agreement that the author was the apostle: Irenaeus, Justin Martyr, Tertullian, Hippolytus.
   C. Some later scholars began to assign it to another John.
      1. The language was said to be much more crude than John's Gospel.
      2. Where the Gospel of John speaks of love, Revelation spends much time on the wrath of God.
      3. The author seems to be speaking of others when he mentions the apostles in 21:14.
   D. Present day students have swung back somewhat to the older view.
      1. One would not expect the same style in: a. A personal letter like the short books of John. b. A biography like the Gospel of John. c. A prediction written under the circumstances of Revelation.
      2. Also it might be well to note that this is Jesus' style, not that of the apostle.
      3. Tradition tells us John was exiled to Patmos at the proper time to have written it.

4. There are certain similarities between the Gospel of John and the Revelation: a. The Gospel uses the term "Lamb of God." b. Revelation uses this term over 20 times. c. There is an emphasis on salvation through the blood of Christ in both. Compare John 1:29, 36 with Revelation 7:14; 12:11.

E. Regardless of whether John the apostle or some other John wrote the book God and Christ authored it. (1:1.)

4. *When was it written?*

A. Almost unanimously the scholars agree that it was written under severe persecution from the Roman Empire.
   1. Sources outside the Bible would indicate this was true.
   2. Such phrases as "To him that overcometh" used repeatedly show the mood of the entire book to be one of victory by endurance.

B. For three hundred years the Church did battle with Rome.
   1. This was especially true of the first century.
   2. Both Judaism and Rome attempted to annihilate Christianity.
   3. At first the threat was only to the Jews but later Christians refused to worship the emperors.

C. The number of martyrs for Christ was enormous.

D. The symbolism of the book is thought to be a means of giving comfort to those familiar with the scriptures while meaningless to the Romans.

E. A list of the Roman emperors through Domitian follows: Augustus, Tiberius, Caligula, Claudius, Nero, Galba, Otho, Vitellius, Vespasian, Titus, Domitian.
   (Before the persecution was halted by the Edict of Toleration in the reign of Constantine there had been over forty emperors.) For a list see World Book Encyclopedia.

F. There are strong arguments made for two dates about thirty years apart.
   1. Before the destruction of Jerusalem. (About A.D. 68.)
   2. In the last years of the apostle John. (About A.D. 96.)

G. Fierce persecution raged at both of these times.
   1. Under Nero Caesar in the earlier date.
   2. During the reign of Domitian at the later date.

H. Those who argue for the earlier date say:
   1. The Syriac version states that John was exiled by Nero.
   2. The temple was still standing. (11:1.)
   3. Nero was the sixth king of 17:10-12.

4. Nero Caesar's name totals 666.
    N-50 R-200 0-6 K-100 S-60 R-200
5. There must have been more than seven churches in Asia by this time of A.D. 96.
6. John would have been an extremely old man by A.D. 96. One source says he was so feeble that he had to be carried into the building and then could speak only a few words.
7. There are passages in Galatians 4 and Hebrews 12 which seem to have reference to Revelation. Both these books are of early date.
8. Jerusalem was truly an apostate city and a harlot Babylon which deserved to be destroyed. See Revelation 17:5; Isaiah 1:21.
    a. Jerusalem had once been faithful. b. Rome never had been.

I. Those who argue for the later date say:
1. Irenaeus claims it appeared during the reign of Domitian.
2. Laodicea had been destroyed during Nero's reign. It was now rebuilt and boasting.
3. Ephesus had had time to lose their first love.
4. Sardis had had time enough to die.
5. Caesar worship did not grow enough to cause persecution in Asia Minor until the later date.

5. *To whom was it written?*
    A. Particularly to the seven Churches of Asia. (1:4.)
    B. However the number seven is associated with completeness as in creation.
       1. Three is a complete heavenly number. (The Godhead)
       2. Four is a complete earthly number. (Four corners of the earth)
       3. Adding the two we arrive at seven.
    C. Thus we have overriding eternal principles which apply to all Churches for all time.
    D. Such dual application is true of many of the scriptures.
       1. Paul wrote to the Corinthians, but we make use of the truths.
       2. Isaiah wrote to fleshly Israel while simultaneously foretelling of the coming Christ.
    E. Revelation was then written for encouragement to persecuted Christians until the end of time.

6. *What was the purpose of the book?*
    A. To show that God rules ultimately in the affairs of men.

222

B. To reveal to the Christians of Asia Minor those things which must shortly come to pass.
C. To show persecuted Christians that:
1. God sees their tears. (7:17.)
2. Their prayers make a difference. (8:3, 4.)
3. Death is not the end. (14:13; 20:4.)
4. Victory belongs to the faithful. (15:2.)
5. Their persecutions will be avenged. (6:9; 19:2.)
6. They *do reign* (1:6), and they *will reign* married to Christ. (21:9.)

7. *There are several methods of interpretation.*
A. The literary method which says:
1. The book is simply another uninspired apocalypse.
2. It is not only uninspired but it is a literary monstrosity.
3. It is amazing to find religious leaders holding this view.
B. The Praeterist method which says:
1. The book was written before the destruction of Jerusalem.
2. Nearly all of it was fulfilled at that time.
3. Some would even include chapters 21 and 22 in the fulfilled.
C. The Continuous Historical method which says:
1. The entire period from the first coming of Christ to his second coming is covered.
2. The symbols represent various events such as the first world war.
3. There is great disagreement among interpreters over the meaning of the symbols.
4. The Year-Day theory is accepted by many of these.
D. The Futuristic method which says:
1. The book deals mainly with events of the future.
2. Much of it has to do with the second coming of Christ and the judgment.
3. Many of these are premillennialist.
E. The Progressive Parallel method which says:
1. The truth is a blend of the Continuous Historical and the Praeterist.
2. There are seven sections each covering the Christian dispensation.

AN OUTLINE OF THE BOOK OF REVELATION

1. *Christ walks among the lampstands.*
2. *Christ opens the sealed book.*

3. *Christ warns of the danger of disobedience.*
4. *Christ is persecuted by the dragon.*
5. *Christ's angels pour out plagues of God's wrath from seven vials.*
6. *Christ's enemies are defeated.*
7. *Christ reigns with his bride over a new heaven and a new earth.*
8. *Conclusion*
9. *Comments on the text of Revelation*

Chapter 1

1:1—
A. The order of revelation is God—Christ—angel—John—Churches of Asia—all mankind.
B. Others have also called themselves servants. (Rom. 1:1; James 1:1; 2 Pet. 1:1.)
   1. This servant is more than a simple employee.
   2. The word indicates a slave (doulos).
C. God's messages are clearer to those who *pray, study* and *act.* See John 8:32.
D. The things must either all happen shortly, or else start shortly. Compare 2 Timothy 4:9. Would Paul wish to wait centuries?
E. Angels often acted as intermediaries. (Acts 7:38; 7:53; Gal. 3:19; Heb. 2:2.)

1:2—
A. The true Christian like John is a witness bearing testimony of Jesus. (1 John 1:1.)
B. Notice the general similarity between the first chapter of John's Gospel and this verse.

1:3—
A. There is a list of beatitudes in Revelation just as in Matthew. (1:3; 14:13; 16:15; 19:9; 20:6; 22:7; 22:14.)
B. Jewish services included the reading of the scriptures.
C. The reader who is to be blessed here could be either:
   1. A special reader who read because few copies were available.
   2. Any reader, including ourselves. See James 11:23, 24.

1:4—
A. This same type of introduction is found in many of the prophets:
   Isaiah, Jeremiah, Ezekiel, Hosea, Joel, Amos, Obadiah, and Jonah.

B. At this point the student should consult a map and locate each of the seven churches as well as to locate Asia Minor.

C. There is a strong relationship between grace and peace.
1. Peace comes when one is no longer at enmity with God.
2. Grace allows forgiveness of sins and thus atonement.

D. The grace and peace come from all portions of the Godhead.
1. From he which is and was and will be. See Exodus 3:14; Psalm 90:2.
2. From the seven Spirits. (Probably the completeness of the Holy Spirit.) See Zechariah 4:2.
3. From Jesus Christ.

1:5—

A. The first part of this verse should go with the previous verse.

B. This and verse 6 contain three characteristics of Christ and three actions of Christ.
1. Three characteristics of Christ.
   a. A faithful and true witness. See John 3:11; 18:37.
   b. First born from the dead. (Col. 1:15.)
   c. Prince of the Kings of the earth. See Psalm 89:27.
   (Notice that it was precisely the Kingship over the kings of the earth that Satan offered to Christ in the temptations.)
2. Three actions of Christ.
   a. He loved us. (Rom. 5:8.) b. He washed us. (Rev. 5:9.) (Barclay translates it *loosed* us.) c. He made us a kingdom of priests. (We are sons of a King with special access to God.)

1:6—

A. Kings and priests are the two highest offices men hold in political and religious life, unless perhaps the eldership.

B. Compare this verse with the close of the model prayer, Matthew 6:13.

C. 1 Corinthians 15:24-28 should be considered in connection with for ever and ever.

1:7—

A. Daniel saw a similar picture in Daniel 7:13, 14.

B. It was promised he would come in such manner. (Acts 1:9-11.)

C. The emphasis here is upon wailing because of punishment but Jesus also comes to *reward* the faithful. See Matthew 24:30; 26:64.

D. Those who crucify him afresh shall join in the wailing. (Heb. 6:6.)

1:8—

A. Alpha and Omega are the first and last letters of the Greek alphabet.
B. God is both eternal and Almighty. See 21:6; 22:13; Exodus 3:14.
C. All principalities and powers must melt before he who is the whole of all things. See a similar expression in Ecclesiastes 12:13.

1:9—

A. It appears that John felt his name was well enough known throughout the seven churches to need no further description.
B. John can encourage these Christians because he was being persecuted even at the time of this Revelation.
   Matthew 24:13 fits well with the entire theme of Revelation.
C. This banishment could have occurred during Nero's reign but Domitian is said to be more apt to have used banishment.
D. Patmos should be located on the map.
   1. It was about forty miles off the coast of Asia Minor.
   2. A rocky and barren island with mines for slave labor.
   3. Crescent shaped, about 10 miles long and 5 miles wide.
E. Some who were banished there were scourged and then worked as slaves.
F. John was there because of his testimony for Jesus Christ.
G. There is a powerful lesson here.
   1. Paul and John both wrote letters of encouragement during periods of punishment.
   2. Perhaps we also can best comfort others after affliction.
   3. Thus affliction may be turned to glory through endurance. See 2 Timothy 2:12.

1:10—

A. To be in the spirit meant that John was in a condition that allowed the Lord to communicate with him effectively.
   Compare Ezekiel 3:12-14.
   1. Jesus told the woman at the well the time was coming in which men would worship in spirit and in truth. (John 4:24.)
   2. Though we need not expect such a revelation as John had God will communicate more effectively if we worship in spirit.

B. The day of the Lord was a common warning among the prophets.
(Isa. 13:6; Joel 1:15; Zech. 14:1; Ezek. 13:5; Mal. 4:5; 1 Thess. 5:12.)

C. This however seems to be the first day of the week.
1. The Jews had their Sabbath.
2. The Romans had their emperor's day.
3. Christians had their Lord's day:
   a. Upon this day Christ arose; b. Upon this day the Church began; c. Upon this day they met to worship.

D. Moses also heard a voice as of a trumpet. (Ex. 19:16.)

E. If the apostle John is the writer he was once again hearing the voice he had learned to love.

1:11—

A. John is not only to see, he is to write what he sees.

B. Thus all Christians *first receive* and follow this by giving. (Even when exiled on Patmos.)

C. Note the similarity between this verse and verse 8.
1. In verse 8 the description applies to God.
2. Now the same description applies to Christ.

1:12—

A. The voice had sounded behind him.

B. Compare these candlesticks to those found in Exodus 25:31-37.

C. Again candlesticks are found in the temple. (1 Kings 7:49.)

D. They are seen also in Zechariah's vision. (Zech. 4:2.)

E. Candlesticks are associated with a source of light. See Matthew 5:14.

F. Seven may indicate completeness of illumination.

G. The seven candlesticks are explained in Revelation 1:20.

1:13—

A. The one like unto the Son of man is Christ. See Revelation 1:18; Daniel 7:13.

B. The robe reminds us of the clothing of the high priests of the Old Testament. (Lev. 16:4.)

C. Kings also wore such robes. (1 Sam. 24:5.)

D. Prophets also wore them, though sometimes crude in material.

1:14—

A. These verses present characteristics of the risen Christ.

B. The white head and hair symbolize purity. (Isa. 1:18; Dan. 7:9.)

C. The eyes like a flaming fire penetrate the hearts of men to see perfectly both the good and evil which they do.

1:15—

A. There is some similarity between the articles of apparel here and the Christian armor of Ephesians 6:13-18.

B. Those who carry the Gospel do have beautiful feet. See Isaiah 52:7; Romans 10:15.

C. The feet of the cherubim of Ezekiel 1:7 sparkled like burnished brass.

D. A voice of many waters would suggest the idea of power and energy. See Ezekiel 43:2.

1:16—

A. The seven stars are later said to be the angels of the seven churches. (1:20.)

B. The stars are supported and upheld by Jesus himself.

C. Several ideas have been suggested with regard to these angels.
   1. Some believe them to be the messengers from John to each Church.
   2. Some have considered them to be the influence of each church as they illuminate the world for Christ.
   3. Still others see them as the collective elderships at each congregation.
      a. Elders are responsible for seeing that their congregations shine brightly. b. They themselves must be as stars high above all shifting winds of human doctrine. See Daniel 12:3. c. Lenski also suggests that as stars they must never be doormats.

D. The two-edged sword is the Word of God. (Heb. 4:12; Isa. 11:4; Isa. 49:2.) Compare here Revelation 19:15, 21.

E. The word as a sword may be a *life taker*. As the seed it may also be a life *giver*.

F. This same shining countenance seems to have been manifest at the Mount of Transfiguration. (Matt. 17:2.)

G. Perhaps this was the glory seen by Saul of Tarsus on the road to Damascus. (Acts 9:3-5.)

1:17—

A. Jesus is first and last in at least three areas.
   1. In God's revelation

2. In human history
3. In the Church

B. When mortals are faced with a true realization of their impure condition as compared with the glorious purity of God they are often found falling to the ground. (Acts 9:4; Ezek. 1:28; Dan. 8:17.)

C. There shall come a time when every knee shall bow and every tongue confess.

D. Strength from the Lord's right hand *follows* humility.

E. Fear not!—Yet we are told to "Fear God and keep his commandments."

F. Jesus as the eternal Word or "Logos" of God is eternal.

G. One has appropriately said, "It should not be difficult to endure unto the end, for *that is where Jesus stands waiting.*" See Ephesians 1:22, 23.

1:18—

A. Jesus had said, "Destroy this temple and I will raise it in three days."

B. Physical death gives way to either true life or true death.

C. Death has gates. See Job 38:17; Isaiah 38:10; Psalm 9:13.

D. There are keys to a number of places.
   1. The key of David. (Rev. 3:7; Isa. 22:22.)
   2. The keys of the Kingdom. (Matt. 16:19.)
   3. The keys of the bottomless pit. (Rev. 20:1.)

E. In the resurrection even the graves will be unlocked.

1:19—

A. This seems to apply to only the vision which John has already seen rather than the whole history of man.

B. He is to record the conditions of the seven Churches as they are and to reveal the future, and he must be true to the revelation as he receives it.

1:20—

A. The best interpreter of the Bible is the Bible. Compare 1:12, 16, 20.

B. Congregations glow brilliantly when Jesus walks among them.

C. We are now about to be told what Jesus saw as he walked among the seven Churches of Asia.

D. He will see as much in the one where *we* worship.

Chapter 2

2:1—

A. Whatever the identity of the angel or messenger or star of the

229

church at Ephesus, Christ is represented as having it in his right hand.
1. Christ is interested in upholding only true messengers.
2. Ephesus had been having some difficulty with false teaching.

B. Christ is ever present among his churches. (Lo, I am with you —.)

C. In each of the letters to the churches we find similar sections:
1. A salutation.
2. A description of Christ. (Each description has a purpose. It deals with some characteristic of that congregation.)
3. A condemnation of evil.
4. A warning.
5. An exhortation.
6. A promise.

D. Ephesus was a powerful city.
1. Though it was not the capital, it was the greatest city of Asia.
2. It had a great harbor.
3. It was very rich and wealthy.
4. It was oneof the Roman "Free cities."
5. Games similar to the Olympics were held there.
6. It was a center of pagan worship.
   a. Among others it was the headquarters for the worship of Diana.   b. The temple of Diana was one of the seven wonders of the ancient world.
7. Many events of the New Testament took place in Ephesus. (Acts 18:19-26; 19:22-41; 20:17-38.)
8. Ephesus made a true testing ground for the power of the Christian faith.

E. Interestingly, Ephesus is now waste and desolate with its harbor filled and lying six miles inland.

2:2—

A. The eyes like a flame of fire have seen their works.

B. Notice the good is always mentioned first in these letters.
1. The Lord sees the bad.
2. But he would rather see the good.
3. This is also good psychology.

C. The labor mentioned here is the kind that *breaks sweat*.

D. The patience mentioned here is the kind that sees one through to triumph.

E. They had been able and alert to detect heresy.

1. They had been warned that wolves would enter, and they had. (Acts 20:29.)
2. Men of all time are cautioned to test the spirits. (1 John 4:1.)
   a. Weakness is to be forgiven. b. Deliberate false teaching is another, and very serious story.

2:3—

A. They had borne up under the impact of error.
B. They had continued to work without weakening. (Gal. 6:9.)
C. The Christian must bear up under trials and burdens but he is not expected to bear false teaching.

2:4—

A. The first flush of attraction to Christ had disappeared.
B. Love should grow rather than diminish.
C. These are not the only ones in the Bible or otherwise to have lost their first love. (Acts 7:40, 41; Judges 2:7, 10.)
D. It may be that heresy hunting had turned love and fellowship into suspicion.

2:5—

A. There are three steps back: remember, repent, do.
B. Christ reacts swiftly to remove his glory.
C. A church without the light of Christ is absolutely worthless.
D. When the spirits of men or churches fall, these men and churches become like the darkness of the sky after the shooting star has disappeared.

2:6—

A. The Nicolaitanes represent the spirit of compromise.
B. If one loves God he will do *his* commandments. (John 14:23.)
C. Later we find Pergamos also having trouble with this sect.
D. The Nicolaitanes were a sect of the gnostics.
E. They were in error on at least four points.
   1. Community of wives.
   2. Adultery and fornication considered insignificant. (They were said to have lived like goats.)
   3. They destroyed weak brethren by eating meat sacrificed to idols.
   4. They mixed pagan ceremonies with their Christian worship.
F. It is important that God's friends be ours and God's enemies also be ours.

G. Like many today the Nicolaitanes wished to mix the pleasures of the world with the life of a Christian.

2:7—

A. There are some men with physical ears but no spiritual ones. (Matt. 11:15; 13:13-16.)

B. If one is able to overcome he will regain access to the tree of life which was lost so long ago in Eden.

C. Paradise means "a pleasure garden."

D. The word paradise is used interestingly in other scriptures. (Isa. 1:30; Prov. 3:18; 11:30; 13:12; 15:4.)

E. One is made to wonder about the comparison between the Garden of Eden and the Paradise of God here mentioned.

2:8—

A. The city of Smyrna was second only to Ephesus in Asia.
   1. It was called the "crown" or "flower" of Asia because of its beauty.
   2. A western breeze off the ocean gave it freshness.
   3. It had been destroyed and rebuilt with splendid planning.
   4. It had been extremely faithful to Rome.
   5. Like Ephesus it had been a center of pagan worship.
      a. Cybele, b. Zeus, c. Apollo, d. Aphrodite.

B. The angel of the church was responsible for seeing that the message of Revelation was received by that congregation.

C. The Church may have been established at Smyrna during Paul's third missionary journey. See Acts 19:10.

D. Citizens of Smyrna were said to have been proud of being "first."
   1. It is good to excel.
   2. We must remember Christ is both "first and last."

E. Just as Smyrna had been destroyed and reconstructed, Christ had been laid to rest in the ground to be later resurrected. (Note the connection between this and the promise to Smyrna.)

2:9—

A. Again the penetrating eyes like a flame of fire have seen all.

B. Both the righteousness and the unrighteousness are known.

C. Christ knew of their tribulations both from without and within.
   a. Jews and pagans as well as Rome had tormented them.
   b. Read the story of Polycarp's death in many commentaries. (There is a good account in Barclay, p. 93.)

232

D. Christians were poverty-stricken for two reasons.
1. Many had come from the lower classes of people.
2. There was a general sharing with none having much. (Hebrews 10:4 indicates that what they had as Christians was sometimes stolen from them.)

E. They could be rich and yet in poverty because of the difference between God's concept of poverty and ours. (Matt. 6:20 and 19:21; Luke 12:20, 21; James 2:5; Rev. 3:17.)

F. The Jews who persecuted the Christians made mockery of the word Jew.
1. He is a Jew who is one inwardly; and circumcision is that of the heart. (Rom. 2:29.)
2. A Jew is a chosen one of God.
3. These men were of Satan's synagogue or assembly and served men, not God.

2:10—

A. They are to suffer a variety of persecutions, but "Blessed are ye when men shall persecute you . . ."

B. Christ who conquered death itself is with them to cast out fear.

C. The devil only casts the body into prison. God can cast the soul into hell.

D. Interpretation of the "ten days" varies.
1. Some believe it means innumerable persecutions. (Gen. 31:7; Num. 14:22; Neh. 4:12.)
2. Those who hold the year-day theory suggest it is ten years.
3. It could well mean only a relatively short time.

E. The crown of thorns today becomes a crown of glory tomorrow. (Matt. 24:22; 2 Cor. 4:17, 18; 1 Pet. 1:7.)

2:11—

A. Again we have admonition to LISTEN to the Spirit's message.

B. If one chances to be killed for the testimony of Jesus it makes no difference for he is then immune to the second death.

C. The last enemy to be conquered is death; then comes true life! (Matt. 10:22; 1 Cor. 15:26.)

D. The second death is the lake of fire. (Rev. 20:14.)

2:12—

A. The spelling Pergamos is feminine, Pergamum is neuter and is more common.

B. Pergamos or Pergamum had a very illustrious history, a capital for almost 400 years.

233

C. It was built upon a high and majestic hill giving a panoramic view.

D. It had a library second only to Alexandria with about 200,000 parchment rolls.

E. It was here that parchment was first used.

F. This city also had much pagan worship.
   1. There was a giant altar to *Zeus* with continuously burning sacrifices.
   2. *Asclepios*, the god of healing, had the emblem of a serpent.

G. Pergamos was the first city in Asia to become a center of *Caesar worship*.

H. The sharp sword belonging to Christ and coming out of his mouth is certainly the Word of God. (Heb. 4:12; Eph. 6:17.)
   1. The Word of God will bare the soul and destroy the wicked.
   2. At the same time it will protect the interest of the righteous.

I. The Roman governor had the "right of the sword" but Christ's sword is far more effective.

2:13—

A. We begin to suspect Christ is going to say, "I know thy works" to each of the seven churches. (Check it out.)

B. Though Christians are only sojourners the word here used means permanent abode.

C. Sometimes it is easier to run away than to be a Christian where Satan's seat is.
   1. The word *martus* from which martyr comes could also be translated witness.
   2. To be a witness for Christ in those days was often synonymous with martyrdom.

D. The phrase "where Satan dwelleth" may mean at least three different things.
   1. The general abundance of false and pagan religion.
   2. The serpent emblem so closely reminiscent of the serpent in Eden.
   3. The Satanic influence of a religion which required men to say "Caesar is Lord."

E. These people were proud of the name CHRISTIAN and would not deny it.

F. Little is known about Antipas except that he had been brought to death by Satan's power.

2:14—

A. Again the Church is a mixture of the good and the bad.
B. They have allowed persons to remain among them who place stumbling blocks in their way.
C. The stumbling blocks were in the form of advice to:
1. Eat meat sacrificed to idols.
2. Commit fornication. (See Numbers 25:1, 2; 31:16 for Balaam.)

2:15—

A. Pernicious doctrine such as that of the Nicolaitanes is dangerous to entire areas since it spreads from congregation to congregation.
B. When the Christian starts on the way he is to be *Hagois* or separated and sanctified. (2 Cor. 6:17.)
C. What God hates in Ephesus he also hates in Pergamos.

2:16—

A. Lack of action will bring sorrow.
B. The sword is not for all—only for the Nicolaitanes.
C. God will destroy those who destroy his flock.
D. Notice it is with the sword of the Word they are destroyed.

2:17—

A. Again the message is for those who are spiritually discerning.
B. The primary message on overcoming is to the Church at Pergamos.
C. Nevertheless the message seems to be addressed to *any* who have spiritual ears.
D. By refusing to fill himself at the feasts of the heathen the Christian becomes eligible for the hidden manna.
E. The hidden manna may well be Christ himself.
1. There are stories of manna which was hidden in Old Testament times.
2. When the Messiah came he was expected to reveal its location.
3. The spiritual nourishment of Christ shall always be hidden to the carnal-minded.
4. Christ is the bread of life to them that come to him. (John 6:31-58.)
F. There are three explanations of the white stone which merit our attention.
1. A white stone of acquital was given to indicate a verdict of not guilty for accused criminals.

235

2. The white stone may be the pure and solid character of the *new* man.
3. The white stone may represent special access to Jehovah.
   a. People of that time carried anything from a pebble to a precious gem for access to their gods. b. They considered it more effective if only they knew the name of the God.

G. The new name also has various explanations.
1. B.W. Johnson says that any pondering is useless since it comes only after a man overcomes and cannot be known in this life. He believes that it implies the new relationship to God and Christ in the glorified state. Like Abram's new name Abraham this new name would be used in a new era of glorification.
2. Adam Clarke believes the new name is *child of God*. Only God's children could understand its value.
3. Hendrickson states emphatically that the new name is CHRIST.
   a. The priests of the Old Testament wore a miter on their forehead with the name of Jehovah. HOLY TO JEHOVAH. b. The mark of the beast is to be written upon the forehead of the unbelievers. (Rev. 20:4.) c. The Father's new name will be written on the foreheads of those who overcome. (Rev. 3:12; 14:1.)

2:18—

A. Thyatira was the least important of the seven cities, yet the longest letter was written to them.
B. It was a city in a valley connecting two other valleys.
C. A city with many trade guilds each having its own god.
D. The city from which Lydia came. (Acts 16:14.)
1. She was a seller of purple.
2. This may have been the beginning of the church at Thyatira.
E. The idolatry and reveling of the trade guilds put great pressure upon Christians.
F. The description of Christ sounds like the messenger of Daniel 10:6: The penetrating eyes; the beautiful feet.

2:19—

A. Charity, faith, service and patience explain the type of works.
B. They come in pairs: Service follows charity or love; faith leads to patience or endurance.

C. It is an unusual church which is not in need of revival, and whose works grow greater.

2:20—

A. Jezebel may have been only a symbolic name for spiritual fornication. See 1 Kings 16:31; 18:4, 13, 19.
B. It seems more likely that Jezebel was a real woman with strong influence.
   1. She is called a prophetess.
      a. Old Testament prophetesses include Miriam (Ex. 15:20); Deborah (Judges 4:4). b. New Testament prophetesses include Anna (Luke 2:36), and the daughters of Philip (Acts 21:9).
   2. Like Jezebel of old she destroyed God's people.
      a. She taught them to commit fornication. (Isa. 54:5; Jer. 3:20; 2 Cor. 11:1-2; Eph. 5:25; 1 Cor. 6:15, 16.) b. She taught them to eat meat sacrificed to idols. (1 Cor. 8; Acts 15:28, 29.)
C. Jezebel was not one to let the Church get in the way of her "business interests."

2:21—

A. Jezebel and hers are going to run out of time.
B. God is longsuffering but he will punish those who persist.

2:22—

A. Jezebel will find that her bed is uncomfortable and very crowded.
B. There is even now time for repentance.

2:23—

A. The proceeds of her fornication shall come to destruction.
B. The reins or kidneys were the seat of emotion in Hebrew thought. Compare Jeremiah 11:20.
C. The heart was the center of reason in their thought.
D. God was able to see through this outwardly flourishing church to the canker inside.
   1. Sometimes crowded churches are simply hungry for entertainment.
   2. People sometimes want to be petted and soothed rather than challenged.
   3. There is a great difference between Jezebel's club and a healthy congregation.
E. We shall be rewarded according to our works.

2:24—

A. Apparently some had resisted the teachings of this false prophetess.

B. The real Christian knows the "deep things of God."

C. Jezebel and her followers appear to have felt that one must know the "deep things of Satan."

1. Occasionally one hears someone say, "I can speak with authority about this sin because I have overcome it."

2. It does not follow that one should expose himself to produce greater victories.

D. The burdens that the church at Thyatira will have because of Jezebel will be enough without God adding more.

2:25—

A. The Christian must never fall backward.

B. His life must overcome and transform others rather than being conformed to a Jezebelian world.

2:26—

A. The power of a faithful Christian shall extend to heathen nations.

B. Again we have our question whether this ruling comes during life or after death.

2:27—

A. Christ is given this promise in Psalm 2:8, 9.

B. The kingdoms of this world are to become the kingdom of Christ. (Rev. 11:15.)

C. The servants of the Lamb shall reign for ever and ever. (Rev. 22:5.)

D. The potters of Thyatira knew the mastery of the iron rod over the vessel of clay.

2:28—

A. This may be an indication that the rulership of verse 27 is through shedding the light of Christ.

B. Christ is the morning star. (Rev. 22:16.)

C. Again we may see a promise of complete union and fellowship with the true Light. See Daniel 12:3.

2:29—

A. The choice is laid before the members at Thyatira.

B. It comes to us no less.

C. Will we know the depths of Satan or the purity of the Morning Star?

Chapter 3

3:1—

A. Seven hundred years before Sardis had been a proud and rich capital city.

B. It was situated on a spur off a mountain chain and was thus nearly impregnable.

C. The hill was composed of porous rock through which Cyrus' soldiers crawled and conquered.

D. Later Sardis forgot its lesson and history repeated itself.

E. Still later an earthquake suddenly destroyed much of the city.

F. Sardis could then understand the warning that Christ would come "as a thief in the night."

G. The Seven Spirits of God are the source of life, important to Sardis which was dying.

H. The Christ carried the light-giving stars, important because Sardis' star had about set.

I. Sardis carried the life-giving name "Christian" but God knew that they were dead.

J. It is quite possible to be dead while alive. See the following: 1 Timothy 5:6; Luke 15:24; Romans 6:13; Ephesians 2:1-5.

K. Sin may kill: the *will*, causing us to do that which we would not; the *attitude*, causing us to revel in that which we despised; the sense of beauty, turning the desire for fulfillment into lust for power, the desire to serve into worldly ambition and the desire for love into unbridled passion.

3:2—

A. Watchfulness is taught in many portions of the New Testament.
   1. Stay awake. (Rom. 13:11.)
   2. Watch the devil. (1 Pet. 5:8.)
   3. Avoid falling to temptation. (Matt. 26:41.)
   4. Stay sober. (1 Thess. 5:6.)
   5. Watch for false teachers. (Acts 20:29-31.)
   6. Be prepared for Christ.
   [Note: Quotation from Augustine "The last day is a secret, that every day may be watched."]

B. They still have a little life and work going on which they must build up.

C. Their works are begun but not finished.
   1. The word translated perfect generally means complete and pleasing to God as it is used in the New Testament.

239

2. Sardis' works were incomplete with little being accomplished toward completion.

3:3—

A. They had received the gospel readily and joyfully. Do they not remember?

B. They must seize what little is left of their beginning and see that it does not escape.

C. They must repent of their lifelessness and wake up.
   1. Note that they were not bothered with heresies.
   2. Heresy is associated with mental activity, and they had little.

D. They should wake up abruptly if Christ comes as a thief in the midst of their slumber.

E. If one walks arm in arm with Jesus there is little likelihood of being surprised.

3:4—

A. Where other congregations had a few evil persons Sardis was defiled *except* for a few.

B. Apparently God sees our souls either clothed in purity or soiled with sin. (James 1:27.)

C. God knew the *names* of the faithful.

D. If we keep our garments clean here we shall have new white ones later.

E. If we walk proud and clean with the Lord here we shall walk with him later in our white robes. (Enoch had this experience.) See Isaiah 61:10; Revelation 6:11; 7:9, 13, 14; 19:8; Genesis 5:22-24; Matthew 22:1-14.

3:5—

A. The bright clothing reminds us that "the righteous shall shine forth as the sun." (Matt. 13:43.)

B. God himself is said to be clothed with light. (Psalm 104:1, 2.)

C. Solomon said, "Let thy garments be white." (Eccl. 9:8.)

D. Some of the words associated with white garments are purity, festivity and victory.

E. Names on the roll books of earth mean little compared with God's book of life.
   1. Heaven is the greatest city of all.
   2. Only those whose names are in the book of life will enter. (Rev. 21:27.)
      a. If the sins remain the name is blotted out. b. If the

240

sins are blotted out the name remains. c. Both cannot be recorded in God's book.

F. If we praise the name of Christ here he will praise ours to the heavenly host, and to God.

G. Men fail in their promises—God never does.

3:6—

A. The things written here as warnings are for the Sardis church.

B. No man at any time may escape this same advice.

3:7—

A. The word Philadelphia is taken from two Greek words meaning brotherly love.

B. Ancient Philadelphia received its name from the love of Attalus for his brother Eumenes.

C. Philadelphia is the youngest of the seven cities.

D. It was located on soil formed from volcanic rock and was thus extremely fertile.

E. Earthquakes were common, leading to considerable insecurity.
   1. Note that Sardis was geographically secure, yet spiritually asleep.
   2. Philadelphia was insecure, but in much better spiritual shape.
   3. Too often temporal security leads men to spiritual risks.

F. Philadelphia had acted as a missionary for the spread of the Greek language.

G. This church stood when many of the others lay in ruins.

H. There are still a number of nominal Christians in this location today.

I. Christ is *completely* HOLY—set apart—hagio. Compare Hebrews 7:26.

J. Christ is the way, the truth and the life, particularly as he pours forth the revelation produced here.

K. The key of David is related to the governorship of God's people.
   1. Eliakim was once given this key. (Isa. 22:22.)
   2. Christ is now governor of spiritual Israel. (See Matthew 16:18, 19; Luke 1:32, 33.)

L. No man or set of men may alter the lock or change the keys for entering the Church!

3:8—

A. The one who possesses the key of David had opened the door.

241

B. The door is an entrance to greater opportunity.
  1. When Christ died the veil of the temple was rent symbolizing the opportunity of entering the Church and Heaven.
  2. But even beyond this the door of opportunity is opened for us if we will see it. (Paul saw this open door.) (2 Cor. 2:12.)
C. When one uses the little strength which he has God will add more. (Parable of the talents.)
D. These had not denied Christ's name even under pressure from the Jews. (See the next verse.)
E. They went beyond confession of his name and kept his Word.
F. Always the reward for serving God is the opportunity for greater service.
  1. To some this seems a foolish cycle.
  2. To the truly wise it is the reason for living. (Rev. 4:11.)

3:9—

A. Jews who deny Christ are no longer God's chosen people.
B. This type of person will be placed in a position of subservience to the circumcised of heart.
C. If God be for us who can be against us?

3:10—

A. They had been faithful in smaller trials.
B. Jesus would keep them in the greatest hour of trial.
C. This hour of temptation was not centuries later.
  1. The Christians at Philadelphia were to be protected *during* it.
  2. They were being braced for terrible persecution and also for punishment that God was to bring upon the Roman world.
  3. At the same time Jesus will keep every man in the raging conflict between good and evil—if that man keeps his Word.

3:11—

A. They must maintain the strength they have and add to it.
B. Once again we remind that the coming of Christ means different things to various people.
  1. A crown is laid up for those who hold fast and overcome.
  2. The crown may be taken away—let him that thinketh he standeth take heed lest he fall.
C. The Bible tells of many who lost their place to someone else.
  1. Esau. 2. Reuben. 3. Saul. 4. Judas. 5. Jews.

3:12—

A. We are all living stones, some are to be pillars.

B. Pillars are at the same time useful, beautiful and durable. Compare Galatians 2:9.

C. If one is a *pillar* he is immovable and will not be a failing portion of the house of God.

D. We are priests of God and the priests of old wore an inscription, "Holiness to the Lord."

E. We are members of the Church of Christ which is the beginning of the City of God.

F. We shall have the new name of Christ.
1. Christ has had many names: Immanuel, Prince of Peace, Savior, etc.
2. In heaven we shall be married to him and receive his new name.
3. The name is as yet a secret. (Rev. 19:12.)

3:13—

A. This is not idle talk.

B. God's aye is aye and his nay is nay.

3:14—

A. Laodicea was named after a woman, Laodice.

B. It was located near warm springs on the most important road in Asia.

C. Laodicea was:
1. Financially secure.
2. A center of clothing manufacture.
3. A medical center which made eye salve.
4. Supposedly beyond need for Jehovah.

D. The Laodicean church is the only one who receives absolutely no praise.

E. The Amen is the *Be it so* with no words wasted. (Translated *Verily, Verily* in John 1:51.)

F. A faithful witness must:
1. Observe personally.
2. Declare accurately.
3. Speak clearly.

G. Christ fits all three of these in the present letter.

H. Christ was present and instrumental in the creation of heaven and earth. See John 1:3; Colossians 1:15, 18; Hebrews 1:2.

I. Also Christ is the beginning of the new creation.

J. The Laodiceans were in need of being recreated and Christ could help.

K. All things begin and end in Christ, the Alpha and the Omega, the beginning and the end.

3:15—

A. God knows the degree of zealousness within our heart.

B. The words used here mean *very* hot and *very* cold.

C. Intensity is more easily overcome than indifference.

D. Antagonism is at least a degree of attention.

E. Evangelism today must contend with massive indifference.

3:16—

A. Cold food or hot food is appetizing whereas tepid food can be nauseating.

B. The Laodiceans were familiar with warm water spewing from the springs.

C. Some say it was tepid when it arrived in the city.

D. The Holy Spirit has no difficulty getting the point across.

3:17—

A. A man approaching Laodicea would have observed fantastic prosperity.

B. Jesus, the true witness, saw the most abject poverty.

C. Rich in material goods, yet poor in faith.

D. A center of clothing manufacture, yet naked.

E. A manufacturer of eye salve, yet blind to their own condition..

3:18—

A. The treasures laid up in heaven by righteous deeds is much more valuable than yellow metal. See Isaiah 55:1.

B. Nakedness was a greater shame in Biblical times, and fine clothing a greater honor. (Nah. 3:5; Ezek. 16:37-39; Mic. 1:8, 11; Luke 15:22.)

C. White raiment of righteous deeds of the saints.

D. Without the light of the world no man can see.

E. Before progress can be made one must be able to see himself which Laodicea could not do.

F. An ugly character cannot be covered with beautiful clothing.

3:19—

A. God's chastening should be prized.

B. Discipline is a vital part of the Biblical plan.

Proverbs 13:24; 23:13, 14; 27:6; 29:15, 17; Psalm 94:12; Job 5:17; 1 Corinthians 11:32; Hebrews 12:5-8.

C. When God leaves a man alone it is a last resort. (Hos. 4:17.)

D. The athlete, the scholar and the child all profit by discipline.

E. God's chastisement is an illumination of conditions more than a revealing of wrath.

F. He had said I *will* spue thee out; there was still time for repentance.

3:20—

A. Jesus had been expelled.

B. The Son of God stands as close as the door of *your* heart.

C. There is a sense of tender affection in the picture. See Song of Solomon 5:2-6.

D. Christianity is the only world religion in which God seeks out man.

E. Jesus does not break in: he must be invited by an open door.

F. The word used here indicated an unhurried evening meal with intimate friendship.

3:21—

A. Christ sits upon *God's* throne.

B. He invites us to sit upon *his* throne.

C. Therefore we have invitation to sit upon God's throne.

D. This was the most wicked of the churches, yet it received the highest promise.

E. Therefore *whosoever will* may come.

F. The promise extends as it has before only to those whose faith conquers and overcomes.

G. One sits upon a throne to judge. (1 Cor. 6:1-5; Matt. 19:28.)

3:22—

A. This means you, Laodicea.

B. This means you, honest seeker of the truth.

NOTE: The seven churches are seven lampstands or candlesticks. The darkness is attempting to snuff out their light. It succeeds to varying extent today as it did in those early Christian days. CHRIST WILL OVERCOME! Will YOU be a part of the victory, or will you be found faint and fallen by the wayside?

245

THINGS CHRIST SAW IN HIS CHURCHES

The Good	The Evil
Ephesus	
Patience	Left first love
Labor	
Testing of false teachers	
Endurance	
Hates the Nicolaitanes	
Smyrna	
Richness of spirit	Hypocritical Jews
Willingness to withstand hypocrisy of the Jews	
Pergamos	
Holding fast Christ's name	Permitted false teachers
	To teach
	Eat meat offered to idols
	Commit fornication
	Nicolaitanes tolerated
Thyatira	
Charity	Jezebel permitted to remain
Service	Fornication
Faith	Meat sacrificed to idols
Increasing works	Proud of knowing the depths of Satan
Sardis	
The few pure among many defiled	Nearly dead
Philadelphia	
Use of opportunities	Nothing
Hast not denied his name	
Kept his word	
Laodicea	
Nothing	Naked
	Blind
	Poor
	Indifferent

It might be well for us to include the following compilation of scriptures and thoughts on overcoming as expressed in the New Testament.

246

THOUGHTS ON OVERCOMING

1. *What is meant by overcoming?*
   A. It is to resist Satan. (1 John 2:13, 14.)
   B. It is to do battle with the Antichrist. (1 John 4:4.)
   C. It is to die to worldly desires and be born again. (1 John 5:4, 5.)
   D. To overcome is to follow Christ. (Rev. 3:21.)
   E. It is to escape corruption. (2 Pet. 2:19, 20.)

2. *We have certain assistance in overcoming.*
   A. Jesus set an example.
      1. He said "I have overcome the world" just before he died.
      2. Satan is said to have *fallen* twice.
         a. At the casting out of devils. (Luke 10:17-19.)   b. At the crucifixion. (Luke 12:31, 32.)
   B. The martyrs of Revelation set an example.
      1. They were slain for the Word. (Rev. 6:9-11.)
      2. They would not worship the beast nor receive his mark. Thus they overcame him. (Rev. 13:7, 15-17.)
   C. The blood of the Lamb helps overcome. (Rev. 12:11.) (Even unto death.)

3. *There are precious rewards for overcoming.*
   A. Eat of the tree of life. (Rev. 2:7.)
   B. Shall not be hurt of the second death. (Rev. 2:11.)
   C. He shall have hidden manna—a white stone and a new name. (Rev. 2:17.)
   D. If he endures to the end he shall have power over the nations. (Rev. 2:26.)
      1. Rule with a rod of iron.
      2. Possess the morning star.
   E. Shall walk with Christ. (Rev. 3:5.)
      1. Dressed in white.
      2. With name written in the book of life.
   F. Becomes a pillar in God's temple. (Rev. 3:12.)
      1. Names will be written on the pillar.
      2. There will be three of them.
         a. Name of God's city.   b. Christ's new name.   c. Name of God.
   G. He shall sit with Christ on his throne. (Rev. 3:21.)

4. *To fail is to fall to the Lake of Fire.* (Rev. 20:15.)

Chapter 4
4:1—
A. John had been told to write the things which he had seen, the things which now are, and things which shall be hereafter; he is now ready for the things which must be hereafter. Compare Revelation 1:19.
B. In chapters 1-3 Christ walked among the lampstands evaluating their works.
C. Now in chapters 4-7 Christ opens the sealed book.
D. A new vision now begins to appear to John.
E. The door simply indicates a means of entry to heaven.
F. Three doors are mentioned in chapters 3 and 4 of Revelation.
   1. The door of opportunity. (3:8.)
   2. The door of the heart. (3:20.)
   3. The door of heaven. (4:1.)
G. The heavens open for important occasions.
   1. Visions. (Ezek. 1:1.)
   2. Descent of the Spirit. (Mark 1:10.)
   3. The coming of Christ. (Rev. 19:11.)
H. The voice may be the voice he heard in 1:10 or it may just be the first voice he heard from the opened heavens.
I. When God speaks people are reminded of trumpets and thunder. (Sinai)
J. So we are invited along with John to pass through the door and stand in awe.

4:2—
A. He had to be lifted above the powers of mortal men to view this scene.
B. Others who had seen the throne of God include
   1. Stephen. (Acts 7:56.)
   2. Ezekiel. (Ezek. 1:26.)
   3. Isaiah. (Isa. 6:1.)
C. The importance of the throne here is shown by the use of the word "throne" 17 times in chapters 4 and 5.
D. It is interesting to compare the entire scene with the Old Testament Holy of Holies. (2 Chron. 3:8; 1 Kings 6:16-38; Ex. 25:22.)

4:3—
A. Each of the stones mentioned emit a different kind of light.
   1. The jasper was like a diamond, clear as crystal. (Rev. 21:11.)

2. The sardine was red.
3. The emerald is green.

B. These stones were also found:
1. On the breastplate of the high priest. (Ex. 28:17.)
2. On the king of Tyre. (Ezek. 28:13.)
3. In the foundations of the Holy City. (Rev. 21:19.)

C. John describes only the radiant glory of God, not his form.

D. God is often directly associated with light.
1. He is light and in him there is no darkness. (1 John 1:5.)
2. He is the father of lights. (James 1:17.)

E. An emerald rainbow reminds us of God's promise of peace in Genesis. The God of Peace.

F. Ezekiel also saw the rainbow. (Ezek. 1:28.)

4:4—

A. The twenty-four elders could be:
1. Permanent heavenly spiritual beings. (Isa. 24:23.)
2. The elders of the 24 courses of priests. (1 Chron. 24:5.)
3. The twelve apostles and the twelve patriarchs.
   (Later these make up the gates and foundations of the Holy City.)
4. They may represent all the faithful with their robes, crowns and thrones.

B. Regardless of their identity they have crowns indicating power and white robes of purity.

4:5—

A. Compare Ezekiel 1:13; Psalm 77:18; Job 37:4; Exodus 19:16 for connections between God, thunder and lightning.

B. The seven lamps here seem to be the same as the seven spirits mentioned in Revelation 1:14.

C. This number seven has been associated with completeness from the creation which required seven days, including God's rest.

D. Thus the seven lamps or spirits burning with fire may be the complete and perfect Holy Spirit.

4:6—

A. The sea of glass being crystal clear gives the impression of an area of purity surrounding God and preventing the approach of any evil.

B. The word translated beasts here is not the same word as beast in Revelation 13:1.
1. The beast of Revelation 13:1 carries an ominous meaning.

249

2. The word used here could as well be translated as "living beings."

C. The beasts seem to move from the midst of the throne to the immediately surrounding area.

D. The many eyes surely indicate unusual powers of observation.

4:7—

A. Similar creatures are found in: Ezekiel 1, 10; Isaiah 6; Genesis 3:24.

B. In the book of Revelation these creatures are mentioned again and again. (Rev. 4:6-8; 5:6-8; 5:14; 6:1; 6:7; 7:11; 14:3; 15:7; 19:4.)

C. There are many similarities between the creatures of Ezekiel and those of John:
   1. Four living ones.
   2. Man, lion, ox and eagle.
   3. Surround the throne.
   4. Studded with eyes.
   5. Multiple wings.
   6. A rainbow present.

D. Ezekiel called his creatures cherubim. (Ezek. 10:20, 22.)
   1. Cherubim is the plural of cherub.
   2. Cherubim were found in the presence of God at several times.
      a. In Solomon's temple. (1 Kings 6:25.) b. On the veil separating the Holy and Most Holy. (Ex. 26:31.) c. On the mercy seat or lid of the ark. (Ex. 25:18.) d. At the corners of the garden of Eden. (Gen. 3:24.) e. Either supporting or surrounding Jehovah. (Psalm 99:1.)

E. The four living creatures have been interpreted many ways.

1. Strength	1. Africa	1. Love	1. Higher animals
2. Service	2. America	2. Justice	2. Tame animals
3. Intelligence	3. Europe	3. Power	3. Wild animals
4. Swiftness	4. The Orient	4. Wisdom	4. Birds

F. Some feel the twenty-four elders represent the faithful among mankind, and the four beasts the faithful among the non-human living world.

G. They could well be permanent heavenly spiritual beings.

4:8—

A. There are differences between the creatures of Ezekiel and those of John.
   1. There are four wings in Ezekiel 1:6.
   2. Each has four faces in Ezekiel.

B. A second emphasis upon the numerous eyes reminds us of Hebrews 4:13.

C. The song praises three characteristics of God:
  1. His Holiness.
  2. His power.
  3. His everlastingness.

4:9—

A. The one who sits on the throne and lives for ever and ever is Jehovah God.

B. Regardless of the identity of the four living creatures they adore and worship God.

4:10—

A. The elders carry the picture of prestige among religious men, but with their prestige they still glorify God.

B. This will always be the attitude of true leaders of God's people.

C. All the power they possess came from God so they acknowledge it by casting their crowns before him.

4:11—

A. Note the similarity between this verse and the conclusion of the model prayer suggested by Jesus.
   "Thine is the kingdom and the power and the glory forever."

B. Whether man or beast the purpose of their creation is the pleasure of God.
  1. Real fulfillment of self will come only when our purpose is service to him.
  2. Self-glorification *must* be temporary and unsatisfying.

Chapter 5

5:1—

A. Chapter 4 had presented the eternal God seated upon his throne.

B. Chapter 5 describes the entrance of the risen Christ upon the heavenly scene.

C. The picture here is similar to that of Ezekiel 2:9, 10.

D. Ezekiel's scroll was filled with lamentations, mourning and woe.

E. The right *hand* of God is the first indication of anything more than glory and a voice.

F. The book is a scroll representing the mysteries of God. (Rev. 10:7.)

251

G. There is writing both within and on the back because there is much to reveal.

H. The seals were usually placed on the knots of strings wound around the scroll.

I. Some believe this scroll was unwound a little and another seal broken in consecutive order.

J. Seven seals would indicate complete security.

5:2—

A. A strong angel may have been an important angel, or simply one who would be able to cry out to many who needed to hear.

B. God's messages are not entrusted to anyone available.

C. If God's revelations are to be understood they must come through worthy messengers to an audience mature enough to receive them.

5:3—

A. No angel or other spiritual being in heaven was worthy.

B. No man living upon the earth met the mark.

C. Neither devil nor dead man could prevail.

D. If the book could not be opened it could not be looked upon and read.

5:4—

A. John is disappointed since he had been promised in Revelation 1:19 he would see things to come.

B. This breaking of the seals is to reveal a number of things:
   1. Protection in tribulation.
   2. Judgment upon evil-doers.
   3. Triumph of the righteous.
   4. New Heavens and a New Earth.

C. We should weep also if such mysteries remained hidden.

5:5—

A. Once again the words "Weep not" are associated with the Christ, as they were in Luke 7:13 and 8:52.

B. Men often weep before they know all the circumstances as John did in this case.

C. John is instructed to look at a LION who is about to take the stage. (Gen. 49:9, 10.)

D. Both we and John are led to look for the majestic king of beasts.

E. Though David had been cut down his root appears as the king of spiritual Israel. Compare Isaiah 11:10.

E. There is someone worthy.

5:6—

A. Is something wrong?? We look for a LION and we see a LAMB.

B. Not at all. This is the king who reigns through service and humility instead of force.

C. Over and over again Jesus is called the Lamb in Revelation and again in Acts 8:32; 1 Peter 1:19; and Isaiah 53.

D. The horns represent power or honor.
   1. They represent power in Deuteronomy 33:17; 1 Kings 22:11; Psalm 75:4.
   2. They represent honor in 1 Samuel 2:1; Psalms 89:17; 112:9; 148:14.

E. The seven eyes of God run to and fro over the whole earth in Zechariah 4:10.

F. Jesus has power and honor within his Kingdom and he knows what is happening.

5:7—

A. Past the angels, the twenty-four elders and the cherubim marches the slain Lamb to the very throne of God.

B. We are reminded of Peter's description in the sermon of Acts 2:31-35.

C. Only Jesus is worthy to reveal the mysteries of God.

D. He has proven worthy only upon completion of obedience unto death.

E. The drama rises as he prepares to open the sealed book.

F. What will happen now that Jesus has taken his place reigning at the right hand of God?

5:8—

A. Suddenly the adoration which has been directed toward God is focused upon the slain Lamb.

B. Christ takes his rightful place above the spiritual beings of both heaven and earth. (Eph. 1:20-22.)

C. The harps are connected with happiness. (Psalms 147:7; 98:5.)

D. The golden vials or bowls of incense are the prayers of the saints.
   1. As incense they provide a sweet savour to God. (Cornelius)

2. Not only the prayers of Saints of Asia, ours also! (Psalm 141:2; Rev. 8:2, 3.)

5:9—

A. There is a new song ready for the new creation.

B. New songs in Israel were often songs of deliverance.

C. It was victory over death which renders Christ worthy to open the book.

D. The twenty-four elders are among the redeemed from the earth.

E. The four living creatures may not be included in this redemption.

F. The Kingdom of Christ transcends every petty boundary between races, nations and languages.

5:10—

A. Every redeemed man becomes a son of God, a prince upon the earth, and reigns supreme.

B. It is not political or material reign but real triumph. Ex. 19:6; 1 Pet. 2:5, 9; Deut. 7:6.)

C. We reign over:
1. Self.
2. The circumstances which beset us.
3. Sin and the devil.

5:11—

A. The song moves from the cherubim to the elders to the angels and then spreads in verse 13 to every creature in the universe as it swells into a great crescendo of praise.

B. Ten thousand times ten thousand is 100 million. In addition to this there are thousands of thousands.

5:12—

A. He is to receive the same type of praise as God himself.

B. God has not stepped down from the throne. The throne now belongs to both God and the Lamb. (Rev. 22:1.)

C. It is interesting that there are seven types of adoration given here. (Complete worship)

5:13—

A. The swell of the heavenly chorus reaches from Heaven to Hades.

B. God and the Lamb reign in one perfectly harmonious picture.

C. They not only reign presently to John but they are due this praise eternally.

5:14—

A. The reader of Revelation must take comfort for God rules in the affairs of the universe. Any interruption must be temporary.

B. Regardless of what the scroll is to reveal the Lord and the Lamb are sufficient to guard the lives which we commit unto them. (2 Tim. 1:12.)

Chapter 6

6:1—

A. The Lamb is now to begin revealing the things which should shortly come to pass.

B. Seven seals are to be broken with each revealing another portion of the mystery.

C. One of the living creatures speaks with the voice of thunder because of the importance of what he is to reveal.

D. The words *and see* are not found in many of the ancient manuscripts.

E. If this is the correct reading this may be a command to the horse and rider rather than John.

6:2—

A. We have seen the conditions of the seven churches. Now we shall examine the difficulties which they must overcome to receive the promises.

B. Again we find similar pictures in the Old Testament. (Ezek. 5:17; Zech. 1:8-10; 6:1-8.)

C. There are at least three explanations of the white horse and his rider.
1. He could be the lust for conquest and victory.
2. He could be Jesus Christ with his conquering Gospel.
3. He could be the victorious Roman Empire at its zenith.

D. Those who believe it to be the Christ and his Gospel see this horse as the same mentioned in Revelation 19:11-15.

E. We pause for a moment to present some arguments for and against the position that this is the Christ and his cause.
1. Arguments in favor of this position.
    a. It is supposed to be a fulfillment of Psalm 45:4-7. b. Christ has just been described as the conquering Lamb. (Chapter 5.) c. The picture seems to agree with that of Revelation 19:11. d. Both the color of the horse and the crown worn indicate Christ. e. Christ is said to bring a sword in Matthew 10:34. f. The rider on the

white horse in Zechariah, chapter 1, may be Christ. (Zech. 1:8.)

2. Arguments against this position.
   a. There is a discrepancy in the details of this picture and that of Revelation 19:11. b. The entire set of seven seem to be woes. If this be the cause of Christ it breaks the unity of the picture. c. It appears inappropriate for Christ to be both the Lamb of God who is breaking the seals and at the same time the rider of the white horse revealed by the first seal.

F. We do know that the Bible uses the symbols of verse 2 to mean certain things.
   1. The horse is normally a warrior in the Bible and not a beast of burden.
   2. The bow is a symbol of power to conquer.
   3. The crown represents authority to reign.

G. It is wise here to compare Matthew 24; Mark 13; Luke 21.

H. It does seem clear that we have a picture intended to contrast with the complete harmony of worship found in chapter 5.

I. Note that with the breaking of the seventh seal in chapter 12 we find Satan cast out of heaven as though the entire vision is a depiction of Satan's effort at rebellion and resulting failure.

6:3—

A. Each of the cherubim is to summon another horse of a different color.

B. What new event will now be unfolded?

6:4—

A. The sword this time does not come from the mouth and the results are not those of the sword of the Word.

B. Again we shall present a set of three explanations for the red horse and rider.
   1. This red horse represents the bloodshed which naturally follows the lust to conquer.
   2. This is the internal strife beginning to eat away at the Roman Empire.
   3. This is the blood of persecuted Christians.

C. In any event the sword is a symbol of strife and not of peace.

D. Proper human relationships have dissolved in hatred and murder.

E. How tragic it is that men cannot or will not see the folly of leaving the worship and service of God for their own ways.

6:5—

A. The third cherubim calls forth his horse. What will be the consequences?

B. Black is the color of sadness, sorrow and mourning.

C. Here are the corresponding three explanations of the black horse.

   1. It could be the injustice which always accompanies strife.
   2. It could be the famine which existed within the Roman Empire as a result of internal division.
   3. It could be the poverty and famine which afflict Christians while their persecutors live in affluence.

   (Note: The result of persecution against the cause of Christ may at first strike primarily the Christians. Later as the corruption spreads the persecutors themselves are struck by the end results of their own foolishness.)

D. The balances are a sign that something is about to be weighed.

6:6—

A. A measure was about a quart.

B. The word penny is misleading. It was the denarius which amounted to a whole day's wages.

C. If a man fed his family the undesirable barley they could just barely hold body and soul together.

D. Do not hurt the oil or the wine may mean at least two things.

   1. Since there is such a scarcity of food one must not waste or damage anything.
   2. The rich shall have their luxuries of oil and wine, etc. while the poor starve.

E. During famine, food is doled out by weight. See Leviticus 26:26; Ezekiel 4:16, 17; Matthew 24:7.

6:7—

A. The last of the four living creatures calls forth his horse and rider.

B. We are reminded of the ancient story of Pandora's box. What will now be released?

6:8—

A. This pale color is not the white of the first horse. This one has the pallid color of the sick unto death.

B. The three interpretations follow.

1. It could be the slaughter which naturally follows conquest, division and injustice.
2. It could be the millions who died of starvation and disease in the Roman Empire following their internal wars.
3. It could be the death of both believers and unbelievers resulting from persecution of the saints.

C. The four calamities brought by the pale horse are the same as the judgments described in Ezekiel 14:21. See also Ezekiel 5:17; Jeremiah 15:2, 3.

D. John Hinds believes the four horses and riders cover a period of history from A.D. 64 to A.D. 284.

At this point I would like to pull together and summarize briefly the three different schemes of interpretation we have been comparing above.

No. 1

God has just been pictured reigning with the Lamb in heaven with everything in harmony. Selfish lust for victory and conquest then rises up to challenge God's supreme rulership. The natural consequence of this is disappearance of peace from the earth in conflict between men. As result of wasting their energies upon strife rather than productive labor there arises a scarcity of the necessities of life. The end result is the loss of life for a large portion of the men on earth.

No. 2

The Roman Empire reached such a zenith of power shortly after John wrote that it was difficult for the people back home to believe the rate of its victorious conquests. Within a short time after this the tide began to change. Civil war began to break out and racked the empire. This resulted in famine and hardship, and was followed closely by pestilence and death of millions.

No. 3

Christ has just been crowned the conquering Lamb and seated at the right hand of God in heaven. Now his cause moves out to ride over the earth. Soon opposition bathes the land in blood as severe persecution takes place. Christians are barely able to continue alive while their oppressors live in luxury. Not only Christians but non-Christians lose their lives in large numbers.

Note: Whether it be the seven churches of Asia, the Church throughout the Christian dispensation, or the individual Christian, a pattern can be seen. The crown of life does not come without overcoming. Christ reigns. His cause rides into the lives of men. The masses reject and fight against the truth even to bloodshed. When

Christ is rejected men starve to death both physically and spiritually. Tragically some Christians lose their lives while this needless battle rages between Christ and antiChrist!

6:9—

A. In verse 8 death and Hades had claimed one-fourth of all men.

B. These souls under the altar seem to be the unfortunate Christians who have lost their lives for the cause of Christ.

C. There was an altar for *sacrifices* in the earthly tabernacle, also in heaven.

D. These saints have been sacrificed on the altar of the cause of Christ.

E. As did Abel's blood cry out, so does theirs from the foot of the altar. (Lev. 17:11-14; 4:7; 2 Tim. 4:6; Psalms 79:5-10.)

6:10—

A. Tertullian has a very vivid statement about his feelings when God takes vengeance on them that know not the Lord. See Barclay.

B. This appears at first to be an unchristian spirit.

C. The question, however, is not *whether* vengeance will be taken. It is only *How long?*

D. Vengeance belongs to God. (Heb. 10:30; Luke 18:7, 8.)

E. Notice the souls cry out while men still dwell upon the earth.

F. Later we shall see these same souls avenged.

6:11—

A. The white robes are a partial consolation while they wait.

B. Others must have an opportunity to accept or reject the cause of the Lord before the plan is complete.
Interesting references here are: Matthew 24:14; Mark 13:10; Daniel 12:4; Luke 21:12-14.

C. Is it possible from this verse that God intends a number of faithful children to be brought up, defying the efforts of Satan and bringing to completion the size family he intended in Eden? See Ephesians 1:9-11.

6:12—

A. Other references to the shaking of the earth are: Amos 8:8; Ezekiel 38:19; Joel 2:10; Haggai 2:6; Matthew 24:29.

B. The sun and the moon are disturbed in the following. (Amos 8:8, 9; Isa. 13:13; 50:3; Ezek. 32:7; Joel 2:31; Luke 23:45; Jer. 4:28.) Compare Luke 23:45 with Acts 2:20.

C. Those who have been involved in severe earthquakes tell of bloodcurdling fear.

D. It is impossible to read the above references without making the connection between this verse and the Great and Terrible Day of the Lord.

6:13—

A. Foy Wallace believes the stars which fall are deposed Jewish officials.

B. See Isaiah 34:4 and Matthew 24:29.

C. Overriding discussion of symbolism is the magnitude of the entire scene. The universe is shivering under the awesome power of God.

6:14—

A. Other verses speaking of the folding of the heavens are: Isaiah 13:13; Isaiah 34:4; Psalm 102:25, 26.

B. Some believe the entire picture here to be the upheaval and disintegration of political powers, the mountains and islands being seats of power. Compare Jeremiah 4:24; Nahum 1:5, 6; Isaiah 2:2.

C. Whether the interpretation be literal or symbolic, the rolling up of the heavens is a joy to the righteous and a horror to the evil-doer.

6:15—

A. There are six calamities under the sixth seal, and there are in this verse six classes of men who are caused to tremble:
   1. Supreme rulers.
   2. The Princes under them.
   3. Mediocre officers.
   4. Rich men.
   5. Strong men.
   6. Lower classes.

B. Men find neither political organizations nor physical mountains and caves fit places to hide from the wrath of the Lamb.

6:16—

A. This whole description sounds like Christ's description of the destruction of Jerusalem. (Luke 23:26-30; Isa. 2:1, 2, 10, 17-21.)

B. This is the day of the Lord and God describes the victims thus.
   1. Like a woman in labor. (Isa. 13:6, 8.)
   2. Inhabitants tremble. (Joel 2:1.)

3. God will witness. (Mic. 1:1-4.)
4. A refiner's fire. (Mal. 3:1-3.)
5. Who can abide? (Joel 2:11.)
6. Mountains cover us! (Hos. 10:8; Luke 23:30.)

6:17—

A. Shakespeare once said, "War is a game, which were their subjects wise, kings would not play at."
B. Under the above set of conditions the kings will be sorry they played anyway.
C. Since the Garden of Eden men have felt they could hide from God. In this great day there will be no place that even seems appropriate.
D. What an odd picture of the *wrath* of the *Lamb*. Even now it is presented in anticipation of our own edification.
E. There is still *one more seal*. Are things to become even worse?

Chapter 7

7:1—

A. There is a pause in the tribulation of the sixth seal.
B. God's angels hold back the winds of destruction. See Psalm 83:18; Amos 1:4; Jeremiah 49:36.
C. The four corners of the earth are mentioned in Isaiah 11:12 and Ezekiel 7:2.
   1. They do not imply stupidity on the part of the writer.
   2. What they do imply is the breadth of God's control.

7:2—

A. John's vision is occurring in heaven, the angel ascends from earth, and from the east.
B. The seal of the living God may do a number of things.
   1. A seal prevents tampering. (Dan. 6:17; Matt. 27:66.)
   2. A seal shows ownership. (Song of Sol. 8:6.)
   3. A seal certifies quality.
C. He is the *living* God:
   1. Not made of wood or stone.
   2. Both powerful and effective.
   3. Embodying both a threat of death and a promise of life.
D. The loud voice tells us of the urgency of postponing the destructive winds.

7:3—

A. Ezekiel 9:4-8 required a pause in the punishment of Jerusalem until foreheads are marked.

B. God seals Christians. (2 Cor. 1:21, 22; Eph. 4:30; Eph. 1:12-14.)

C. Paul spoke of the seal of his apostleship. (1 Cor. 9:1, 2.)

D. B. W. Johnson thinks the seal could as well be the confession as it is of public nature as is the seal on the forehead.

E. The slaves of that time were often branded on the forehead with the owner's name.

F. Revelation 13:16 informs us that the beast also caused a mark to be placed on the forehead or on the right hand.

7:4—

A. John hears the number rather than seeing them as they are on earth, he in heaven.

B. The sealing does not exempt them from the coming terror, it brings them through.
Note: The seal of the Spirit will bring any man through tribulation.

C. The hundred and forty-four thousand are not all the redeemed, only the ones from the twelve tribes, and this may be only from the ones living at the time.

D. An argument can be made that the hundred and forty-four thousand is the church.
   1. They were sealed. (Rev. 7:14; Eph. 4:30.)
   2. They were redeemed. (Rev. 14:4; Eph. 1:7; Eph. 1:14; Rom. 8:23.)
   3. They were without blemish. (Rev. 14:5; Eph. 5:27.)

E. This does not appear to be all of spiritual Israel because there is a multitude in white robes in addition to these.

F. Some believe these to be:
   1. Those alive at the time John writes as opposed to the faithful before and after.
   2. Others see this as those responding from Judaism as opposed to the multitude coming from all the earth.

G. The twelve tribes mentioned in three comparative lists follow.

Genesis 35	Ezekiel 48	Revelation 7
Reuben	Reuben	Reuben
Simeon	Simeon	Simeon
Levi	Ephraim	Levi
Judah	Judah	Judah
Issachar	Issachar	Issachar
Zebulun	Zebulun	Zebulon
Dan	Dan	Manasseh

Genesis 35	Ezekiel 48	Revelation 7
Naphtali	Naphtali	Naphtali
Gad	Gad	Gad
Asher	Asher	Asher
Joseph	Manasseh	Joseph
Benjamin	Benjamin	Benjamin

H. Dan may have been left out because this tribe became very idolatrous. See Genesis 49:17.

I. The number, 12,000 for each tribe sounds symbolic since-it is hardly likely that the exact number would be identical for God's faithful from each tribe.

J. The 144,000 are mentioned again in Revelation 14:1.

7:5—Of the tribe of Juda were sealed twelve thousand. Of the tribe of Nepthalim were sealed twelve thousand. Of the tribe Gad were sealed twelve thousand.

7:6—Of the tribe of Aser were sealed twelve thousand. Of the tribe of Nepthalim were sealed twelve thousand. Of the tribe of Manasses were sealed twelve thousand.

7:7—Of the tribe of Simeon were sealed twelve thousand. Of the tribe of Levi were sealed twelve thousand. Of the tribe of Issachar were sealed twelve thousand.

7:8—Of the tribe of Zebulon were sealed twelve thousand. Of the tribe of Joseph were sealed twelve thousand. Of the tribe of Benjamin were sealed twelve thousand.

7:9—

A. The 144,000 included only those from the twelve tribes of Israel.

B. Now we have a multitude including all the Gentile nations.

C. It pleases us to see the beauty of God's impartiality. Would that men could be the same.

D. Could this multitude be the same as the one mentioned in Hebrews 12:22, 23 to which we come?

E. Though the number is innumerable it must still be few compared with the unfaithful, since Jesus said, "Few there be that enter."

F. The white robes symbolize victory and purity.

G. The palm leaves in their hands are for praise and thanksgiving to God.

   1. Used in the feast of the Tabernacles. (A feast of thanksgiving.)

   2. Used to spread in front of Christ upon his triumphal entry into Jerusalem.

7:10—

A. God does not need saving, this is their song of salvation with hearts full of thanksgiving.

B. Both God and the Lamb receive their adoration.

7:11—

A. This is the same order in which they were found in the picture of Revelation 4 and 5.

B. If angels in heaven rejoice over one sinner who repents think about this multitude!

7:12—

A. Thanksgiving and might are included here in place of riches and strength as found in the song of Chapter 5.

B. There may be sorrow elsewhere, here there is only happiness.

7:13—

A. The elder does not ask for information, he wishes to focus John's attention.

B. Now the Bible interprets the question which we also find fascinating.

C. Perhaps the biggest question involved is, "Am I included in this number?

7:14—

A. The American Standard translation has the word *the* before great tribulation. It is there in the manuscripts.

B. The result of sin is great tribulation followed by death.

C. This multitude has found their way out of the affliction of the world. See Hebrews 12:22, 23.

D. Notice that it does not say God washed their robes. They washed their robes.

E. God made the blood of Christ available for them to make their robes white.
   See Hebrews 9:14; 1 John 1:7.

7:15—

A. The faithful have endured.
   1. The tribulation is certain.
   2. The chosen will pass through.
   3. The tribulation will turn to bliss.

B. The church is called the temple of God, but this seems to be the churches delivered.

C. Christ dwells among Christians today, but *this dwelling* appears to be the consummation of the earnest of the Spirit.

7:16—

A. They shall escape the very things which oppressed them in tribulation.

B. This is almost a direct quotation from Isaiah 49:10.

C. God knows how to satisfy.
1. (Matt. 5:6) They which hunger and thirst after righteousness shall be filled.
2. (John 6:35) He that cometh to me shall never hunger; and he that believeth on me shall never thirst.
3. (John 4:14) But whosoever drinketh of the water that I shall give him shall never thirst; but the water that I shall give him shall be in him a well of water springing up into everlasting life.

7:17—

A. God will lead men as a great Shepherd. (Psalm 23; Isa. 40:11; Ezek. 34:23; 37:24.)

B. Jesus was the Great Shepherd. (John 10:11, 14; Heb. 13:20.)

C. These faithful shall continuously be led to greater pleasures in the continual night and day service of Jehovah.

D. The word used to speak of God's wiping away tears indicates complete removal. Sorrow is gone!

E. Compare this passage with Revelation 21:3-7.

Chapter 8

8:1—

A. In each of the other cases a voice is heard; this time only silence.

B. The silence may mean two things.
1. The entire heavenly chorus is held in awe are the horror of what is to happen.
2. God has time to listen to the prayers of saints in the midst of all the praise of heaven.

8:2—

A. The trumpets are for the purpose of announcing the impending disaster. (Joshua 6.)

B. A battle is about to begin.

8:3—

A. In the temple incense was burned before the first sacrifice and after the last sacrifice of the day. It is here added to the prayers of the saints. (Ex. 30:6.)

B. The prayers of Cornelius and of all the saints ascend with sweet savor to God.

C. The golden altar here is the altar of incense as in the Old Testament temple.

8:4—

A. It was when the smoke of the incense filled the most holy place that God made himself known.

B. Pray without ceasing.

8:5—

A. There seems to be a connection with the prayer of the souls beneath the altar, "How long?"

B. The prayers of the saints go up and the fire of chastisement comes down.

C. The saints have been sealed, perhaps vengeance is nearer now.

D. There is a similar picture of fire from the altar in Ezekiel 10:2.

E. The voices, thunderings and lightnings indicate a gathering storm.

F. Some think these come from men about to be disturbed, but it appears more likely they proceed from God himself. (Rev. 4:5.)

8:6—

A. Some of the apocryphal books give the names of seven archangels.
1. Michael 2. Michael 3. Raphael 4. Uriel 5. Raquel 6. Remiel 7. Sariel. See Tobit 12:15.

Note: We do not place equal value upon apocryphal sources but it is interesting to see where some of the names of such as Raphael originated.

B. The trumphets are ready now to sound.
1. Trumpets often sound a call to battle.
2. They also provide warnings which may be the case here.

C. There are similarities between the seals and the trumpets.
1. The first four in each case are naturally separated from the last three.
2. The last seal and the last trumpet have special significance.

8:7—

A. The hail and fire is apparently hail and lightning which bring death as shown by the blood.

B. Notice only the earth is affected.

C. Of this earth only a third part is afflicted.

D. The question is now "Will evil men repent after this warning?"

8:8—

A. The burning mountain reminds us of a tremendous volcano blowing into pieces and falling into the sea.
B. A mountain sometimes indicates a political force in the scriptures, as in the case of Mount Zion.
   See Jeremiah 51:25; Zechariah 14:4.
C. All of nature is involved in the warnings.
   1. First, the earth.
   2. Then the sea.
D. The picture is much like that of the plagues of Egypt as God warned Pharaoh with increasingly difficult affliction.

8:9—

A. This is not the end of the world as only a third part is destroyed.
B. Not only the sea, but its contents, suffer destruction.

8:10—

A. There are other scriptures where stars fall from heaven. (Rev. 9:1; Matt. 24:29; Mark 13:25.)
B. Other scriptures which may well be related are: Isaiah 14:12; Luke 10:18; John 12:31 and 16:11.
C. This star brings to mind the interpretation of the angels of the seven churches as stars.
D. Something or someone which has been providing guidance loses its previous place of eminence.
E. The fresh water and its fountain sources are now ruined in the third part.

8:11—

A. Wormwood is sometimes connected with gall, and bitterness. (Deut. 29:18; Jer. 9:15; Lam. 3:19.)
B. The gall associated here is sometimes thought to be hemlock, a poison!
C. It is unwise to interpret the bitter waters as people here because the people *drink of* the waters.
D. One after another God's wonderful environment is drying up, burning up, etc.
E. Whether these destroyed surroundings are physical or spiritual there is an awful lesson here as each warning becomes necessary for an impenitent multitude.

8:12—

A. The sun, moon and stars illuminate the earth, and now one third is to be removed.

B. God is affording plenteous opportunity for repentance and recognition of his rightful power to guide.

C. Life always suffers when light is insufficient.

1. Animals and vegetables perish without physical light.

2. Men die just as quickly and more permanently when they do not receive spiritual illumination.

D. This is reminiscent of the plague of darkness. (Ex. 10:21-23.)

8:13—

A. Commentators have very grave doubts as to the translation of the word angel here since the better manuscripts have "eagle."

B. The eagle flies in the midst of heaven that he may be heard.

C. Surely men will repent if they know greater afflictions are to follow! But they do not!

D. So far the warnings have been directed against man's surroundings.

E. Now the picture will change.

Chapter 9

9:1—

A. Stars are supposed to shed light but this star descends from grandeur to degradation.

B. This power fallen from heaven is given the key to the bottomless pit.

1. Christ opened the door to heaven through the key of David.

2. This angel or star can allow entrance or exit from the portals of the abyss.

See Jude 6, 13; Isaiah 14:12.

C. Perhaps verse 11 of this chapter identifies this fallen star as Satan by naming the *angel* king as Apollyon or destroyer.

D. As Christ has the power to allow men a taste of the heavenly gift this fallen star has the ability to allow men on earth a taste of hell.

E. Three points should be noticed.

1. He is not given the power to hurt men with the seal of God on their foreheads.

2. Jesus said, the gates of hell should not prevail against his Church.

3. There are keys to the Kingdom of Heaven and to the Gates of Hell.

F. This abyss appears to be a place of torment until the judgment. See 9:1, 2, 11; 11:7.

G. The ultimate place of punishment for the fallen angels, the demons, the false prophet, the beast and the Serpent is the lake of fire. (Rev. 20:13-15.)

9:2—

A. The murk and darkness of hell are allowed to overshadow the light of the heaven.

B. Satan is allowed to release the demonic pollution of hell upon these men who will not repent.

9:3—

A. From the smoke of hell come consuming, destructive locusts.

B. It is not just a matter of quick death. They bring slow torment.

9:4—

A. These are most unusual locusts who hurt men rather than vegetation.

B. This time the affliction is imposed directly upon these evil men.

C. Again those who have the seal of God are immune.

9:5—

A. Death is not always the worst fate. (Job 3:21; Jer. 8:3.)

B. Five months of such torment should bring about a penitent attitude from the evil-doer. It does not!

C. It is of little consequence whether the locusts last five months or their sting does. The torment is real and men should have turned in their ways.

9:6—

A. This description sounds similar to 6:15 and also Mark 13:19.

B. When one opposes the will of God life can become worse than death.

9:7—

A. It is not surprising that the locusts are difficult to interpret. Their origin is the bottomless pit which belches destruction.

B. It is possibly a mistake to grasp here for specific symbolism.

C. They have conquering crowns of those accustomed to victory.

D. They are wiser than locusts, as indicated by their human faces.

9:8—

A. Wild, waving hair would render their appearance more ferocious.

B. One suggestion is that there is deception in their having the hair of women who are normally more docile while they have the teeth of lions indicating their true ferocity.

C. All parts of the description seem to add to their unpleasantness.

9:9—

A. The locusts not only have offensive weapons; they are protected by their breastplates from counterattack.

B. The sight of these creatures is bad enough.

C. Now we hear them also and the sound is as fearsome as the sight.

D. Barclay gives a very good description of the destruction of a visitation of locusts on pp. 60, 61 of his Daily Bible Study servies (Vol. 2) on Revelation.

9:10—

A. Some see in this verse various kinds of implements of war.

B. It is very clear that they have the ability to inflict pain for a considerably longer time than a wasp or bee sting pains one.

9:11—

A. Satan is the greatest destroyer we know. He seems to be their leader and king.

B. The entire picture is that of a consuming, destructive horde overrunning evil men at the will of he who goes about seeking whom he may devour. See 1 Peter 5:8.

C. Joel pictures an invasion of locusts in Chapters 1 and 2 which should be read at this time.

9:12—

A. The flying eagle had proclaimed three woes. The locusts were only the first.

B. The warnings have now begun to hurt men directly as the locusts sting them.

C. What new chastisement will be brought upon the opposers of God?

9:13—

A. Some believe the voice here to be the prayers of the saints since it comes from the horns of the altar.

B. Others believe it to come from God himself as he releases the evil forces over mankind.

C. At any rate it is the signal for a renewed taste of torment.

9:14—

A. From beyond the Euphrates had come the Chaldeans as well as the Medes and Persians.
B. Notice God is able to control these forces until he desires their release.
C. Some commentators assign these angels to men in history but such pinpointing is presumptuous.
D. Speculation is beginning to run wild by this time among the scholars, and the warning of 22:18 might well be remembered.

9:15—

A. God had restrained them until the time that exactly suited his purpose.
B. The third part of the sea, the earth, the fresh water and the heavens had been destroyed. Now the third part of men are killed.

9:16—

A. Two hundred thousand thousand is two hundred million.
B. The overwhelming number is too great to count and John *hears* the number.
C. There can be no avoidance of destruction and death.

9:17—

A. The men riding the horses have breastplates fashioned in the bottomless pit.
    1. Red from the furnace of fire.
    2. Blue from the smoke arising above the fire.
    3. Yellow from the burning sulfur or brimstone.
B. The mouths of the horses emit fire, smoke and brimstone to match the breastplates of their riders.
C. Something is to be trampled and burned.

9:18—

A. It is most interesting that it is the fire, smoke and brimstone which kill, rather than the riders of the horses.
B. Some have seen airplanes, tanks, etc. with gunpowder and bombs doing the actual killing. We must be cautious.
C. The main lesson is that God is still chastising that men may repent.

9:19—

A. The student is left to his own devices to interpret this horror.

9:20—

A. It is strange that men will deliberately worship devils, yet they do.

B. The reactions to God's chastisement are varied.
   1. Some hide their heads like ostriches.
   2. Some curse him for their misfortune.
   3. Only a few repent in the face of his power.
C. The worship of the creation rather than the Creator is a mark of grossest ignorance.
D. Our God is a LIVING God.

9:21—

A. Men's lust and love of self usually rises higher than their fear of Jehovah.
B. There are many who will fight God to the point of self-destruction.
C. There is a sense in which both Genesis and Revelation tell the story of every man.
   1. All men must fight to keep from falling to sin as did Adam.
   2. Even so all men must struggle to repent of their sins as they are chastised and guided by the Father.
D. When we compare the patience of God toward Pharaoh and toward these evil-doers we can only be amazed at his longsuffering.
E. We fail to sympathize with those who criticize Jehovah for punishment in a lake of fire. Only when there is no hope are men doomed.

Chapter 10

10:1—

A. The first mighty angel was seen in 5:2.
B. This angel is thought by some to be Christ, yet the Bible speaks of Christ as being superior to the angels. (Heb. 1:5.)
C. The angel does appear to have come directly from the presence of God.
   1. The presence of God is sometimes shown by a cloud. (Ex. 14:24.)
   2. It is also indicated by a pillar of fire. (Ex. 14:24.)
   3. Moses' face shone brightly when he had been in God's presence.
   4. The emerald rainbow surrounds the throne of God. (Rev. 4:3.)

10:2—

A. The angel in 5:2 proclaimed a sealed book; this book is open.
B. There is apparently some message written upon the book which John is to read.

C. This angel rather than having an effect upon one third of the earth, etc. seems to have power and influence over both the sea and the land in their entirety.

10:3—

A. There are three views as to the identity of the seven thunders:
1. Hinds believes they are the voice of Rome which was built upon seven hills opposing the righteous influence of the mighty angel.
2. Some believe them to be rumblings from the evil of the earth at the difficulties which have befallen them.
3. Others believe the seven thunders are the voice of God himself, since often when God spoke persons described it as being thunderous, and since seven is associated with perfection.
4. Thunder normally implies an approaching storm.

10:4—

A. There are secret things which men are not supposed to know.
1. There are secret things which belong to God. (Deut. 29:29.)
2. Paul said some things were unlawful for him to reveal. (2 Cor. 12:1-4.)
B. If these thunders are rumblings from Rome, God might not care for their utterances to be recorded in his divine revelation.
C. It is interesting that when one is told he is not in on a secret his curiosity often becomes much keener.
D. It is possible that we shall never know what the seven thunders uttered, even after the judgment and the resurrection.

10:5—

A. All has ceased as John waits what is to come.
B. The angel raises his hand in readiness for an important announcement.

10:6—

A. Him that liveth for ever and ever could be either God or Christ.
B. We are told not to swear by heaven, however this angel is allowed to swear by God or Christ, since there is no higher authority.
C. Evil and unrepentant men have no more opportunity. Time for mercy is now gone. Justice will now prevail.

10:7—

A. God's plan for mankind will become clear as the seventh trumpet begins to sound.

B. No longer will it appear that evil may reign and destroy.

C. God had long declared to his prophets that he had a plan which would come to fulfillment.

D. Job will have his answers to such burning questions as "Has God forsaken me?"

E. The Mystery of God is a recurring theme. (Eph. 1:8, 9; 5:32; Col. 1:26; Rom. 16:25.)

10:8—

A. The sealed book of Chapter 5 was offered only to Christ.

B. This open book is entrusted to John.

C. Why does God wish for John to take the little book?

10:9—

A. There is a similar passage in Ezekiel 3:1-4.

B. In both this passage and Ezekiel the prophet is to devour and swallow the book.

C. In both he finds the book sweet to the taste but bitter to the belly.

D. Both prophets were to prophesy to a rebellious people after eating the book.

E. Too often preachers and Christians who attempt to take the Gospel to those who need it worst find it sweet to learn, but bitter to teach.

10:10—

A. God's predictions come true.

B. Something which John will dread revealing is going to happen.

10:11—

A. Now that John has devoured the book he has something to speak.

B. He has already prophesied much. Now he has new information to bring forth.

Chapter 11

11:1—

A. The angel which had the little book now gives John a measuring instrument.

B. Some believe that this is strong indication that the temple still stood in physical Jerusalem.

C. Those who argue for the later date around A.D. 95 completely symbolize this passage.

D. The Church is several times referred to as the temple of God. (1 Pet. 2:5; 1 Cor. 3:16; 2 Cor. 6:16.)

E. The picture is one of impending judgment and judgment begins at the house of God. (1 Pet. 4:17.)

F. Ezekiel Chapter 40 and following present a detailed picture of measuring the temple.

G. Also Amos' plumbline, Amos 7:7-9, and Zechariah 2:1 are similar prophetic pictures.

H. This is similar to the sealing of the saints (Rev. 7:3) with only the Holy to be protected.

11:2—

A. The old Jewish temple had four courts.
  1. Court of the Gentiles—No Gentile could pass this court without fear of death.
  2. Court of the women—Women were forbidden beyond this court.
  3. Court of the Israelites—The common people were forbidden beyond this court.
  4. Court of the priests—The most Holy place where only the high priest could enter was located in this area.

B. One measures in order to determine what is within and what is without a piece of property.

C. Here only the true Church or temple of God is found worthy of preservation and protection.

D. The forty-two months is the same as the time span found in Daniel 7:25 and 12:7.

E. It is also three and one half years or 1260 days. See verse 3.

F. Many commentators agree that Antiochus Epiphanes, the Syrian, desecrated the Jerusalem temple for exactly this amount of time.

G. The Holy city may be trampled but the temple is immune, sounding like the protection mentioned when God's servants were sealed previously.

H. The Jewish feast of Hanakkuh is today a memorial of the cleansing of the temple after Antiochus Epiphanes was driven out by the Maccabees.

11:3—

A The two witnesses may have been the law and the prophets. (Rom. 3:21.)

B. They sound like persons and could have been Moses and Elijah.
   1. The things which these witnesses did are found in Exodus 7:14-18 and 2 Kings 1:9, 10.
   2. God always sends witnesses to preach before he exacts vengeance.
C. It appears that the two witnesses prophesy to the Gentiles during the time they tread underfoot the holy city.

11:4—
A. The mouth of two or three witnesses was required to verify testimony.
B. Olive trees are sources of oil and candlesticks use the oil to produce light. (Zech. 4:11-14.)

11:5—
A. Impenitent men always try to torment God's witnesses.
B. Whenever this happens these foolish men bring death upon themselves from the fires of hell.

11:6—
A. Elijah prayed that it not rain and it failed to rain. (1 Kings 17:1.)
B. Moses had the power to turn water into blood and smite with plagues.

11:7—
A. After the 1260 days, not during it, the beast shall overwhelm them.
B. The beast from the bottomless pit may be the world which opposes the witnesses as the Church.
C. At any rate the *beast* indicates an undesirable malicious anti-Christian influence.

11:8—
A. This city is spiritual Jerusalem, the supposedly faithful city of God.
B. Egypt was known for its persecution of God's people.
C. Sodom was known for its sexual laxity.
D. God's city is then so infiltrated by the world that it kills God's own witnesses.

11:9—
A. These seem to be the same group that John was told that he was to prophesy again before. (Rev. 10:11.)
B. Three days and a half is a short time compared with the time

of their witnesses of 1260 days. (Note Ezekiel 4:6 for the year-day proof text.)

C. The fact that the bodies were left unburied shows the complete contempt in which the world held the witnesses.

11:10—

A. Men are so shortsighted that they cannot look beyond the immediate present.

B. The world seems to be winning on all sides over the excellence of character which is Christ, but the victory is for a day only.

C. The bristles of the antiChristians always stand up when they are tormented by the witnesses of Jesus.

D. It is a time of great rejoicing to the worldly when the influence of Christ lies slain and ready to be buried.

11:11—

A. This sounds a little like Ezekiel's dry bones. (Ezek. 37:5.)

B. God's Spirit is the source of all the motion of righteousness in existence.

C. That which the world thought was dead has risen just as it did from the tomb of Jesus.

D. Now the worldly influence within the Holy city is awestricken.

11:12—

A. God is the source of the great voice.

B. Only the true witnesses, the pure in heart, shall see God.

C. Jesus ascended up into the cloud and is to return in like manner.

D. The wicked shall have the opportunity of knowing those they persecuted are receiving a reward.

11:13—

A. The earthquake is probably spiritual commotion rather than a real earthquake.

B. The disturbance is still within the Holy City.

C. Seven thousand killed could be the influence of many influential persons within supposed Christianity.

D. There is major difference of opinion as to whether the giving God glory indicates repentance. Nebuchadnezzar gave God glory without repenting. (Dan. 2:47; 3:28; 4:1-4; 4:34-37.)

11:14—

A. Revelation 8:13 spoke of the three woes which were to come upon the inhabitors of the earth.

B. When the seventh angel sounds his trumpet the third of the three woes will come.

11:15—

A. Whereas there was one great voice heard from heaven in verse 12, now there are several.

B. Is this the opening of the Kingdom to all nations of the world?

C. Or is it the crumbling of all nations before the growing stone cut out of the Mountain? (Dan. 2:44; 7:18, 27; Isa. 11:9; 1 Cor. 15:24-26.)

D. It is God that shall reign for ever and ever. Christ shall deliver up the Kingdom to his Father after he has put down all authority. (1 Cor. 15:24.)

11:16—

A. The same 24 elders which surrounded the throne of God when everything appeared to be harmonious back in chapter 5.

B. The great news that Christ has overcome causes rejoicing in heaven. Every time righteousness is victorious the elders give praise to God.

C. They are apparently very prestigious, still they fall on their faces and off their thrones in worship to the King of the Universe.

11:17—

A. It is time for rejoicing when God ends the march of evil and rebellion.

B. God could have taken this power before but he chose to give time for repentance.

C. Now time has ended and justice will be had.

11:18—

A. The anger of the nations who disbelieve will be to no avail against God's consuming power.

B. Death is no escape from the punishment of God for rebellion against his will.

C. This is the time of reward as well as the time of punishment as both prophet and lowly saint, the great and the small receive according to their works.

D. Now those who serve the serpent, devouring and destroying, shall themselves be destroyed.

11:19—

A. John now sees a new activity in the heaven he has been allowed to see inside.

B. After the judgment God's temple is opened, not on earth as in the case of the Church but in heaven where the place that Christ prepared for the faithful exists.

C. Here is the Father's house with many mansions.

D. The ark was always representative of the immediate presence of God.

E. Are the great disturbances the prelude to the war in heaven discussed in 12:7-9 or are they the storm of destruction visited upon the wicked in the pouring out of God's wrath?

Chapter 12

12:1—

A. John is of couse still in heaven and sees the woman appear there.

B. The sun, moon and stars are all luminaries emitting light.

C. There is perhaps a connection between the crown of twelve stars and either the twelve apostles or the twelve partriarchs, possibly both.

D. The general context indicates that God's glory rests upon her.

12:2—

A. The woman is going to bring forth a child but she suffers in doing so.

B. We are caused to wonder about the importance of this blessed event.

12:3—

A. As opposed to the glorious appearance of the woman of verse 1 we see the fearsome picture of a dangerous monster.

B. Heads represent authority, horns represent power and crowns represent glory. This dragon must command our attention.

12:4—

A. What power! He is able to sweep through the very stars of heaven disturbing them in their positions.

B. Now he stands before the woman and it makes us tremble for the safety of her child.

C. He must have some purpose for wishing to devour her child.

12:5—

A. There are now three characters introduced in this chapter in verses 1-12, the woman, the dragon, and the man child.

B. One interpretation says that the woman is the chosen people of God, including both Old Testament Israel and the New Testament Church. (Isa. 54:5; Jer. 3:6-10; Hos. 2:19, 20.)

 1. The stars are said to be the glory of the Patriarchs.

 2. The moon is the increased glory of the Law of Moses.

3. The Sun in which she is clothed is the brilliant light of the New Covenant.

C. Another interpretation sees her as the apostate church of post New Testament times, ready to bring forth the true Church which would lead men back to God.

D. A large number of commentators believe the woman to be the New Testament Church. (Gal. 4:26; Eph. 5:32; 1 Cor. 11:3; 2 John 1.)

E. The man child also has more than one possible interpretation.
1. He may be the Messiah. (Psalm 2:9; Gen. 3:15; Gal. 4:4; Rev. 12:5; 12:10.)
2. The man child may be all Christians including Christ. (Rev. 2:27.)
3. He may be the restored New Testament Church.

F. The dragon is interpreted by the Bible itself as the Devil, Satan, that old Serpent. (Verse 9.)

G. Nevertheless the dragon works through various agents on earth.
1. Some see the dragon as any evil force which stands ready to devour God's offspring.
2. Some see him at work in the crucifixion of the Lord.
3. Still others believe the Roman Empire's efforts to destroy newborn Christianity fit the description accurately.

H. The dragon is foiled. He has been unable to destroy the woman. Now her child is snatched away to the protection of God's throne.
1. This may be the ascension of Christ to the right hand of God. See Acts 2:34.
2. It may also be the protective power of God preventing the destruction of his Church.

I. There is an eternal lesson involved here as we reminisce over the many times the dragon has almost but not entirely snuffed out God's children.
1. At the time of the flood
2. Baby Moses
3. Christ into Egypt
4. The crucifixion
5. The persecution of Nero

12:6—

A. God's woman is placed on the defensive by the dragon but God has anticipated the problem and prepared a place to prevent her destruction and at the same time provide nourishment for her.

B. Some scholars believe the 1260 days here, the 42 months of 11:2 and the times, time and a half a time of 12:14 are all the same period of time.
  1. Foy Wallace sees here the siege of Jerusalem.
  2. Some see it as the period of time the Bible was kept out of the hands of the common people, from the declaration of a universal bishop at Rome until the announcement during the French Revolution that "liberty and reason are the only true worship."
     a. This is the time period from A.D. 533 to A.D. 1793. b. The latter announcement is taken as the killing of the two witnesses. c. Hinds, Barnes and Elliot like this interpretation.
C. Regardless of the meaning of the symbols we are safe in saying that neither the woman nor her seed can be eliminated by the persecuting dragon.

12:7—
A. The dragon cannot afford to see the survival of the woman or her seed and so he gathers all his forces to make war against God's angels who protect the man child in heaven.
B. Michael appears to be the protector and defender of God's people. (Dan. 10:13, 21; Dan. 12:1; Jude 9.)
C. The dragon is also the eternal accuser, ready always to prove God's children will not be faithful.
D. Through the ascension of Christ and the birth of Christianity the dragon loses his case. There is nothing to base his accusations upon. He must fight!

12:8—
A. The dragon finds it impossible to change the organization in heaven; he cannot dislodge the man child.
B. A great deal depends here upon whether the heaven mentioned is the heaven where God has his throne with the emerald rainbow, or whether this heaven is the place of governments on earth.
  1. Wallace believes it to be the latter.
  2. If it is the former, the battle looms much wider in scope.

12:9—
A. One cannot help but recall such passages as Isaiah 14:12-15; 2 Peter 2:4; Jude 6.
B. Among the higher spiritual powers of heaven the devil and his angels have destroyed their influence.
C. It is important to notice that if one takes his shelter within the

281

Kingdom of God as did the man child the dragon is helpless.
(Matt. 16:18.)

D. The dragon must now make his efforts within the carnal and
earthly realms.

12:10—

A. The voice is loud again because of the importance of the announcement.

B. The man child will live in spite of the efforts of the dragon.

C. With the victory and continued existence of the man child
comes:
1. The Kingdom of God.
2. Salvation and strength.
3. The power of Christ.
4. The end of accusations against the brethren.

12:11—

A. The brethren removed the power of Satan by cleansing themselves in the blood of the Lamb, and obedience to him.

B. Their willingness to declare the Christ and to lose their lives
in him leaves the dragon in defeat.

12:12—

A. The influence of Satan had been divided between heaven and
earth before, but now he is cast out of the heavenly places
and those who enter there may rejoice at victory.

B. In the earthly places he will redouble his efforts which will result in great anguish.

C. He will thrash about like a prizefighter who has been stunned;
who knows he is about to be knocked out.

12:13—

A. He cannot attack the man child who has been taken to heaven
for he has been thrown out.

B. It is clear that if he cannot persecute the man child he will
persecute its mother.

C. We notice that the woman is still upon the earth. Earthly Israel has given way but the Church still stands.

12:14—

A. There are other places where God has employed eagles' wings
to bring his own to safety. See Exodus 19:4; Deuteronomy
32:11, 12; Isaiah 40:31.

B. Whatever the meaning of the woman we recognize that she
brings forth fruit for God and God protects this fruit-bearing
woman from the attacks of Satan.

C. The wilderness would seem to be a place of separation from the multitudes.

D. It may be a mistake to try to make all of the 1260 day periods cover the same time span.

E. Note that it speaks of the woman fleeing to *her place* as though it is talking about the same place as mentioned in 12:6.

F. Some see this as the entire gospel dispensation.

G. Others see it as the time the Church appeared to be almost nonexistent for a literal twelve hundred and sixty years.

12:15—

A. Water often indicates people and if true in this case would mean the devil was trying to overwhelm the Church by number of servants.

B. Satan would like nothing better than to wash away the Church with that which pours forth from his mouth.

12:16—

A. The earthy, carnal nature of Satan's teaching is self destructive.

B. The very nature of good and evil requires the swallowing up of wickedness.

C. The efforts of the dragon are wasted, since God's fruit-bearing woman will live on, nourished and protected by her husband.

12:17—

A. The dragon cannot destroy either the woman or her man child.

B. The portion of the woman's seed who loved not their lives unto death have defeated him with the blood of the Lamb.

C. Now he will focus his attention upon those left who are faithful to God upon the earth.

D. What new weapons will he bring forth?

Chapter 13

13:1—

A. It is well established by now that John's visions bear many likenesses to passages in the prophetic books of Daniel, Ezekiel, Jeremiah, Isaiah, etc.

B. The dragon goes to the sea for an agent to fight for him.

C. The sea is often the people as it is used in prophecy. (Isa. 60:5; Jer. 51:42; Rev. 17:1; Rev. 17:15.)

D. Daniel saw four beasts rise up out of the sea. (Dan. 7.)
    1. One like a lion.
    2. One like a bear.

3. One like a leopard.
4. One diverse from the rest and having ten horns.
E. The beast from the sea in this verse is a composite of Daniel's beasts.
F. Daniel was told that his ten horns were ten kings. (Dan. 7:24.)
G. Daniel's fourth beast was a kingdom. (Dan. 7:23.)
H. This fourth kingdom's eleventh king was to be replaced by the Saints of the Most High who will possess the kingdom and reign eternally. (Dan. 7:27.)
I. This fourth kingdom's eleventh king should wear out the Saints for a time, times and a half a time.
J. John saw a scarlet-colored beast with seven heads and ten horns in Revelation 17:3.
1. At this point the ten horns are said to be ten kings.
2. The seven heads are said to be seven mountains.
   a. This might make little sense if we did not know one of the names for the Church is Mount Zion. b. Here then are seven sources of power and influence.
K. John's beast in verse 1 has blasphemy or ridicule of God written upon his seven heads.
L. Let us rephrase the verse with the interpretation as follows: "As I stood at the edge of the tumultous people I saw a kingdom arise from among them, having seven sources of power and influence and ruled by ten kings, and the authority of the kingdom was evil and ridiculed God."
M. Most Protestant commentators believe the beast from the sea is the Roman Empire.
1. The several visions of Daniel are blended to give this interpretation.
   a. The image with the head of gold, breast of silver, legs of iron, and feet of iron and clay. (Dan. 2.) b. The four beasts. (Dan. 7.) c. The ram and the he goat. (Dan. 8.)
2. This interpretation is given strength because the Church arose within the time of the Roman Empire and because most prophecy has an immediate application as well as an eternal lesson.

13:2—
A. Leopards are stealthy, bears are strong, and lions are devourers.
B. Since this beast is a composite several commentators believe it represents a series of powerful empires:

1. Egypt
2. Assyria
3. Babylon
4. Persia
5. Greece
6. Rome
7. The British Empire

C. Some such as Jehovah's Witnesses and David Lipscomb believe it to be all political organizations which they believe to be dominated by Satan and methods of force rather than love.

D. The dragon will now work through the beast to make war against the remnant of the Saints.

13:3—

A. It is possible that the wounding of the head had a connection with the defeat suffered when the earth swallowed up the flood which the dragon sent upon the woman.

B. This does not sound like the seven heads are the literal hills upon which Rome was built since they could hardly be wounded.

C. Wm. Barclay sees the death of Nero as the wounding of the head which was healed when later emperors resumed persecution of Christians.

13:4—

A. The authority and the power of the beast cause people to be astonished.

B. It is possible for the Devil to still receive adoration through his agent or instrument.

C. The beast is also worshipped.

D. If this is the evil in political organization people place more importance upon political leaders than upon God.

E. If it is the Roman Empire the Caesar worship which was given by the people fits nicely.

F. Persons were convinced no one dared to oppose the power of the beast.

13:5—

A. It sounds like the mouth was given unto the beast by the dragon and not by God.

B. He has seven heads but a single mouth.

C. Blasphemy is written upon his heads and spouts from his mouth.

D. He is allowed to operate by God but he receives his power from Satan.

E. He persecutes the Saints the same time period as in Daniel 7:25.

13:6—

A. There is nothing sacred and Holy to this beast.

B. Some have said the heaven of Revelation is the realm of the Roman rulers. If so and if this beast is the Roman Empire we have a strange situation in which the beast blasphemes against them that dwell in his own realm.

C. The blasphemy against God takes three forms.
1. Against his name. (Some say by calling the Roman Empire Holy.)
2. This tabernacle of God seems to be the Church.
3. Those that dwell in heaven may be two things.
   a. The martyrs who had died for the cause of Christ. b. The angels and heavenly host who were present even at creation.
4. It is tempting to see those who dwell in heaven as Christians who live on earth but have entered the Kingdom of Heaven but this may be more than the heavenly places of Ephesians 1:3 where all spiritual blessings are found.

13:7—

A. Job was at the mercy of the Devil when God granted him power to test this faithful man.

B. It is possible for the Devil to kill saints and overcome them but it is not possible for him to defeat the spirit of the saints.

C. The kindred and tongues and nations, etc. are found several other places, each time being a place of conflict between God and the Devil. (Rev. 7:9; 5:9; 11:9; 17:15.)

13:8—

A. The influence of the Devil becomes overwhelmingly accepted.

B. In the midst of a world of evil worshippers the true Christians refuse to bow down.

C. The sacrificial death of the Lamb of God was planned from the beginning.

13:9—

A. It has been some time since we heard this statement repeated over and over at the end of each of the letters to the Churches.

B. This time the one who has ears for spiritual things is to turn

286

away from the worship of the beast and make sure one's name is written in the book of life.

13:10—

A. Here are two characteristics of the first beast.
   1. He restricts the freedom of men.
   2. He kills with the sword.
B. These effects are temporary and he himself will be punished in like manner.
C. The saints must endure and overcome through patience and faith. God will punish. (Rev. 14:12.)

13:11—

A. The first beast was said to have come up from the sea. This one comes from the earth.
B. As used in Revelation the term "earth" often carries a meaning of *earthly* as opposed to *heavenly*.
C. Thus one could read the verse to say a beast arises out of the ungodly world.
D. It appears like a peaceful, gentle, perhaps even Christlike entity.
E. Undernearth it breathes devouring fire like the dragon which it represents.

13:12—

A. Some believe the second beast to be the organization which enforced Caesar worship.
B. Some believe it to be the worldwide political organization, controlled by Satan.
C. Others believe it to be the Roman Catholic Church.
D. This second beast spreads the power of the first beast over the world.
E. The end result is that men are caused to pay worship to the first beast.

13:13—

A. Apparently this beast is able to work miracles, but see the following scriptures:
   Revelation 16:14; 2 Thessalonians 2:9; Matthew 24:24.
B. James and John once asked if fire should be called down on a Samaritan village. (Luke 9:54.)
C. If this second beast is the Catholic Church the miracles they claim to perform would fit this description.
D. At the same time Barclay points out magic and trickery were resorted to in the enforcement of emperor worship.

287

13:14—

A. Some love the truth, others love a lie.
B. God will send a strong delusion if a man wishes to believe a lie.
C. The lying wonders and miracles performed by the second beast deceive those who love not the truth.
D. There is a serious problem here as to how literally we are to take the "image of the beast."
   1. If the image is literal it could refer to such images as that of Caligula, set up in the Holy of Holies in Jerusalem.
   2. If the image is symbolic as the beasts are, then it may be something one can see, yet not the beast itself, for example statues of the dead.

13:15—

A. We are dealing with four different things here.
   1. The dragon
   2. The beast from the sea
   3. The beast from the earth
   4. The image of the beast from the sea
B. The people who are deceived are the ones who make the image of the beast.
C. The beast from the earth then gives it the power to speak.
D. When the image of the beast speaks it commands the death of those who will not worship it.

13:16—

A. The power of the beast's image reaches all kinds of men.
B. God's people were sealed with his Holy Spirit. In their foreheads. (Rev. 7:3.)
C. Those who worship the beast's image are sealed or marked in two appropriate ways.
   1. In their foreheads because they accept his philosophy and teach it.
   2. In their right hands because they willingly work for the beast.

13:17—

A. Any man who does not accept the image of the beast will be cut off from social transactions.
B. Every man makes a choice between the mark of the Devil and the mark of God.
C. The name of the beast has a number.
D. He who would prosper in the earth while the beast controls must have either his mark, or his name, or the number of his name.

E. It is possible that his mark, his name and the number of his name are all the same.

F. Adam Clarke believes that the image of the beast is the Roman Catholic pope.

13:18—

A. One has the strong feeling that those early Christians may have had an easier time of deciphering the number of the beast than we have today.

B. The blessing of God is pronounced upon those that read and understood the words of this book. We are sure the people of that day could interpret the meaning of this number.

C. We present here a few of the schemes which have been used to try to determine the identity of the beast.

1. Julius Caesar was the first of the Caesars. Nero Caesar was ruling when John wrote the Revelation. He persecuted the Christians as a beast. The Latin letters of one form of his name represent numbers which can be totaled.

N	50
E	6
R	500
O	60
N	50
	666

2. Again the Greek name Euanthas totals the same number.

E	5
U	400
A	1
N	50
TH	9
A	1
S	200
	666

3. If the letter A of the English alphabet is given the value 100 and each following letter is one higher we have an interesting result.

H	107
I	108
T	119
L	111
E	104
R	117
	666

4. A form of the word Latin which is used in the worship services of the Roman Catholics totals correctly.

L	30
A	1
T	300
E	5
I	10
N	50
O	70
S	200
	666

5. One explanation accepted by many is that the number 6 is representative of imperfection as compared with the number 7 which represents perfection.
   a. Repetition of the number emphasizes it. b. Therefore this number 666 indicates the foolishness of man emphasized over and over again.

Chapter 14

14:1—

A. The Lamb is without doubt Jesus Christ.

B. Mount Zion was the location of the earthly Jerusalem. It is to this Holy Mountain that people of all nations must flow according to Isaiah.

C. The writer of Hebrews says that we are come unto Mount Zion—to the Church of the Firstborn.

D. Now the Lamb is surrounded by those who loved not their lives unto death, those who were sealed from the twelve tribes of Israel.

E. They are also those who were sealed with the Holy Spirit before the angels were allowed to harm the earth. (Rev. 7:3, 4.)

F. All 144,000 are still here, without the Dragon capturing one.

14:2—

A. It seems that the 144,000 are singing praises unto God.
   1. The voice is powerful like great Niagara.
   2. The voice is attention drawing like thunder.
   3. The voice is sweet like the melody from the harp.

B. The fact that harps are mentioned here has little to do with the argument over use of mechanical instruments in worship on earth. This is heaven and symbolic.

14:3—

A. Whenever the Church is victorious songs of praise arise in heaven.

B. Only the redeemed of Israel can learn and sing this song.

C. When one is called out from the tongues and tribes and nations there is good reason to sing a new song.

14:4—

A. This appears to be spiritually pure behavior rather than physical purity.

B. God describes this kind of fornication among his people in Jeremiah 3:1-10.

C. The fact that these virgins are men seems to mean that it includes both male and female.

D. Just as a faithful maiden follows her fiance these faithful follow their Lord.

E. God chose them from among the multitudes because of their character.

F. They are the part worth offering to the Lord, just as God was satisfied with only the finest of the harvest in the Old Testament days.

See Exodus 23:19; Numbers 15:20; 18:22; Deuteronomy 26:2.

14:5—

A. There are three things true of these 144,000.
   1. They are a sacrifice to God.
   2. They love the truth and hate the lie.
   3. They are faultless before God. (Cleansed by the blood of Jesus.)

B. One is reminded that it was said of Jesus that there was no guile found in his mouth.

14:6—

A. The gospel was to be preached unto all the world before the end came. See Matthew 24:14.

B. This was not the feat spoken of by the apostle Paul in Colossians 1:23 because the end did *not* come then.

C. This is an everlasting gosple; the world may fall in ruins but this gospel shall continue.

14:7—

A. As though this were one last final call for men to recognize their folly. The warning is similar to that in Acts 14:15.

B. Here is the essence of all loyalty to Jehovah—fear him—glorify him—worship him, for there is little time.

C. His hour of reward and punishment is here.

14:8—

A. Every time an angel appears another momentous announcement is ready.

B. This time Babylon (which means confusion) is announced as fallen.

C. This is a preview much as the headline of a newspaper, for Babylon's fall is described in later chapters.

D. Babylon was the greatest city of the Babylonian empire which opposed and persecuted God's chosen people in the times of the Kings of Israel.

E. God's great city was Jerusalem—Satan's was Babylon.

F. Babylon's fornication was clearly her spiritual filth.

G. Ancient prostitutes of the time of Revelation gave those they seduced intoxicating potions of wine mixed with other materials.

H. These victims then became insensible and were at the mercy of the prostitute.

I. Some suggest that the wrath of her fornication here may mean the wrath which comes upon those who share her flouting of God.

J. Men from every nation under heaven fall to Babylon's temptation.

14:9—

A. The fate of those who worship the beast or his image is about to be declared.

B. It is announced in a loud voice to insure the announcement is heard.

14:10—

A. Drinking from the cup of God's wrath is mentioned other places. (Jer. 25:15; Job 21:20.)

B. This cup is undiluted wrath and will be a very bitter potion.

C. Fire and brimstone were used in the destruction of Sodom and Gomorrah.

D. The Lamb and the angels will be responsible for the destruction.

E. Remember that the rich man was in sight of Lazarus while he was being tormented.

14:11—

A. The torment lasts as long as the reward of the righteous.—The same word is used.

B. Not only does it last eternally, there is no respite, even for a second.

C. Those who worship the beast have a bleak future.

14:12—

A. The saints have three characteristics:
1. They have the patience necessary to be true until death.
2. They demonstrate faith in Jesus Christ.
3. They keep the commandments of God.
B. The patience of the saints will keep them from the worship of the beast.

14:13—

A. Those who qualify by having the characteristics of verse 12 may look forward to the rest and reward of this verse.
B. Possibilities as to the identity of the ones who die in the Lord are:
1. The 144,000.
2. The man child caught up to God.
3. The redeemed from the earth.
4. Those who loved not their lives unto the death.
5. Martyrs found at the foot of the altar.
C. After great labor the rest is sweeter.
D. Even though the labor ceases the effect and influence continues after death.

14:14—

A. This picture is of one like unto the Son of man, there seems to be little doubt however that this is the Christ himself returning for his own.
B. The picture of Christ returning on the clouds is also given in:
1. Acts 1:9-11
2. Daniel 7:13, 14.
C. The golden crown indicates his victorious kingship.
D. The sickle is an instrument used in reaping the wheat—this one is sharp and ready.
E. Joel spoke of the use of the sickle in reaping the harvest. (Joel 3:14.)

14:15—

A. The command comes through an angel but it is the command from God himself.
B. This is the end, now God will harvest his crop.
C. There is no more time to produce. The growing season has concluded.
1. Man knows when it is useless to allow the crop to remain in the field.
2. God also will harvest at precisely the right time to accomplish his ends.

D. This harvest has been anticipated by Christ while in the flesh. See Matthew 13:24-30, 37-43; Mark 4:29; Matthew 3:12; Joel 13:13.

E. There could be no more appropriate picture of this time than the harvest.
1. The good is gathered into the bins.
2. The useless is thrown away or burned.

14:16—

A. The dead in Christ will now be united in the air with the living Christians. See 1 Thessalonians 4:16; 1 Corinthians 15:18.

B. How beautifully simple the description—"The earth was reaped."
1. God often used simple descriptions which are later elaborated.
2. Note the similarity to—"In the beginning God created the heavens and the earth."

C. The earth is cleared of the faithful, then the wicked await.

14:17—

A. The first angel has reaped only the faithful, now we have the appearance of an angel to reap the wicked.

B. It would be improper with the information presented here to say how much time elapses before the second angel comes forward.

14:18—

A. This angel seems to have come from the altar where the ones who were beheaded for the cause of Christ cried out, How long, how long must we wait, and who were answered, Wait until the number of saints who are to be killed as you have been fulfilled.

B. God's number has now been fulfilled—the wait is ended.

C. Normally grapes were a sign of prosperity, this time the reverse is true and the grapes represent the tares, the chaff, the fruit of wickedness on the earth.

D. Verse 10 of this chapter tells us that those who have the mark of the beast are to drink of the wine of God's wrath.

E. This verse makes it the grapes themselves which are to be trampled under the feet of God.
See Lamentations 1:15; Isaiah 63:3.

F. As in the time of the flood of Noah wickedness is fully ripe. This time there will be no seed of Satan left.

14:19—

A. Adam Clarke believes that the winepress is Hell.

B. Those who refuse to believe that God will punish severely must ignore this passage.

14:20—

A. The punishment of the wicked will take place outside the City of God, the New Jerusalem.

B. There is an interesting passage in Hebrews 13:10-15.

C. The wine flowed from an upper vat to a lower container when the grapes were pressed and crushed. Here the quantity of the juice indicates the magnitude of the wickedness at that time.

D. Sixteen hundred furlongs is said to have just about covered the land of Palestine.

Chapter 15

15:1—

A. Another picture is now added to the seven seals, the seven trumpets, the praising multitude, etc.

B. These are the last plagues because they represent God's change from patience to wrath.
   1. God begins by preaching the Word.
   2. Next the world persecutes the truth.
   3. God bring minor judgments upon the persecuting world.
   4. The war rages between the seed of woman and the dragon.
   5. God's patience gives way to wrath.
   See Exodus 10:27; Matthew 12:32; Romans 1:24; 1 John 5:16.

15:2—

A. This is the same sea of glass mentioned in Revelation 4:6 but this time the intermingled fire indicates the coming wrath of God.

B. Each time that Revelation discusses the punishments of God we are presented a picture of the safety of those who are faithful to the end. God cares for his own.

C. It is not enough to defeat the beast himself, one must overcome his image, his name, and his number.

D. The harps mentioned here in *heaven* have no bearing on the argument over instruments of earthly worship other than the voice.

15:3—

A. This reminds us of the song that no one else can sing in Revelation 14:3; no one can appreciate God's greatness like those who have used his strength to overcome the beast.

B. God's fleshly Israelites sang the Song of Moses in Exodus 15:1-19 when they had been delivered by the hand of God from the Egyptians.

C. Now the spiritual Israelites sing the Song of the Lamb since they have been delivered by the hand of God from the beast.

D. The entire song here is quotations from Psalms. (Psalms 92:5; 145:17; 86:9; 99:3; 98:2.)

E. The song is about God, not men; we forget ourselves in praise of God in heaven.

15:4—

A. Both the wicked and the righteous shall someday recognize the holy power of God.

B. God's judgments will be impressive before the entire world.

15:5—

A. The temple and the tabernacle have always been a source of God's pronouncements.

B. The temple or tabernacle is here opened and ready for the emergence of the angels with instructions from the King of Kings.

15:6—

A. Though the mission of the angels is destruction the garments they wear reveal their own righteousness.

B. They have the golden girdle and the white linen of truth and purity.

15:7—

A. The beast here is not associated with the dragon; it is instead one of the four living creatures who serve God around his throne.

B. The angels are now given the means of fulfilling their mission.

C. God's enemies will shudder before him while he himself lives eternally.

15:8—

A. God's glory filled the place of worship with smoke several times:
  1. Mount Sinai (Ex. 19:18).
  2. The tabernacle (Ex. 40:34).
  3. The temple (1 Kings 8:10).
  4. In Isaiah's vision (Isa. 6:4).

B. It is too late now for men to repent: God will adopt no more children while the harvest of the grapes of wickedness are trampled.

Chapter 16

16:1—

A. The voice from out of the temple seems to be that of God himself.
B. There is disagreement about whether we are still under the seventh seal, as well as the seventh trumpet.
C. Here all seven angels are told to pour out their vials on earth. Later only the first angel pours out a vial upon the earth.
1. The earth in the first verse must mean earth as opposed to God's heaven.
2. This points up the difficulty of interpretation in this book as words change their meaning from verse to verse and chapter to chapter.

16:2—

A. There are three lists which need comparison.
The plagues of Egypt—
water into blood, frogs, lice, flies, murrain on cattle, boils and blains, thunder and hail, locusts, darkness, death of firstborn.
The terrors of the Trumpets—
on the earth, on the sea, on the fresh water, on the sun, on the seat of evil, on the Euphrates, on the air.
The plagues of the vial—
on the earth, on the sea, on the fresh water, on the sun, on the seat of evil, on the Euphrates, on the air.
B. There are several similarities above.
C. One great difference is in the completeness of the destruction with the vials.
D. We are made to remember Job's boils which covered him from head to toe, as now the wicked suffer a like fate.

16:3—

A. Not one third this time—every living soul.
B. The blood of a dead man differs from the blood of a live man since the separation or coagulation occurs because of a lack of oxygen in the system.

16:4—

A. There is now nothing to drink besides blood.
B. These wicked are in far worse condition than a world with polluted streams.

16:5—

A. Do you accuse God of injustice in such severe punishment? The angel says, "Not so."

B. How serious is the crime of rejecting the will of Jehovah?

16:6—

A. There are some men who have a thirst for others' blood.

B. God is saying, "You are so bloodthirsty, now drink up."

C. The angel declares that this is just punishment for them.

16:7—

A. The saints who cried out, "How long?" agree with the angel of the waters.

B. God is just.

16:8—

A. It was darkness in Egypt, now it is the reverse.

B. The sun which is such a major blessing to mankind is now turned against these rebellious men.

16:9—

A. We have little concept of the results if the temperature were to rise even an average of 25 degrees over the entire earth.

B. Like children, some adults take punishment whereas others grit their teeth and castigate the one who attempts to guide them.

16:10—

A. It was from beyond the Euphrates that many of the invading hordes entered the land of Palestine.

B. The river Euphrates was dried up when Babylon was conquered in the time of Nebuchadnezzar. (Cyrus.)

C. God several times used his power to dry up waters. (Ex. 14:21; Josh. 3:17; Isa. 11:16; Jer. 51:36.) Also related is Zechariah 10:11.

16:11—

A. The seat of the beast must be the source of his authority.

B. The beast and his kingdom are faced with confusion and lack of ability to see where they are going.

C. We would probably say that they gritted their teeth for pain. This pain may have been mental anguish at seeing the beast's kingdom in darkness.

D. Jesus said that there would be gnashing of teeth in outer darkness.

E. While the sun scorched men, the beast's kingdom is filled with darkness.

16:12—

A. Some men will walk directly into the fires of hell sticking out their tongues at the God of heaven.

B. It is the energy and spirit of the devil which energizes his children for such foolhardiness.

16:13—

A. Since these evil spirits come from the *mouth* they are associated with speech of some kind.

B. The dragon, the beast and the false prophet act with the same purpose so that we are not surprised that these spirits come out of all three.

C. Frogs were associated with loathsome conditions during the Egyptian plagues.

16:14—

A. The forces of evil are beginning to assemble for an all-out pitched battle against the power of Jehovah.

B. These powers are even powerful enough to rise above natural law.

C. The tension mounts but there is only one conclusion which can come—God must be victorious.

16:15—

A. Paul also warned that Christ should come as a thief, suddenly.

B. It will be expected that every man be adorned with garments of righteousness. Without such garments every man walks in shame.

16:16—

A. Armageddon is probably the "Mount of Megiddo" where Deborah defeated Sisera.

B. Many battles were fought at this site. See 2 Kings 9:27; 23:29, 30.

C. Compare here Ezekiel's Gog and Magog. (Ezek. 38:8, 21; 39:2, 4, 17.)

16:17—

A. The last angel now pours out his woe upon evil men.

B. God's own voice speaks from the throne as he initiates the beginning of the end.

C. The contents of the vials will finish the work.

16:18—

A. This may possibly be a physical earthquake in which case we are awed when we recall disasters like the Lisbon earthquake.

B. It is much more likely that these thunders and voices and the earthquake are descriptions of the horrible state of confusion among the society of men when the fruits of rebellion are harvested.

16:19—

A. Here is a great city made of nations. Great Babylon is divided into three camps before its final destruction. National organization begins to crumble before the power of the Almighty.

B. God is not slack concerning his promises as some men count slackness. He will reckon with the opposing city.

C. Babylon has a preference for drinking (the blood of the saints), so God shall provide for her a cup.

16:20—

A. The islands are likely small concentrations of power which now melt away.

B. The mountains upon which Babylon sits can no longer be found.

16:21—

A. This hail was unbelieveably large. A talent is about 96 pounds.

B. Still, wicked men cling to their blasphemy and pride.

C. It is not that they cannot repent. THEY WILL NOT.

Chapter 17

17:1—

A. John is to observe and record for those of us who read, both the rewards of the faithful and as of now the gruesome destruction of the wicked.

B. He is to follow the angel to where he will witness the judgment of the great whore.

C. Verse 18 tells us that the unfaithful woman is the great city which reigns over the kings of the earth.

D. Verse 15 interprets the waters upon which she sits as the peoples, multitudes, nations and tongues.

E. A city as used here is not a geographical location with streets and sidewalks, buildings, etc. It is a group of people gathered with a unifying purpose.

F. Babylon has one purpose, that is to seduce individuals from the service of the true God.

G. We have the choice of serving as a part of the unfaithful whore city of Babylon, or we can serve as a part of the espoused and true Bride of the Lamb.

17:2—

A. Pleasure-loving Babylon of old was described as having a golden cup from which she made the nations of the earth drunken. This Babylon has also caused men to lose their senses.

B. Her cup contains anything which is able to turn men's hearts from the God of heaven to reveling and lusts, pride and vanity of the world.

17:3—

A. The wilderness seems an odd place to witness a city but spiritual encounters often took place in the wilderness.

B. The beast upon which she rides is of course subject to her.

C. He is a beast of scarlet color because of the dangerous viciousness he exhibits.

D. The blasphemy indicates his wickedness, the heads his wisdom, and the horns his power.

E. It is our belief that the beast has been in existence since the time of Nimrod, appearing and disappearing with various world kingdoms as they rose and fell in opposition to God.

F. And so they ever go together, the heads, the horns, the blasphemy, and the pleasure of this world as they combine their efforts to defeat the true Bride, the city of God.

17:4—

A. Would it be expected that the great harlot would be clothed otherwise? She is trying to look as attractive as possible.

B. Not only is she attractive to the pleasure seeker, she is able to offer the promise of riches.

C. The golden cup in her hand at first glance sparkles as precious metal, inside however it contains only nauseating filthiness as it is seen by the spiritually discerning.

D. Shall we go after the golden cup of filthiness offered by Babylon, or shall we adorn ourselves with the white robes of the Bride of Jesus?

17:5—

A. The ancient prostitutes often had their names written on their foreheads.

B. The word mystery is often used in the Bible to describe something which is hidden at the moment but is later to be explained. The rest of the chapter goes on to tell the mystery.

C. She is Babylon the great because of her power, her riches, her beauty and her ability to ride the beastly kingdoms which arise from the multitudes who know not God.
D. Christ is the Bridegroom, the Church is his Bride, and *from this union* is born all that is pure and righteous and good among mankind.
E. The Devil is the father of liars. *He consorts with Babylon* to bring forth harlotry and abominations of every sort among the hordes who tread the wide road to hell.

17:6—
A. There is nothing the frightful woman enjoys more than drinking out of her cup which she has filled through the ages with the blood of the Christians whom she has helped to persecute and kill. (A woman spurned.)
B. As John looks at her he is astonished. Verse 7 helps us to understand the true feeling which John had toward her.

17:7—
A. There is no need for John to wonder about the picture which he sees.
B. Both the woman and the beast are to be discussed.
C. The beast will be considered first, followed by the woman.

17:8—
A. There is little point in attempting to find out when the beast is and when it is not since the beginning of the verse says it is not and the end of the verse says it is.
B. The point seems to be that this beast has the ability to rise up from the bottomless pit to do his dirty work and when descend back into the depths. He is here now and gone tomorrow, but is always ready to appear anew.
C. His source is the great abyss from which comes every evil influence.
D. His destiny is the lake that burneth with fire and brimstone.
E. He is able to capture the admiration of all those who love this world.

17:9—
A. As in the explanation of the number 666 wisdom is needed to understand this.
B. The mountains mentioned here are like those mentioned in Revelation 16:20. They are concentrations of tremendous power. The woman would fall but she rides these power structures.

17:10—

A. The word kings and kingdoms is sometimes used interchangeably in prophecy. This may well mean powerful kingdoms, five of which are gone by. In Revelation 13:3 one of this same beast's heads was wounded and thus cannot be a literal mountain.
B. The sixth king reigned as John beheld. This without much doubt refers to the Roman Empire which may be only the sixth king, or may be all seven of them.
C. The seventh king or kingdom is still to come and will have short endurance.

17:11—

A. This verse makes the beast that was, and is not, and yet is, to be not only the whole beast, but also the eighth head.
B. This is explained by the fact that he is also of the seven. The eighth head is no more the beast than are any of the others.
C. The beast rises from the bottomless pit. His destiny is perdition and hell fire.

17:12—

A. This verse causes us to feel that the kings mentioned in verse 10 are really great kingdoms or world powers and that these ten kings are lesser and are men who shall reign rather than organizations.
B. Their power was to be exerted after John saw his vision.
C. They should have their very short moment in the sun.

17:13—

A. The only way that these ten kings have one mind is in their opposition to God. (Rom. 8:7.)
B. It is possible that these ten kings are actually political kings who support the antiChrist.
C. It is also possible that they are various forms of aggrandizement such as science, art, philosophy, and music which are twisted to objects of worship.

17:14—

A. The ten kings will fight against the Lamb through the beast.
B. There is no power or combination of powers that can defeat the Lamb of God.
C. The ten kings need to learn like Nebuchadnezzar that God rules in the affairs of men and kings.
D. All those who oppose the beast and the kings are God's faithful.

17:15—

A. Jesus informed us that the multitudes would travel the broad way and would support evil with their carnal mind.
B. The beast arises out of the multitudes and nations and he is ridden by the great harlot.
C. Without the aid of vicious forces and seductive powers both beast and rider would fall.
D. Note that this verse is very comprehensive covering every people of the earth, and not the Roman empire only.

17:16—

A. Now we see a strange thing happen; the beast turns upon the rider.
B. We recall Christ's words that a kingdom divided against itself cannot stand.
C. The eating of her flesh indicates extreme hatred for the seductive powers she has used. (Psalm 27:3.)
D. They should like to see nothing left but her ashes. (Lev. 21:14.)
E. The harlot is to be left desolate without her admirers.

17:17—

A. God allows these powers their freedom of will and yet they are used by him.
B. The word of God shall not return unto him void.

MYSTERY BABYLON THE GREAT

1. Babylon was founded by Nimrod who was the great grandson of Noah. He was the grandson of Ham and the son of Cush.
2. There is strong evidence that the passage which says that Nimrod was a mighty hunter before the Lord is actually telling us that Nimrod was a man who loved the thrill of the kill in opposition to God.
3. The early followers of Nimrod built the tower of Babel as a means of making a name for themselves and asserting their independence of Jehovah.
4. God took note and confused their powers of communication, preventing them from organizing further.
5. The same location later became the city of Babylon, the capital of Nabopolasser's kingdom in 625 B.C. From here the entire Babylonian Empire arose.
6. Nebuchadnezzar was Nabopolasser's son. It was he who captured Jerusalem and took the Jews captive for a period of 70 years.

7. Nebuchadnezzar built the hanging gardens of Babylon which are only one of the indications of the splendor of this ancient city. (One of the seven wonders of the ancient world.)

8. God warned his people many times that they would be punished as captives in a foreign land.

9. Then he turned to prophecies about the ultimate destruction of this wicked city which he had allowed to exist as a tool to chastise his people.

   A. Daniel predicted the fall of Babylon to Belshazzar. (Dan. 5.)

   B. See the following passages regarding the fall of Babylon.
   Jeremiah 50, 51; 25:9-14.
   Isaiah 13:17-22; 47:1-11.
   Psalm 137.

   C. Make comparisons between

Isaiah 47:8	Revelation 18:7, 8
Isaiah 21:9	Revelation 14:8; 18:2
Jeremiah 50:38, 39	Revelation 18:2
Jeremiah 50:38; 51:13	Revelation 17:1; 17:15
Jeremiah 50:29	Revelation 18:6
Jeremiah 50:40	Revelation 18:22, 23
Jeremiah 51:8, 9	Revelation 18:15-19; 17:4-6
Jeremiah 51:60-64	Revelation 18:21

10. Daniel's beasts and John's beasts seem to have heads, horns and blasphemies in common.

11. The ten toes of Daniel's image are like the ten horns of John's beast.

12. After Babylon falls God paints a beautiful picture of a new heaven and a new earth. (Rev. 21.)

WHAT IS BABYLON?

Hendrickson—Babylon then, is the world as center of seduction at any moment of history. p. 202.

Wallace—The symbolic name Babylon is applied to the fallen city of Jerusalem. p. 364.

Jehovah's Witness—Babylon is the entire world empire of false religion, including all those religions which are based upon a resemblance to ancient Babylon. p. 499.

Clarke—We have shown that the woman sitting upon the seven-headed beast is a representation of the Latin Church. p. 1043.

Hinds—The great city of Babylon must be understood figuratively as meaning the Papal Church. p. 260.

Barclay—The mystery in this case is that the name Babylon means Rome. p. 187.

Johnson—The Scarlet Harlot is the symbol of a faithless, apostate Church, the mother of all the other false churches which have followed her.

Lipscomb—The point before us is that Babylon was, and is, not the false Church, but the human governments that have grown up in rebellion against God. p. 101.

Campbell—The Roman Catholic Church is the Babylon of John. Witty, p. 79.

Witty—Babylon includes all of the organized political and ecclesiastical confusion that has opposed the Church of God and cursed the children of men from the first century of the Christian era. p. 147.

Chapter 18

18:1—

A. The angel comes from the presence of God and is clothed in his glory.

B. There is a suggestion by some that the enlightenment of the earth is a result of the message the angel carries.

18:2—

A. This is a repetition of the message of Revelation 14:8.

B. The doom song of ancient Babylon was sung in Isaiah 13:19-22 and in Jeremiah 50:39; 51:37.

C. Doom songs were also sung for Edom (Isa. 34:11-15), and Nineveh (Zeph. 2:13-15).

D. When an ancient city was destroyed wild animals found convenient places of refuge.

E. We speak of haunted houses today; only evil spirits were left.

F. The use of the prophetic past indicates the absolute surety that Babylon will fall.

18:3—

A. The all nations reminds one that the beast upon which the great city rides is arisen from the peoples, multitudes, nations and tongues, thus from all the earth.

B. This sounds more inclusive than the city of Rome, Jerusalem, or the early Catholic church, although it still might fit the apostate church of later times.

C. Those who are power-hungry and profit seekers love Babylon for what she offers them.

18:4—

A. The admonition to "come out" is given to God's people many times.

   1. Abraham was instructed to get out of his own land.

   2. Lot was told to get out of Sodom.

   3. Other verses teaching the same principle are:

      Isaiah 48:20; Jeremiah 50:8; 51:6, 45; Romans 12:2; 2 Corinthians 2:16-18.

B. Although God's people may be in Babylon at the time of his call, they will hear his voice and hearken if they are truly his people.

C. Every care is taken that God's own will not partake of the coming destruction of the wicked city.

18:5—

A. The sins of Babylon reach unto heaven in similar manner to the prayers of Cornelius.

B. God's longsuffering is at an end for this shameful city and it now turns to justice.

C. God is not slack concerning his promises.

18:6—

A. Reward is used in an unusual sense here since what is about to happen to Babylon is not pleasant. The meaning is clear however.

B. The Old Testament principle was justice, an eye for an eye.

C. Christ said, have mercy, pray for your enemies.

D. There is a time of vengeance coming, at the hands of God's angels.

E. She has poured out suffering upon God's children from her cup.

F. Now she shall have *two* cupfuls.

18:7—

A. For every pleasure she has had at the expense of God's children she shall now receive a double portion of grief.

B. Those who revel in evil are always shortsighted, thinking that their exultation shall see no end.

C. This passage is almost identical with the statement about earthly Babylon found in Isaiah 47:7-9.

D. The queen is pictured as carefree and sitting on top of the world, while the widow sits in sorrow.

307

18:8—
A. Whether or not this be a twenty-four hour day the point is the same, *sudden* and *complete* loss of all.
B. In addition to the famine, mourning and death of the widow, Babylon will be burned to ashes.
C. She may be strong in the eyes of men—the Lord is strong enough to dethrone her.
D. The queen shall now become less than the widow.

18:9—
A. The mighty men of the earth who have such great affection for the harlot queen will see the source of their pleasures in smoking ruins.
B. They surely did not expect the object of their affections to come to this pitiful end.

18:10—
A. The kings are in grief over the loss of their pleasures, yet they dare not come close for fear of sharing in her torment.
B. It is hard for them to believe that such a mighty and great city lies in ruins.
C. The suddenness of the fall seems to preclude either Rome or the Catholic church as more than symbols of Babylon since neither of them came to ruins in *one hour*, or even with great suddenness.
D. The seductive power of worldly attractions stands just as haughtily as ever awaiting the final judgment of the God in heaven.

18:11—
A. Not only the men of power but the men of profit are horror-stricken as their selfish merchandising grinds to a halt.
B. One can hardly glory in his riches when there is no city in which to sell.
C. Previously one had to have the mark of the beast to buy and sell but now the mark is useless.

18:12—
A. This collection includes materials from the mineral kingdom, the animal kingdom, and even later the souls of men, the spiritual kingdom.
B. It would be difficult to prepare a more complete list of precious baubles.

18:13—
A. The beasts of burden are now included.

B. Any man who follows the great harlot has sold his soul to the devil, the devil will play with it as he pleases.

18:14—

A. Every outcome of Babylon's efforts is now turned to nothing.

B. Everything which she prized is gone.

C. Worse than in Job's case, they shall never be found again.

18:15—

A. A repetition of verse 10, they grieve but not to the extent of lending any assistance.   There is no way they could alter the outcome anyway.

B. Riches are fleeting and the wailing and weeping are all that are left.

18:16—

A. The fine linen of the saints endures, this fine linen burns to ashes.

B. The beautiful ornaments are now gone.

C. The beautifully-dressed woman has become a shabby hag.

18:17—

A. Again we are reminded that the disaster is to be within a very short time.

B. Three groups have now mourned Babylon.
   1. The mighty men of political power.
   2. The merchandising profiteers.
   3. Now those who provide the goods for the merchants are grieving.

C. But again they stand afar off as did Peter when the Lord was taken to trial.

18:18—

A. In addition to losing her ornaments the great harlot is now smoking in ruins.

B. The lamenters still cannot believe that any city could match the once mighty Babylon.

18:19—

A. All the attractions of the world have turned to despicable ashes.

B. Selfishness is receiving its just reward.

C. Once again we find it takes but a single hour.

18:20—

A. It is wrong for men to take vengeance—this is GOD!

B. Blessed are ye when nmen shall revile you and persecute you. . . .

309

C. The apostles and prophets above all have been mistreated and abused.

18:21—

A. The mighty angel adds his own force to that of gravity in throwing Babylon down.

B. The harlot city does not fall simply because of her own weakness; God sees that the city is thrown down.

C. She is to disappear completely. This phrase, no more at all, is found a number of times in this chapter.

18:22—

A. All happiness and joy shall disppear.

B. The food supplies shall cease.

18:23—

A. There will be no light. The darkness will be complete.

B. All marriage and procreation shall cease.

C. The term "great men of the earth" sounds suspiciously like the description of Nimrod, the founder of the original Babylon.

D. Babylon shall bring down her mighty men with her.

E. She has deceived the masses of every nation who ever existed.

18:24—

A. She has drunk the blood of God's people from her cup.

B. As Babylon hath caused the slain of Israel to fall, so at Babylon shall fall the slain of all the earth. (Jer. 51:49.)

Chapter 19

19:1—

A. The saints had been told in 18:20 to rejoice, now they do so.

B. The word "Alleluia" means *praise God*.

C. It is interesting that Clarke reports the North American Indians as using this word in exactly the same manner during their worship.

D. God is the sole source of salvation, and of all power.

E. God is therefore due glory and honour.

19:2—

A. Only God is perfect in judgment.
   1. Only God sees the heart.
   2. Only God has no prejudice.
   3. Only God knows the correct punishment.
   4. Only God knows the gravity of sin.

B. The crime Babylon committed was a most serious sin.

C. The cry for vengeance in 6:10 is now answered with respect to Babylon's drinking of the blood of Christians.

19:3—

A. Waves of praise sweep over the heavenly host.

B. This time they are rejoicing over the permanence of Babylon's destruction, as the smoke arises *forever.* (Isa. 34:9, 10.)

19:4—

A. At each impressive victory of righteousness we find the praise from all the host of heaven.

B. We are inspired to fall upon our own knees and join them in adoration.

19:5—

A. This is a quote from Psalm 135:1, 20.

B. From the cherubim to the most unimportant angel the praise is called forth.

19:6—

A. The swell of praises is like:
1. The din of a massive crowd.
2. The roll of thunder.
3. The roar of Niagara.

B. God has been reigning all the time. It now becomes evident to all and impossible to ignore. See Psalm 97:1.

19:7—

A. Marriage is used in the New Testament to teach four different lessons.
1. Guests (Matt. 22:1-14; 25:1-13.)
2. Engagement (2 Cor. 11:2.)
3. The Ceremony (Rev. 19:7, 8.)
4. Married (Rom. 7:14; Eph. 5:22-32.)

B. The Jewish wedding had several elements, (betrothal) (the dowry interval). See Genesis 29:2 (the feast).
1. We are here dealing with the time after the dowry has been paid.
2. The bride is arrayed and the feast will last forever.

19:8—

A. The harlot Babylon was also arrayed in fine linen but it was a sign of her luxury, not her purity.

B. God had promised the people of Sardis that if they overcame they should walk with him in white. They are ready.

C. We are even told to "put on Christ." (Eph. 4:24.)

311

19:9—

A. Foy Wallace believes the marriage supper to be the continuous fellowship of Christians with the Lord.

B. It is unusual here that the Christian seems to be both the wife and the guest.

C. We are assured that in the security of God's own promises these blessings are awaiting the faithful.

19:10—

A. It would be most natural to worship one who brought such tidings of joy as did this messenger.

B. The messenger quickly informs John that only God is to be worshipped.

C. The end of all the prophets was to testify of Jesus as the Word of God. (Acts 10:4.)

D. Revelation 22:8, 9 records a similar event and in this place the angel is said to be of the prophets.

19:11—

A. There was doubt in Revelation 6:2 but this time there is none. This rider is the Christ.

B. He speaks always in harmony with reality.

C. When he judges it is done with perfection.

D. Like the knights of King Arthur he will defeat the dragon and claim his bride.

E. The white horse was associated with victory, and victory he shall have.

19:12—

A. The eyes as a flame of fire represent his consuming power and his infinite ability to perceive the situation.

B. He has many crowns to indicate the sure victory over all enemies.

C. He had promised the faithful at Smyrna a crown of life.

D. Those of Smyrna had also been promised a new name if they overcame.

E. It may be a sign of foolishness to discuss the new name mentioned here since only Christ knows it.

19:13—

A. The Word of God is obviously not the new name mentioned.

B. The blood in which his clothing is dipped is the blood of his enemies. (Isa. 63:3.)

C. There is some possibility that the word "knew" of verse 12 is used in the same sense that Joseph "knew not" Mary.

D. If that is the sense here it would mean that only Jesus knows the Word of God to perfection. This, however, seems to be straining at straws. See and compare Revelation 2:17.

19:14—

A. Compare the armies which accompany him now with the legions of angels which he said were available in Matthew 26:53.
B. Those who follow also ride the victorious white horses.
C. The armies of heaven are now clothed in white linen. They must be at least a portion of the Bride.

19:15—

A. The sword proceeding from his mouth is the same as:
   1. The two-edged sword of Hebrews 4:12.
   2. The sword of the Spirit of Ephesians 6:17.
   3. The sword mentioned in 1:16 of this book.
B. The rod of iron indicates absolute control and authority. See Psalm 2:9.
C. The enemies of the Lord shall be trodden under his feet. See Hebrews 10:13; 1 Corinthians 15:23-28.

19:16—

A. This sounds as though the name is written on his clothing at the thigh area.
B. He is not just a king *among* kings; he is the king *of* kings.
C. From him come all authority and all blessings.

19:17—

A. The angel is so bright that he can be seen standing in the sun.
B. All the despicable scavengers of the air are invited to clean up the mess which is about to be produced.
C. When God gets through with the men who oppose him there will be a need for beautifying the environment.

19:18—

A. Kings often escape the bloodshed while the underlings die—not this time.
B. All the rebellious from all the nations, great and small, will feel the results of their foolishness.

19:19—

A. The great city Babylon has already sunk beneath its own ashes but the beast with his political power still commands the kings of the earth.
B. What a pitiful sight, men against their maker; most ludicrous and tragic to behold!

313

C. Man cannot win.

19:20—

A. Now that the seductive power of Babylon is gone we witness the demise of the forceful action of the beast, and the lying deception of the false prophet.

B. The air becomes even more polluted as the smoke from the beast and the false prophet are added to that of Babylon.

C. Burning brimstone is about as vivid a torture as one can conceive. Still this is likely symbolic, and only representative to the degree that our finite minds can comprehend.

19:21—

A. One by one they have gone: that great city—the beast—the false prophet, and now those who serve the beast.

B. Only the dragon is left, stripped of all his agents.

C. Satan's deception and persecution of the Church of Jesus Christ is reeling before the onslaught of the rider of the white horse.

Chapter 20

20:1—

A. This sounds much like the same angel who loosed the locusts from the pit in 9:1-3.

B. Some claim this angel is Christ, since he is described as having the keys of hell and death. (Rev. 1:18.)

C. It is difficult to accept Christ as being an angel, as Hebrews clearly states that he is normally higher than the angels but was made lower when he came in the flesh. (Heb. 2:9.)

D. Whoever the angel is he faces a gigantic task of tying Satan with the chain and containing him in the abyss.

20:2—

A. No details of the battle to subdue the Devil are given here.

B. This is the same old serpent who had been deceiving men since Eden.

C. Satan's activities are to be hindered. There is no indication here that he is completely inactivated.

1. One may be bound and still do a lot of damage.

2. A dog on a chain can still bite.

20:3—

A. Even with the devil subdued as above there are some men who are evil without the devil's aid. There could still be evil in existence.

314

B. Here we shall note three positions with regard to this thousand years.
1. The premillennial position.
   a. Abraham was made a promise by God that through him all nations should be blessed. b. Although the Jews are scattered today they will be restored to Palestine and will rule over the Gentile nations. c. The world is becoming progressively more evil with no promise from either Christ or the apostles that a period of blissful peace should occur before the return of the Lord. d. Since the prophets spoke of such a period it must be that it will be ushered in at Christ's second coming. e. Christ will come the first time to gather his faithful to meet him in the air. This will be the first resurrection. f. While the saints are in rapturous honeymoon with the Bridegroom in the air the man of sin will be revealed on earth and there will be terrible tribulation. g. Christ will then return with his saints to cast Satan into the abyss. h. Christ will set up his kingdom in Jerusalem and reign in person from the throne of David over a world where the knowledge of God covers the earth as the waters cover the sea. This reign to last for one thousand years. i. There will then be a violent outbreak of wickedness as the Devil is loosed for a little season. j. The wicked dead will then be raised, the judgment will take place. k. The wicked shall be tormented in hell and the righteous shall live in a heaven on earth similar to the original Garden of Eden.
2. The postmillennial position.
   a. The Old Testament prophesied fully of a period of peace on earth. b. The ancient Jewish nation and its temple saw destruction. c. The Church is present-day Israel and is established for the purpose of teaching the Devil the folly of disobedience to God. d. As yet the world has not seen a victorious Church. e. But Christ will reign until he has made every enemy his footstool. f. The preaching of the gospel will result in a major breakthrough in spiritual affairs. g. Through the power of the Gospel, Christ will symbolically reign over the world where men have beaten their swords into plowshares, etc. h. Then the influence of the Devil will break out again followed by God's intervention at which time the Devil shall be completely defeated. i. The judgment will take place with the wicked sent to

315

everlasting punishment and the righteous kingdom being turned over to God in Heaven.

3. The amillennial position.

   a. The world is to be blessed through spiritual Israel. b. Christ sits upon David's throne today reigning along with all those who are willing to lose their lives for him. c. The Devil was partially bound in the lifetime of Christ and he continues to be further bound today as the Gospel tears men from his grasp. d. The first resurrection is the rising from the grave of baptism every time a Christian crucified the old man and is born anew. e. The thousand years is the entire period of time between Christ's first coming and his second. f. Christians find themselves today in a condition somewhat like the engagement period of the Biblical times. g. Christ shall come back to judge all men at which time the wicked will be condemned to the lake of fire along with the devil, and the righteous will see the consumnation of their marriage in all its fulness.

C. The scholars of the religious world have debated these ideas from the first centuries of Christianity.

1. Justin Martyr and Irenaeus vs. Augustine.
2. The Scofield Bible.
3. Alexander Campbell.
4. David Lipscomb.
5. H. Leo Boles vs. R. H. Boll.
6. Hall Calhoun's son.

D. Certain principles can be ascertained without doubt.

1. After the Devil has lost his agents, Babylon and the beast and the false prophet, he will find himself restrained in his deceptions.
2. This period of restraint shall last for an extended time.
3. He will not escape, he will be loosed and taught the lesson one final time.

20:4—

A. The Christians of Laodicea were told that if they overcame a throne awaited.

B. Notice that John did not see the bodies of those who were beheaded, only the souls.

C. These who were beheaded may be all those who willingly offer their lives to the cause of Christ since there were Christians who died even more horrible deaths than beheading.

D. This is probably all those who had died to the world and died in Christ.

E. Christians never die, they join the body of Christ and reign until Christ comes and raises all the dead in bodily form at the general or second resurrection.

20:5—

A. It is clear that the ones who take part in the first resurrection are a select group whereas the rest of the dead may, or may not include righteous persons.

B. We can hardly be dogmatic in asserting that this thousand years is a literal thousand years when we find it imbedded in such an environment of symbolic and figurative language. It is most surely a long time.

   1. To some it is blasphemy to think it could be anything other than literal.

   2. To others it represents the entire gospel dispensation from Christ's first coming to his second, regardless of actual length.

   3. Foy Wallace believes it to be the time of reduced persecution of the Church immediately following the victory over the Roman Empire.

C. The first resurrection includes only those who are going to live and reign with Christ during this time.

20:6—

A. The second death is defined in Revelation 20:14. It is separation from all that is connected with God by being cast into the lake of fire.

B. Then those who take part in the first resurrection are safe from the fires of hell. The second general resurrection and the judgment hold no fears whatsoever.

C. Perhaps the fact that they have overcome and endured unto the end with no more opportunity for Satan to seduce them explains why they will not find the lake of fire.

D. Revelation 5:10 speaks of the redeemed by the blood of Christ as being *already* made Kings and priests.

E. The premillennialists believe that this reign is a reign of fleshly Jews over Gentile nations.

F. Since Christ reigns today it may be that by becoming one with Christ every faithful Christian shares in his reign.

20:7—

A. For a short time or a little season the Devil shall be released from his bound condition.

317

B. It is almost as if God were giving him a chance at reform after having shown him though the power of the Church that divine wisdom cannot be opposed.

20:8—

A. There are still nations on the earth at the end of the thousand years reign.

B. Gog and Magog are evil forces which respond to the leadership and deception of Satan. Ezekiel calls upon the Son of man to prophesy against Gog which is against the land of Israel. (Ezek. 38.)

C. Satan seems to have lost none of his seductive power nor his vigor in evil.

D. The phrase "sand of the sea" is a favorite expression for vast multitudes.

E. Some believe that after passing through many centuries of relative freedom to teach the word of God we are now entering the little season when Satan again prevents men from exposure to the teaching of the gospel.

20:9—

A. There is no place where the saints of God can be free from the presence of the forces of Gog and Magog; they cover the breadth of the earth.

B. Just when it appears that they are going to eliminate the saints God steps in.

C. It is not water which drowns this time, it is fire which devours.

20:10—

A. It has been thousands of years since the Devil began his reign of terror among men. Now it ends, not in triumph, but in the lake of fire.

B. Babylon was thrown down into the sea.

C. The beast and the false prophet are awaiting the company of their mentor.

D. Though some passages speak of eternal destruction leaving room for an interpretation of annihilation this scripture presents a picture of eternal *torment*.

20:11—

A. The great white throne is the seat of Jehovah, God.

B. The old heaven and earth have now served their purpose and are now to be removed.

C. The Devil had corrupted the original creation. He is gone

and now his stained and sin-scarred world is to be replaced.
See Psalm 102:25-27; Isaiah 51:6; Mark 13:31; 2 Peter 3:10;
Hebrews 12:26, 27.

20:12—

A. The first resurrection of verse 4 included only righteous persons.
B. This gathering includes all men of all times, except for those who have taken part in the first resurrection.
C. It will not be before the courts of fallible and foolish men that these stand.
D. The books which are opened could be:
   1. The Old and New Testaments.
   2. The book in which your deeds are written.
   3. The book of life in which are written the names of those with which God is pleased.
E. This judging by the works is not contrary to the teaching of Romans. The faithful will have works written in the book of deeds. Without them faith is dead.

20:13—

A. It will matter not a whit where a man's body was laid to rest.
B. Nor will it matter that the atoms of his body were used to produce the body of another man.
C. The one who became the first fruits of the grave will now unlock the doors of every grave and death shall lose his victory.
D. What sort of reward would the works which God has written bring to you?

20:14—

A. The word for hell here is the abode of the dead. It shall no longer be needed.
B. There shall be no more physical death, nor a place for the dead to be.
C. The first death is separation from the body. The second is separation from God.

20:15—

A. This is not the first time we have heard of the book of life. (Phil. 4:3; Rev. 3:5; 13:8; 17:8.)
B. We shall hear of it again in Revelation 21:27 and 22:19.
C. Is your life secure? Can your name be found in the list in the book of life?
D. If not the company of all the opposers of God for all time waits to greet you.

Chapter 21

21:1—

A. There are many interesting comparisons between Genesis and Revelation:

Genesis	Revelation
Paradise lost	Paradise regained
The devil begins work	The Devil finishes work
The tree of life lost	The tree of life regained

B. John has seen the doom of the wicked, now he is shown the bliss of the blessed.

C. When God's people escape from Babylon it is to a new heaven and a new earth. See Isaiah 65:17; 66:22; 2 Peter 3:13.

D. The sea was a source of fear to the ancients, representing a boundary limit beyond which man was in great danger.

E. The sea seems to represent people in turmoil, as when the beast arises out of the sea. Now it shall melt away along with the old heaven and earth.

21:2—

A. Wallace believes that since it came out of heaven that it is not heaven, nor in heaven. He holds it to be the Church, victorious.

B. In one sense it is possible to say that since the pattern for the temple and the tabernacle came from God, they too came down out of heaven.

C. Hebrews speaks of Mount Zion, the Holy city, the Church of the firstborn as though Christians already possessed it. (Heb. 11:10; 12:22, 23.)

D. The Church is to adorn herself with white linen which is the righteous deeds of the Saints. (Rev. 3:4, 5.) Here the adorning appears to be finished.

21:3—

A. Notice that nearly everything said of the New Jerusalem is at least partially true of the Church today. Here the list of blessings seems to be perfected.

B. We are reminded of 1 Corinthians 13:10 where the part is replaced by the perfect.

C. It is also interesting to note that the Church is to grow to perfection. See Ephesians 4:10-16.

D. Recall that Jesus said, "I go to prepare a place for you."

E. The prophet's dream is coming true:
   1. Isaiah 54:12; 60:11-22.

2. Haggai 2:7-9.
3. Ezekiel 40 and 48:31-35.
F. Jerusalem meant "abode of peace." This is God's new "abode of peace."
G. Though God dwells within us now, this dwelling takes away all sorrow and he personally wipes away the tears.
H. The glory of the Lord had been with men before. (1 Kings 8:11.) Now it stays with them permanently.

21:4—

A. This mortal shall have put on immortality.
B. The Satan corrupted, sin-stained heaven, earth and sea takes its pain, sorrow and crying with it as it flees away.
C. Death which had claimed so many of the early Christians would be replaced with the crown of life.

21:5—

A. Here is the new creation. I will make a new thing. (Isa. 43:18, 19.)
   1. New creatures. (2 Cor. 5:17.)
   2. A new earth.
   3. A new heaven.
   4. A new city.
   See Romans 11:36 and Ephesians 4:6.
B. Man rearranges and restructures, whereas God truly makes all things new.

21:6—

A. God is from everlasting, to everlasting.
B. God's plan is true and faithful. His will is temporarily hindered, but the end will see God in control.
C. It is God's will that men who desire enough to be faithful shall be able to drink deeply from the fountain of eternal life. Satan cannot stop us.

21:7—

A. Jesus had said that the meek shall inherit the earth. Now God says "all things."
B. All Christians are God's children, but we have now only the taste of the heavenly things. Then we shall come into our full inheritance.
C. How many blessings can we imagine? God promises all things, every possible blessing which shall make life full.

21:8—

A. God's new creation will include none of that which was associated with Satan.
1. The fearful who were too timid to stand for God will not be there.
2. The prejudiced who would not accept the truth will not be there.
3. The polluted who loved the mire will not be there.
4. The ones who placed sexual pleasures above the kingdom will not be there.
5. The false religionists and magicians will not be there.
6. Those who loved the material things and placed them as God will not be there.
7. The lying sons of Satan who is the father of liars will be with their father.

B. Along with the beast, the false prophet, and the devil, they shall be separated forever from God and his new Jerusalem.

21:9—

A. The angel had finished the unpleasant task of pouring out the vials of God's wrath; now a much more pleasant task.

B. Let us also take the unpleasant tasks and watch for the pleasant to follow.

C. This is the second time the angel has said, Come hither.
1. Come, I will show you the judgment of the great harlot. (Rev. 17:1.)
2. Come, I will show you the bride of the Lamb.

D. Wives are very often extremely beautiful at their wedding. This is Christ's wife. He knows how to choose true beauty.

21:10—

A. He had started the Revelation by saying, I was in the Spirit on the Lord's Day.

B. The great and high mountain would provide a clear and unobstructed view of the glory of the city.

C. Is it pleasant for you to be a part of the Church today while it is in the process of adorning itself as Satan hinders? What will it be like fully adorned with no evil of any kind?

21:11—

A. The jasper was a beautiful sea-green.

B. God's throne was surrounded by an emerald rainbow in Revelation 4:3.

C. One gets a picture of the presence of God providing a general glow emanating from the city as a whole.

D. The Saints are now the light of the world because God dwells in them.

E. There in the new Jerusalem shall be thousands of saints with the source of their light, all providing a perfect, flawless as crystal, radiation.

F. This shall require new spiritual bodies, since corruptible eyes cannot stand in the presence of God's glory.
   1. Moses coming down from the Mount.
   2. Saul who was blinded.

21:12—

A. The description of the New Jerusalem shows several characteristics:
   1. Beauty
   2. Love
   3. Light
   4. Worship
   5. Security

B. Isaiah talks of God providing salvation as a wall. (Isa. 26:1.)

C. The great high wall is not to keep out evil, for evil has been cast into the lake of fire.

D. There had been cherubim placed on the Garden of Eden has man was driven out.

E. Now the angel keepers of the gates have welcomed the faithful back to God.

F. As spiritual Israel, men have come into the city as true seed of Abraham.
   1. The old fleshly Jewish family brought us the Christ.
   2. The twelve tribes of the new spiritual Israel were living stones in the great new city.
   3. To get into the city one must be a son of Abraham by circumcision of heart.

21:13—

A. The significance of the gates pointing in each direction could mean that salvation was available to all who would come to Christ.

B. Through the twelve gates have come men of every nation.

21:14—

A. Christ was the cornerstone upon which the city was built. (Eph. 2:20; 1 Cor. 3:9.)

B. As the preaching of the twelve apostles had been spread, the foundation of the imperfect Church was laid. Now the impurities have been purged.

C. The charter members have their names emblazoned on the base of the building.

D. In Galatians 2:9 certain of the apostles are called pillars.

21:15—

A. One would need a golden reed to measure such a precious city. (Ezek. 40:3.)

B. Revelation 11:1 has a picture of John being given a reed and instructions to measure the temple, etc.

C. His measurings will show the immensity of this glorious new city.

21:16—

A. Plato and Aristotle, both Greeks, referred to the good man as "Foursquare."

B. The cube was one of the more desirable geometrical figures of that day.

C. The Holy of Holies in Solomon's temple was a perfect cube. (1 Kings 6:20.)   See also Ezekiel 41:21; 43:16; 45:2; 48:20.

D. Some believe the twelve thousand furlongs was the circumference.

E. It seems much more likely that this is the distance of each side.

F. If so this was so ordinary city, being equal in space to about the size of the United States, east of the Mississippi River.

G. The main idea seems to be that there is plenty of room for all who overcome and qualify to live there.

21:17—

A. The wall would be about 266 ft. high.

B. This would mean that the wall on one side of this city was as long as the Great Wall of China and ten times as high.

C. Angels appeared in the form of men at various times in the Bible.   This seems to be one of them.

21:18—

A. Jasper was not only very beautiful, it was extremely durable.

B. As Solomon's temple was described as almost entirely overlaid with gold, this city would reflect any light which was in its vicinity until it would be an astonishing sight.

324

C. This gold, like the jasper of verse 11 is clear of all blemishes.

21:19—

A. We see a picture similar to Josephus' description of the foundations of the Jerusalem temple, where he said some of the stones were as large as 70 feet.

B. The precious stones provide a wide diversity of colors.

Jasper—green
Sapphire—blue
Chalcedony—yellow-red
Emerald—green
Sardonyx—reddish white
Sardius—blood red
Chrysolite—greenish yellow
Beryl—blue green
Topaz—pale green and yellow
Chrysosprasus—pale green and yellow
Jacinth—red and yellow
Amethyst—purple to violet

C. Eight of these stones were included in the breastplate of the high priest. (Ex. 28:17.)

21:20—

A. Twelve stones, one for each of the twelve apostles.

21:21—

A. Pearls were held to be a very special form of beauty in gems since they held a natural beauty when first beheld, untouched by men.

B. The size of these pearl gates indicates once again the symbolic nature of this book.

C. Now gold is nice to have around to look at, but this city has so much of that which is valuable that one may even walk on the gold.

D. Again notice that this gold is unblemished.

21:22—

A. The temple was a place to commune with God, thus there is no need for a temple here since the city is all temple.

B. Again we have evidence that this is the Church in perfection form, as the Church is the temple of God. (1 Cor. 3:10-16.)

C. We as a Church are the Body of Christ and the temple of God.

21:23—

A. God is light.

B. Even the angels shine brighter than the sun on occasion.

C. Saul saw a light brighter than the sun.

D. We shall only know the full meaning of the Glory of God when we have been brought into his presence.

21:24—

A. A city of God in which all nations and Kings are free to enter is the realization of many Old Testament prophet visions:

   1. Isaiah 2:2-4; 11:12; 45:22; 49:6; 51:5; 55:5; 56:6-8; 66:19.

   2. Jeremiah 3:17; 16:19-21.

   3. Daniel 7:14.

   4. Zephaniah 2:11; 3:9.

   5. Zechariah 2:13; 8:20-23; 14:9.

B. Israel was a chosen people, nevertheless they saw themselves as the nation through which all others might be blessed.

C. Where God is, the night shineth as the day. (Psalm 139:11.)

D. There is no respect of persons with God.

E. Wallace makes an interesting point here that these are still kings as they bring their glory into the city. He therefore says it must be the church on earth, not the eternal home.

21:25—

A. The gates of the ancient cities were shut at night for protection.

B. The gates of this city shall never be shut because it is continual day.

C. One of the great fears of men is darkness. There shall be no darkness here.

D. There shall be no need of rest at night for this shall be the eternal rest.

21:26—

A. All of that which is truly proven to be glorious and honorable shall be able to enter from all ages and all nations.

B. Even some of the Kings of the earth shall be wise enough to submit to the will of God and enter.

C. It might be worth while to note that we are both Kings and priests now.

21:27—

A. It is not the penitent sinner who is barred from God's perfect city. It is the rebellious sinner.

B. Ah! To be free of all influences which would tear us from the eternal presence of perfect love.

C. We are told again that this is not to be ours unless our names are enrolled in the city books.

Chapter 22

22:1—

A. In chapter 21 we have observed the outside of the City of God, now we enter.

B. This is far from being the only reference to a river or fountain of life in the scriptures:

Genesis 2:8-10; Ezekiel 47:1-7; Psalms 46:4; 36:9; Joel 3:18; Zechariah 14:8; Jeremiah 2:14; John 7:38, 39; Revelation 7:17 and 21:6.

C. Its crystal clarity indicates its perfect purity.

D. Some water sources are exhaustible—this is not since it flows from the throne of the Eternal God.

E. We are informed in this verse that God's throne is also the throne of the Lamb, or Christ.

22:2—

A. Students of the original language state that there is a need to place the first portion of this verse with the previous verse. This places the river which flows from God's throne in the midst of the street. It is not the tree which is in the midst of the street, but the river.

B. This could mean that the river, being in the midst of the street is easily accessible.

C. To say the tree of life grew on either side of it is to say both sides of it. Like saying, the pine tree grows throughout Tennessee.

D. The tree of life is also found in Genesis 3:6 and Ezekiel 47:12.

E. There are strong connections between the Spirit of God, the tree of life and the river of life.

   1. The man who possesses the Spirit of God has living waters flowing from his belly, or heart. (John 7:38, 39.)

   2. The Holy Spirit produces a number of fruits, as does the tree of life. (Gal. 5.)

F. Trees which produce fruit twelve times a year are in perpetual production.

G. Not only does the tree of life produce food for spiritual life, it produces medicine.
   1. Here one never grows hungry.
   2. Here there can be no disease and affliction. (How many shall rejoice at this!)
   3. Remember God told the Laodiceans to buy his eyesalve.

22:3—

A. The curse of pain, sorrow, hunger, death, toiling in sweat, etc. entered with sin.

B. Now sin has been removed and the curse is gone.

C. Neither the curse nor the accursed remains.

D. There is now no hindrance to complete service and worship.

22:4—

A. Blessed are the pure in heart for they shall see God. (Matt. 5:8.)

B. Then shall I know even as also I am known. (1 Cor. 13:12.)

C. They shall be granted the privilege of seeing God's face, which even Moses was denied. (Ex. 33:20, 23.)

22:5—

A. Almost as if it were too difficult to believe, it is repeated that there will be no night.

B. God is light and in him there is no darkness at all. (1 John 1:5.)

C. This time there is no need of artificial light either.

D. Those who conquer will share God's throne along with the Lamb. (Rev. 3:21.)
   1. In chapter 20 the reign is for a thousand years.
   2. Now the reign is extended indefinitely.

E. Strangely enough, while in complete submission to God his subjects are reigning.

22:6—

A. Verses 6-21 are confirmation of the divine nature of the Revelation.
   1. The angel confirms. (The same God who spoke to the prophets of old speaks now.)
   2. John confirms.
   3. Christ affirms.

4. Let those who desire ignore the message.
5. Let all who listen come.
6. DO NOT TAMPER.

B. Again we are told that the things revealed were to come to pass shortly.

22:7—

A. There are seven beatitudes in the book of Revelation. (1:3; 14:13; 16:15; 19:9; 20:6; 22:7; 22:14.)

B. There are three kinds of men.
1. Devoted without knowledge.
2. Educated without devotion.
3. Those who read and keep the sayings.

C. The latter are promised a blessing.

D. This is another proof that the book of Revelation can be *understood* and heeded by those for whom it was intended.

22:8—

A. This is the second time John has been told not to worship an angel. (Rev. 19:10.)

B. John has not forgotten this quickly, he is simply overcome with the grandeur of the occasion.

C. This same mistake is made all too often by those who fail to differentiate between the divine message and the frail humans who carry that message.

22:9—

A. The glory for the message of Revelation belongs to God alone.

B. Angels are servants, as are the Old Testament prophets and John of Revelation.

C. The angels are bound to bring about the plan presented in this book. God's plan shall ultimately prove to be the only rule of action.

22:10—

A. Daniel was given opposite instructions. He was to seal up his vision for many days. (Dan. 8:26; 9:24; 12:4, 9.)

B. Now the time is ready for the opening of all the prophetic seals.

C. The work of Christ moves steadily toward its conclusion.

22:11—

A. The word "let" is used in two different ways.
1. Positive—Let the wicked forsake his way.

329

2. Negative—Let him be filthy still.
B. God is not willing that any should perish.
C. There comes a time when God knows it is too late.
  1. The wicked shall do wickedly. (Dan. 12:10.)
  2. He that will refuse to hear, let him refuse. (Ezek. 3:27.)
  3. Like food, a man can refuse the Spirit of God until in the end he cannot take it. Whosoever *will* may come.

22:12—

A. We have not worked hard enough to deserve the reward which Christ brings.
B. His sacrifice *can* bring atonement and the possibility of reward.
C. It is faith and grace which save, still the faith is shown by a man's works.
D. This verse carries a hint of degrees of reward in heaven.
E. Christ is always at hand to come quickly to his servants who need assistance.
F. The final reward will come sooner than we expect.

22:13—

A. As the Alpha and the Omega Christ is:
  1. Complete.
  2. Timeless.
  3. Authoritative.
B. It is said that as the final and complete authority God:
  1. Received his power from no one.
  2. Shares his power with no one.
  3. Delivers his power to no one.
C. Nevertheless Christ was delegated all power in heaven and in earth.
D. And every man has been given enough power to obey or to deny.

22:14—

A. There is considerable controversy over whether the verse should read, "Blessed are those who wash their robes."
B. In the Greek the two phrases are very similar.
C. The older manuscripts seem to lean toward the latter translation.
D. Barclay has an excellent discussion of this problem. Pp. 289-290 of Revelation, Vol. 2.
E. Everyone carries a robe with him.

1. He is always in the process of weaving it.
2. The robe may become splashed and dirty.
3. No power or spot remover on earth can cleanse it.
4. Christ's blood will clean it.
5. Only with a clean robe may one enter the City of God.

22:15—

A. He that telleth lies shall not tarry in my sight. (Psalm 101:7.)
B. This is a repetition of previous lists except for the dogs.
C. Dogs were far different creatures in the land of Palestine than here.
D. They symbolized all that was thieving, treacherous and loathsome.
E. It is also possible that the passage is talking about male prostitutes, as Deuteronomy 23:18 speaks of the price of a *dog*.
F. Adam Clarke believes the dogs to be spiritual Gentiles, or uncircumcised of heart.
G. It is not impossible that the dogs are men who return to the vomit of sin.

22:16—

A. This message is not that of John. It comes from Jesus. (Rev. 1:1.)
B. As the offspring of David, Christ—
   1. Occupies the throne of David. (Acts 2:29-33.)
   2. Brings the mercies of David. (Acts 13:34.)
   3. Sets up the tabernacle of David. (Acts 15:13-17.)
   4. Holds the key of David. (Isa. 22:22.)
C. The morning star ushers in an eternal day of the Kingdom of Heaven.
   1. There shall come a star out of Jacob. (Num. 24:17.)
   2. He that followeth me shall not walk in darkness. (John 8:12.)

22:17—

A. The Spirit had made invitation at the end of each of the letters to the Churches.
B. The entire Bible, the Word, or the tool of the Spirit invites man to Heaven.
C. The invited must become inviters.
D. The found must find others.
E. God provides the water of life freely but he forces no man to drink.

F. In these days men sell unpolluted fresh spring water for physical health.

G. Here God provides the spiritual water of life freely.

22:18—

A. This passage is often misused to apply to the entire Bible.

B. There are enough other passages to prove the point. See the following: Deuteronomy 4:2; Proverbs 30:5, 6; 1 Corinthians 4:6; 2 John 9; Romans 1:22-25; Galatians 1:8, 9.

C. Translations provide a problem as to how literal we must be in addition and subtraction. Sometimes there are words in one language for which there are no single words in another.

D. No man may try to explain away the Divine Revelation as uninspired or spurious.

E. Nor may any man add his own *human* revelation.

22:19—

A. No conscientious man can handle the Book of Revelation in light manner.

B. Among the things a man might lose are:
1. The new name.
2. The new song.
3. The crown of life.
4. Walking in white and reigning with Jesus.
5. The water of life and the tree of life.

C. No sane man should neglect so great salvation.

22:20—

A. The Spirit and the Bride invite men to come to God.

B. Now the promise is I COME TO YOU.

C. Amen means, Be it so.

D. Thus this verse is saying, Come, let it be so in the precise manner predicted.

22:21—

A. It is significant that the last thought in the Bible is the Grace of Christ.

B. Only an inspired writer could provide such a mixture of clarity and obscurity as is found in this book.

C. All believers are agreed on the comfort and encouragement provided by the Revelation.

D. It is interesting to compare the entire book with the second Psalm.

This work is concluded with a prayer of thanksgiving to God for allowing the author the privilege of serving him in this manner. May the student of the prophets receive spiritual edification and instruction. And may all glory, honor, and power be given to the Father in heaven, and to his Son through whom this prayer is made.

A List of Cross References Between the Book of Revelation and the Major and Minor Prophets of the Old Testament.

Revelation

Chapter 1

7	Daniel 7:13; Zechariah 12:10.
8	Isaiah 41:4; 44:6; 48:12.
12	Zechariah 4:2.
13	Ezekiel 1:26; Daniel 7:13; 10:16; 10:5.
14	Daniel 7:9; 10:6.
15	Ezekiel 1:7; 43:2.
16	Isaiah 49:2.
17	Ezekiel 1:28; Daniel 8:18; 10:10.
20	Malachi 2:7; Zechariah 4:2.

Chapter 2

16	Isaiah 11:4.
23	Jeremiah 11:20.
27	Daniel 7:22.

Chapter 3

7	Isaiah 22:22.
9	Isaiah 49:23; 60:14.
10	Isaiah 24:17.
14	Isaiah 65:16.
17	Hosea 12:8.
18	Isaiah 55:1.

Chapter 4

2	Isaiah 6:1; Jeremiah 17:12; Ezekiel 1:26. Ezekiel 10:1; Daniel 7:9.
3	Ezekiel 1:28.
5	Ezekiel 1:13; Zechariah 4:2.
6	Ezekiel 1:5; 10:14.
7	Ezekiel 1:10.
8	Isaiah 6:2-3.

Chapter 5

1	Ezekiel 2:9-10; Isaiah 29:11; Daniel 12:4.
5	Isaiah 11:1.

Chapter 14

5	Zephaniah 3:13.
8	Jeremiah 51:7.
10	Isaiah 51:17; Jeremiah 25:15.
11	Isaiah 34:10.
14	Ezekiel 1:26; Daniel 7:13.
15	Joel 3:13; Jeremiah 51:33.
18	Joel 3:13.
20	Isaiah 63:3.

Chapter 15

3	Hosea 14:9.
4	Jeremiah 10:7; Isaiah 66:22.
6	Ezekiel 44:17.
8	Isaiah 6:4.

Chapter 16

6	Isaiah 49:26.
9	Daniel 5:22-23.
12	Jeremiah 1:38; 51:36; Isaiah 41:2, 25.
18	Daniel 12:1.
19	Isaiah 51:17, 23; Jeremiah 25:15.

Chapter 17

1	Jeremiah 51:13.
2	Jeremiah 51:7.
4	Daniel 11:38; Jeremiah 51:7.
12	Daniel 12:20; Zechariah 1:18, 19, 21.
14	Jeremiah 50:44-45.
15	Isaiah 8:7.
16	Jeremiah 50:41-42; Ezekiel 16:37-44.

Chapter 18

1	Ezekiel 43:2.
2	Isaiah 13:19; 21:9; Jeremiah 51:8. Isaiah 13:21; 21:8; 34:14; 34:11. Jeremiah 50:39; 51:37.
3	Isaiah 47:15.
4	Isaiah 48:20; 52:11; Jeremiah 50:8; 51:6, 45.
5	Jeremiah 51:9; Jonah 1:2.

6	Jeremiah 50:15, 29; 51:24, 49.
7	Ezekiel 28:2; Isaiah 47:7-8; Zephaniah 2:15.
8	Ezekiel 47:9; Jeremiah 50:34.
9	Ezekiel 26:16-17; Jeremiah 50:46.
10	Isaiah 21:9.
11	Ezekiel 27:27-36.
13	Ezekiel 27:13.
17	Isaiah 23:14; Ezekiel 27:29.
18	Ezekiel 27:30-31.
19	Ezekiel 27:30-31.
20	Isaiah 44:23; 49:13; Jeremiah 51:48.
21	Jeremiah 51:64.
22	Isaiah 24:8; Jeremiah 7:34; 16:9; 25:10. Ezekiel 26:13.
23	Jeremiah 25:10; 7:34; 16:9; 38:11. Isaiah 23:8; Nahum 3:4.
24	Jeremiah 51:49.

Chapter 19

3	Isaiah 34:10.
6	Ezekiel 1:24.
8	Ezekiel 16:10.
11	Isaiah 11:4.
13	Isaiah 68:2-3.
15	Isaiah 11:4; 63:3.
16	Daniel 2:47.
17	Ezekiel 39:17.
18	Ezekiel 39:18, 20.
20	Daniel 7:11.

Chapter 20

3	Daniel 6:17.
4	Daniel 7:9, 22, 27.
6	Isaiah 61:6.
8	Ezekiel 38:2; 39:1.
9	Isaiah 8:8; Ezekiel 38:9, 16.
11	Daniel 2:35.
12	Daniel 7:10; 12:1; Jeremiah 17:10; 22:19.

Chapter 21

1	Isaiah 65:17; 66:22.
2	Isaiah 52:1; 54:5; 61:10.
3	Ezekiel 43:7.
4	Isaiah 25:8; 35:10; 61:3; 65:19.
5	Isaiah 43:19.
6	Isaiah 12:3; 55:1.
7	Zechariah 8:8.
10	Ezekiel 48.
12	Ezekiel 48:31-34.
13	Ezekiel 48:31-34.
15	Ezekiel 40:3; Zechariah 2:1.
19	Isaiah 54:11; Ezekiel 1:26.
23	Isaiah 24:23; 60:19-20.
24	Isaiah 60:3, 5, 11; 66:12.
25	Isaiah 60:11; 60:20; Zechariah 14:7.
27	Isaiah 35:8; 52:1; 60:21; Joel 3:17.

Chapter 22

1	Ezekiel 47:1; 14:8.
2	Ezekiel 47:12.
3	Zechariah 14:11; Ezekiel 48:35.
5	Daniel 7:27.
10	Daniel 8:26; 12:4, 9.
11	Ezekiel 3:27; Daniel 12:10.
12	Isaiah 40:10; 62:11.
13	Isaiah 41:4; 44:6; 48:12.
14	Daniel 12:12.
16	Zechariah 6:12.
17	Isaiah 55:1.

BIBLIOGRAPHY

Bales, James D., *Prophecy and Premillennialism*, Bales Pub. Co., Searcy, Arkansas, 1972.

Boles, H. Leo, & Boll, R. H., *Unfulfilled Prophecy*, Gospel Advocate Co., Nashville, 1954.

Clarke, Adam, *A Commentary and Critical Notes*, Vol. 6, Romans to Revelation, Abingdon Press, Nashville, No date.

Erdman, Charles R., *The Book of Jeremiah*, Fleming H. Revell Co., Westwood, NJ, 1955.

Freeman, Hobart, *An Introduction to the Old Testament Prophets*, Moody Press, Chicago, 1968.

Gabelein, Arno C., *The Prophet Ezekiel*, Loizeaux Bros., Neptune, NJ, 1918.

Hailey, Homer, *A Commentary on the Minor Prophets*, Baker Book House, Grand Rapids, 1972.

Hendrickson, Wm., *More Than Conquerors*, Baker Book House, Grand Rapids, 1967.

Hinds, John T., *A Commentary on the Book of Revelation*, Gospel Advocate Co., Nashville, 1937.

Ironside, H. A., *Isaiah*, Loizeaux Bros., Neptune, NJ, 1952.

Jehovah's Witnesses, *Then Is Finished the Mystery of God*, Watchtower Bible and Tract Society, NY, 1969.

Jenkins, Ferrell, *The Old Testament in the Book of Revelation*, Cogdill Foundaiont, Marion, Indiana, 1972.

Johnson, Ashley, *Opening the Book of the Seven Seals*, College Press, Joplin, Missouri, 1900.

Johnson, B. W., *The People's New Testament with Notes*, Gospel Advocate Co., Nashville, No date.

Keil, C. F. & Delitzsch, F., *Commentaries on the Old Testament*, Ezekiel, Eerdmans' Publishing Co., Grand Rapids, 1970.

Laetsch, Theodore, *Bible Commentary—The Minor Prophets*, Concordia Publishing House, St. Louis, Missouri, 1956.

Lenski, R.C.H., *Interpretation of St. John's Revelation*, Augsburg Publishing House, Minneapolis, 1963.

Leslie, Elmer, *Jeremiah*, Abingdon Press, Nashville, 1954.

Leupold, H. C., *Exposition of Daniel*, Baker Book House, Grand Rapids, 1949.

Lewis, Jack P., *The Minor Prophets*, Baker Book House, Grand Rapids, 1966.

Maddux, Roy C., *The Prophets in Outline*, Baker Book House, Grand Rapids, 1967.

McDowell, Edward, *The Meaning and Message of the Book of Revelation*, Broadman Press, Nashville, 1951.

Montgomery, James, *Isaiah*, Vols. I & II, Gussie Lambert Press, Shreveport, 1967.

Murray, George, *Millennial Studies*, Baker Book House, Grand Rapids, 1960.

Newton, Isaac, *Daniel and the Apocalypse*, J. Murray, London, 1922.

Pink, Arthur W., *The Life of Elijah*, I. C. Herendeen, Swengel, Pennsylvania, 1956.

Rice, John R., *The Coming Kingdom of Christ*, Sword of the Lord Publishers, Murfreesboro, Tennessee, 1945.

Robinson, George, *The 12 Minor Prophets*, Baker Book House, Grand Rapids, 1926.

Smith, J. M. Powis, *The Prophets and Their Times*, University of Chicago Press, Chicago, 1941.

Summars, Ray, *Worthy Is the Lamb*, Broadman Press, Nashville, 1951.

Vine, W. E., *Isaiah*, Zondervan Publishing House, Grand Rapids, 1971.

Wallace, Foy, Jr., *The Book of Revelation*, Foy Wallace, Jr. Publications, Nashville, 1966.

Wallace, Foy, Jr., *God's Prophetic Word*, Foy Wallace, Jr. Publications, Nashville, 1960.

Witty, Claude F., *Babylon is Falling*, Detroit, 1940.

Yates, Kyle M., *Preaching From the Prophets*, Harper & Bros., New York, 1942.

Young, Edward J., *The Book of Isaiah, Vols. I, II & III*, Eerdmans Publishing Co., Grand Rapids, 1956.

Young, Edward J., *My Servants, the Prophets*, Eerdman's Publishing Co., Grand Rapids, 1952.

TAPES

Baggett, *Lectures on Isaiah*, Sunset School of Preaching, Lubbock, Texas.

McGuiggan, James, *Lectures on Daniel*, Sunset School of Preaching, Lubbock, Texas.

McGuiggan, James, *Lectures on Ezekiel*, Sunset School of Preaching, Lubbock, Texas.

Rogers, Richard, *Lectures on the Minor Prophets*, Sunset School of Preaching, Lubbock, Texas.

Rogers, Richard, *Lectures on Revelation*, Sunset School of Preaching, Lubbock, Texas.